Class and Labor in IRAN

Modern Intellectual and Political History of the Middle East
Mehrzad Boroujerdi, *Series Editor*

CLASS and LABOR in
IRAN

Did the Revolution Matter?

Farhad Nomani & Sohrab Behdad

SYRACUSE UNIVERSITY PRESS

Library of Congress Cataloging-in-Publication Data

Nu'mani, Farhad.
Class and labor in Iran : did the revolution matter? /
Farhad Nomani and Sohrab Behdad.
p. cm.—(Modern intellectual and political history of the Middle East)
Includes bibliographical references and index.
ISBN 0–8156–3070–0 (cloth : alk. paper)—ISBN 0–8156–3094–8 (pbk. : alk. paper)
1. Labor supply—Iran. 2. Social classes—Iran. 3. Capitalism—Iran.
4. Iran—Economic conditions—1979–1997. 5. Iran—Economic
conditions—1997– I. Behdad, Sohrab, 1943– II. Title. III. Series.
HD5812.56.A6N85 2006
331.10955   2005035197

And in the cloud-covered world
The ney player keeps to his path,
Always playing, making his own way forward.

NIMA USHIJ
(English rendering by Ann Townsend)

Farhad Nomani is a professor and cochair of the Department of Economics at the American University of Paris and was a member of the Faculty of Economics at Tehran University from 1972 to 1983. He is the coeditor of *Islam and Public Policy,* coauthor of *Islamic Economic Systems* and *The Secular Miracle: Religion, Politics, and Economic Policy in Iran,* and author of *The Development of Feudalism in Iran* (in Persian).

Sohrab Behdad is a professor and the John E. Harris Chair in Economics at Denison University and was a member of the Faculty of Economics at Tehran University from 1973 to 1983. He is the former president of the Middle East Economic Association and a member of the editorial board of the *International Journal of Middle East Studies.* He is the coeditor of *Islam and Public Policy* and *Iran: Crisis of Islamic State* and author of articles on the postrevolutionary economy of Iran and the critique of Islamic economics.

Contents

Figures

Tables

Acknowledgments

IN CONDUCTING THIS PROJECT we have accumulated a heavy burden of debt to many colleagues and lifelong friends who have intellectually inspired, encouraged, or assisted us. They have stimulated and challenged us to pursue our work deliberately and persistently. If we were wiser, we would have followed their directions more closely.

We are especially grateful to Professor Erik Olin Wright and Professor Fatemeh Moghadam for reading the entire manuscript and making many constructive suggestions.

We wish to express our gratitude to Professor Bahram Tavakolian, Denison University, and Professor Ali Rahnema, the American University of Paris, not only for reading parts of this manuscript and engaging in fruitful discussions on class and Iranian sociopolitical issues with us but also for being sources of counsel and support throughout the years at Denison for Sohrab and in Paris for Farhad.

We acknowledge the facilitating role of the American University of Paris and Denison University in our project. For Sohrab, Denison University generously provided student assistants, funds for acquiring documents and material, and a semester of leave as an R. C. Good fellow. Moreover, Sohrab is thankful to his departmental colleagues, especially Ross LaRoe and Timothy Miller, for their generosity in sharing their expertise with him on this and many of the previous projects that he has undertaken. We are also grateful for the help of Sohrab's research assistants, Jafar Olimov, Brandon Boettcher, and Jasmine Tan.

Finally, thanks are due to Mehrzad Boroujerdi, series editor, and Mary Selden Evans, executive editor, of Syracuse University Press. They have been the most wonderful sources of support in the preparation of this project.

Needless to say, these acknowledgments do not implicate anyone. All errors and opinions are ours.

Class and Labor in IRAN

1

Introduction

Class and Revolution

OUR BOOK IS ABOUT the reconfiguration of the class nature of the Iranian workforce in the past three decades. This time has been an important period in the modern history of Iran. After two decades of rapid capitalist development, ending with the boom and the bust of the mid-1970s oil bonanza, Iranians experienced a revolution, leading to a theocratic state, the Islamic Republic of Iran. The Islamic state, with fictitiously lofty goals, began its quest for an Islamic utopia, with a hitherto undefined Islamic economic system. It claimed that the Islamic state would eradicate the class of *taghotian* (a Quranic term referring to those driven by the arrogance of wealth and power) and would establish the rule of the *mostazafan* (oppressed), who, after all, "shall inherit the earth," as it says in the Qur'an: "And We desired to show favour unto those who were oppressed in the earth, and to make them examples and to make them inheritors" (28:5).[1] The Islamic Republic declared itself the "Rule of the Oppressed!"

The language of class and the rhetoric of class war entered the Islamic discourse in the decade preceding the 1979 revolution. Ali Shariati, a noncleric Islamic evangelist, a doctor of sociology from Sorbonne, impressed by Sartre, Fanon, and Durkheim, talked class more explicitly than the Marxists under the Shah's strict censorship. He offered an Islamic conception of history in close parallel with the historical materialism of Marxists. The history of humanity since Abraham, the prophet, says Shariati, is the story of oppression of the dispossessed by the propertied class and of the permanent struggle of the oppressed against the oppressors. It all began with the killing of Abel (the pastoral man) by Cain (the landowner). In this interpretation of the Islamic conception of history, the central issue in the Islamic struggle for liberation is

---

1. From translation of the Qur'an by Picktall (1953).

1

elimination of the privileges of the propertied class by eradication of the institution of property. Shariati is unequivocal in stating that Islam is opposed to capitalism, private ownership, and class exploitation. Hence for Shariati and his growing number of followers, Islam of liberation promised a "monotheistic classless society" *(Jame'h-ye bi Tabaqeh-ye Tawhidi),* and Islamic socialism was the historical projectile of the Islamic movement.[2]

Shariati attracted many young urban intellectuals to the Islamic movement, joining the front-line brigade of the opposition to the Shah's regime. An Islamist protagonist noted in 1980 that "many of those who with their blood bought the foundation of the Islamic Republic in this world, and Paradise in the hereafter, were, directly or indirectly, the pupils of Shariati."[3] The Islamic establishment in Iran found Shariati's liberation rhetoric disturbing and his notion of a classless society totally wrong (see Abolhasani 1983). Yet Shariati's widespread appeal among the young Islamic activists made any serious public criticism of him and his ideas politically impossible.

Ayatollah Khomeini, in a famous speech to the seminary students visiting him in 1977 in exile in Najaf, Iraq, refuted those who claimed that social classes had to be abolished. To Khomeini, making people classless is making animals out of human beings. Nevertheless, in the same speech Khomeini asked the seminary students not to denounce those who make such claims because "Islam is for justice . . . [and] for class balance" n.d., 3:222). The ambiguous concepts of justice and balance played a pivotal role in Khomeini's social philosophy, and in the orientation of the Islamic state established in 1979. It was a balance that is supposed to bring inherently contradictory elements into a harmonious whole. Khomeini declared in June 1979, in a speech to "industrialists and bazaaris" in Qum, that "Islam . . . will neither banish capital, nor would it let capital [grow] such that someone will have hundreds of millions of dollars" (8:470). The Islamic state is the arbiter and the grantor of the balance. Khomeini stated in the heat of the revolution in 1979, "Even if we assume someone has legitimate properties but the Islamic judge realizes that an individual's having so much will adversely affect the welfare of Muslims, he can expropriate those properties" (10:481). This justification provides the Islamic state with the power of political expropriation and confiscation of property, a notion to which many senior Islamic jurists were opposed (DHHD 1984, 189).

2. For an analysis of Shariati's notion of class discussed here, see Rahnema and Nomani 1990, Behdad 1994a, and Dabashi 1993. For Shariati's biography, see Rahnema 1998.
3. Hamid Algar in his preface to Shariati 1980, 9.

Khomeini's rhetoric was in tune with the rhythm and tone of the popular revolutionary movement. The Marxist intelligentsia and the growing number of Shariati's Islamist activists had established an anticapitalist agenda for the revolution. In step with the international domination of dependency theory as the explanation for underdevelopment, poverty, and backwardness of developing countries, declarations of the revolutionary organizations and groups invariably condemned dependent capitalists and dependent capitalism in Iran. They also sought an end to the deprivation and poverty of the oppressed *(mostazafan* in the Islamist lingo) and workers and toilers *(kargaran va zahmatkeshan* in the lingo of the Left).[4]

The Iranian revolution was a thundering social eruption. It was populist and spontaneous in that there was no well defined organizational leadership, nor was there any revolutionary program for economic or social reconstruction.[5] In the months that followed the revolution, the slogans of mass demonstrations and the resolutions of the striking workers and various newly formed organizations expressed some relatively uniform demands. Those demands included the nationalization and expropriation of large industries, banks, mines, large landholdings, and real estate. Many of these demands were formulated based on the general framework of dependency theory—for example, "Dependent Capitalism Must Be Annihilated!" *(Sarmayehdari Vabasteh Nabood Bayad Gardad!).* Others were truly spontaneous.[6]

In the revolutionary movement property rights and capital came under attack for being "excessive," for benefiting from close association with the ancien régime, or for affiliation with foreign capital. Being unclear in their def-

4. For slogans of the revolution, consult the Tehran dailies *Ayandegan* and *Kayhan.* A number of collections of declarations, too numerous to list, have been published by various political organizations. *Kar* and *Mojahed* were the official publications of the two most important revolutionary organizations, Sazman-e Fadaian-e Khalq-e Iran and Sazman-e Mojahedin-e Khalq-e Iran.

5. For a review of early experiences of planning and programming in the revolutionary Iran see Behdad 1988b. For Khomeinism and populism, see Rahnema and Nomani 1990 and Abrahamian 1993.

6. One of us observed how an important slogan entered the list of revolutionary demands. Some weeks before the February uprising, a large demonstration passed by the building of the Central Bank of Iran on Ferdowsi Avenue in Tehran. Some personnel of the Central Bank, who were on a "sit-in" strike, appeared at the windows of the bank to express solidarity with the demonstrators. One Central Bank employee shouted, "Banks must be nationalized!" (Bank-ha melli bayad gardad!) Demonstrators shouted approval, and from that day nationalization of banks was added to the list of revolutionary demands. In the summer of 1979, banks along with insurance companies and many manufacturing industries were nationalized.

inition, illegitimacy of property and capital became a relativistic criterion in different places and circumstances. Hence, in a small town a car dealer or a retailer of home appliances could be regarded as an imperialist outpost and a large "bloodsucking capitalist" *(sarmayehdar-e zaloo sefat)*, the owner of a fifty-hectare farm a despicable landlord, and a retired major an associate of the Shah. Takeovers and expropriations were widespread. Economic activities became widely disturbed, and accumulation became seriously disrupted. Iran was plagued by an economic crisis of the postrevolutionary type.

Our Theoretical Conceptualization

We contend that a postrevolutionary economic crisis is a distinct economic phenomenon, resulting from a postrevolutionary structural crisis. It is the result of open social confrontation. It is when sanctity of property rights and legitimacy of capital come under attack. Production and accumulation become disrupted. As the ancien régime collapses, the state becomes unable to protect property rights and unable to facilitate the accumulation process. The crisis continues until the state is fully instituted, an economic order is established, and production and accumulation processes are resumed undisturbed. However, defining and establishing the new economic order will be the subject of an intense political struggle among various social classes and groups pursuing their own particular interests. The path of resolution of these conflicts and the characteristics of the state and the economic order that will be the outcome of this struggle will depend on the configuration and political leverage of various class alliances, not excluding the importance of the impact of external (international) players.

Furthermore, we contend that the outcome of an economic crisis of the postrevolutionary type is more than just a decline in output. The social turmoil will cause capitalist relations of production to wither and petty-commodity economic activities to thrive. These conditions lead to a degenerative process, creating tangles within the existing economic structure, impeding the accumulation process, and intensifying the economic crisis. We call this phenomenon "structural involution." It is manifested in sectoral shifts in production and employment, increased peasantization of agriculture, deproletarianization of the workforce, and an expansion of service activities. Once the state is established, normalization of economic activities begins. Then, the process of structural involution will be reversed toward reconstitution of the capitalist relations of production, restoration of the accumulation process, proletarianization of the workforce, and depeasantization of agriculture. We call this reversal process "deinvolution" of the economic structure.

In our study we recognize two periods in the postrevolutionary years. The first period is the years of revolutionary fervor, characterized by a search for an Islamic utopia. It began in 1979 and came to an end when the burden of inefficiencies of the populist-statist economic policies and the financial cost of the war with Iraq, under international economic sanctions, were exacerbated by the glut in the international oil market. By 1988, the revolutionary project was declared defunct. The search for the illusive Islamic utopia and the claim of establishing the rule of the oppressed quietly died away. The ceasefire resolution of the United Nations was accepted, and hostilities with Iraq ended. As fate had it, Ayatollah Khomeini died soon after, in June 1989. It was a decade of social turmoil, economic disturbances, and crisis, a decade of structural involution. It was the Khomeini decade.

The death of Ayatollah Khomeini marked the beginning of the second postrevolutionary period. This period, extending to the present, is characterized by reorientation of the state and public policy toward economic restructuring, by rejuvenation and reconstruction of capitalist economic relation and institutions. These years are a time of economic liberalization, à la prescriptions of the International Monetary Fund (IMF) and the World Bank. The state pursued the policy of reversing the economic trend of the previous decade. It is the beginning of the process of deinvolution in the economic structure of Iran, a trend that is progressing slowly and painfully as it entails the political transformation of the Islamic Republic from a populist-revolutionary state, claiming a commitment to establishing the rule of the oppressed, to a run-of-the-mill capitalist state.

The postrevolutionary period, from 1979 to the present, constitutes a sufficiently long time, permitting us to identify the decisive structural shifts in the Iranian economy and the reconfiguration of the class nature of the workforce. Variations in the class nature of the labor force are generally effected by long-run socioeconomic, technological, and demographic changes. Yet particular circumstances, such as political reforms, wars, and revolutions, can destabilize, deform, and weaken the existing class structure by creating new opportunities in employment status and position and in the power structure for some population groups, while limiting the opportunities for others. Hence, we can perceive changes in the pattern of employment and the class nature of the workforce as the result of two concurrent processes. First, fluctuations may occur when new positions are created and others are eliminated as socioeconomic conditions promote certain activities and retard others. These changes will increase or decrease the number of persons in various positions and may alter their hierarchical relations, affecting the distribution of employment, pattern of employment status, and consequently the class nature of the workforce. Second, changes may come as the organization of production is modified or as the composition of those individuals holding the positions is modified, without any appreciable difference in the composition of economic activities. In this situation the pattern of employment status and occupational position, and the characteristics associated with each category, may change, too, although the activity distribution of employment has not been altered appreciably.

In this study we seek to explore the changes in the pattern of class division of employment and in the differentiated lifelong opportunities of the Iranian workforce in the context of a long period of revolution and postrevolutionary politico-socioeconomic changes. In particular, we ask this question: how have the revolution, its initial petty-bourgeois orientation, and its subsequent pro-market restructuring in the post-Khomeini period affected the pattern of social inequalities in terms of class divisions and lifelong opportunities of the workforce?

There are important nuances in dealing with the issue of class and class divisions, which require us to define our approach precisely. We contend that *workforce* is not a homogeneous category. The relations between the individuals of the workforce are hierarchical and are based on class interests, which are defined on the basis of relations of production in economic activities. Production relations reflect the way effective ownership rights and power over producers and productive assets are distributed (Cohen 2001, 63). In this sense, the production relationship can be identified as relations of ownership, because those who own resources enter into an asymmetric relation with those who do not. This relationship gives rise to class locations (independent of those who occupy them) in economic structures, or modes of productions, and determines the antagonistic class interests of the occupants. In a capitalist economy a set of these class locations based on the three axes of ownership of resources, organizational assets/authority, and skills/credentials constitute the class structure. This asymmetric relationship results in the appropriation of labor effort in the process of economic activity. The rights and powers of those who own scarce assets, are in a position of wielding control/authority, and are in possession of skills and credentials in economic activities result in unequal lifelong opportunities between those who have and those who do not have these resources. Yet the concept of class as a power relationship is by its nature a relational hierarchy.

This asymmetric and hierarchical relationship, the social hierarchy of work, can be approximated with reasonable certainty in an employment-occupational structure to reflect the three axes of class locations. In this manner, the social hierarchy of work becomes a complex structure that depicts the class nature of the employed workforce. It will also depict the more particular aspects of class divisions, such as gender and spatial divisions in employment-occupational structures in a relational and hierarchical manner.

The operationalization of the class structure in this study is a slightly modified variant of Erik O. Wright's (1997, 23–26) based on the above three dimensions of class relations. The construction of the social hierarchy of work in Iran in 1976, 1986, and 1996 is the result of cross-classification of three matrixes of occupational status–economic activities, occupational status–major occupational groups and major occupational groups–economic activities. The interlacing of these matrixes is based on the three axes of class locations.

We examine the pattern of change in the class nature of the Iranian workforce in two periods, 1976–86 and 1986–96, determined by the timing of the national censuses of population in Iran. Fortunately, these two periods closely correspond to our periodization of the postrevolutionary years.

What Is Ahead

As a point of departure, and because class analyses are varied and entail sensitive theoretical nuances, it is necessary to be explicit about our underlying theoretical approach. We define our approach in class analysis in Chapter 2, recognizing the prevailing void in class analysis of Iran.

We proceed with the analysis of the political economy of the postrevolutionary years. Here we tell our story of what happened to the Iranian economy in the revolutionary movement and in the postrevolutionary years. This story has been told by us and others before, with different focus or emphasis. We offer a theoretical model for explaining the changes in the economic structure in the revolutionary movement and the postrevolutionary period as a distinct phenomenon, called a "postrevolutionary economic crisis." It is characterized by structural involution, as the accumulation process becomes disrupted because of the ongoing social turmoil and the state's inability in protecting property rights. These conditions are tantamount to a shriveling of the capitalist relations of production. We also recognize the reversal of this trend in the subsequent period, when the state begins invigorating capitalist accumulation and rejuvenating the capitalist relations of production. We refer to this reversal trend as the deinvolution process.

Before examining the class nature of the changes in the workforce we need to examine the relevant demographic factors influencing general attributes of the workforce. Chapter 4 focuses on the important secular attributes of population growth and the changes in the participation rates, for men and women, and by age groups. Such a focus enables us to statistically identify major sources of change in the size and structure of the male and female workforce within the socio-politico-economic context of the period and to delineate the implications of these trends for the future changes in the class nature of the workforce.

The next four chapters explore the class nature of the change in the workforce and its differentiated life opportunity at various levels. Based on the theoretical, methodological, and conceptual points raised earlier, and relying on decennial census data on employment, we identify the class structure of the employed workforce in 1976, 1986, and 1996 and demarcate the underlying sources of change in these structures.

Gender relation is an important aspect of inequality in power relations, that is, social stratification. In the vast scholarly studies and debates that exist on the problem of gender under the rule of the Islamic Republic of Iran, a comprehensive empirical study of class, gender, employment, the measurement of the extent of exclusion of women from the labor market, and employment segregation in Iran is still lacking. Chapter 6 presents a statistical analysis of the changes in the market participation of women and the class nature and differentiation of women's employment.

The study of changes in urban-rural division completes the examination of the pattern of change in social inequalities within the Iranian workforce subject to involuntary and deinvolutionary processes. The differential weight and pace of change in the configuration of production relations or modes of production in urban and rural regions reflect the evolving balance of power of the class nature of the workforce at a less aggregate level. Such a focus lays the ground for a more explicit study of factors affecting differentiated life opportunities of the workforce.

Taking into consideration the compound effects of all these factors, we examine the resulting differential lifelong opportunities of the class-divided workforce in urban and rural areas. A thorough examination of differentiated opportunities based on class divisions requires information on income-consumption, wealth, "job" trajectories, and "cultural capital" differentials in mediation with family, gender, and state. Yet a lack of data obliges us to rely on only a few measurable proxies, such as the class nature of employment-unemployment opportunities and distribution of income-expenditures, for the study of the factors that facilitate the reproduction of class inequalities over time.

Finally, we present our overall observations on the class nature of the Iranian workforce and its implication for economic and political conflicts.

Sources of Data

Iran's decennial censuses of population and housing for 1976, 1986, and 1996 by Markaz-e Amar-e Iran (MAI, Statistical Center of Iran) provide a relatively uniform classification of employment in different economic activities and occupations for the country.[7] The timing of these three censuses closely corresponds to the demarcation of the two periods in our study. The *Census 1976* reflects the general disposition of the Iranian population at the height of the monarchic White Revolution, fueled by the oil bonanza of those years. The *Census 1986,* on the other hand, reflects the conditions at the depth of the postrevolutionary decline, aggravated by a world oil glut. Certainly, comparison of these two periods will accentuate the magnitude of changes in the initial postrevolutionary period. Similarly, keeping 1986 as a benchmark for the comparison of the impacts of the Islamic Republic's economic-liberalization effort will also exaggerate the impact of these policies in the second decade of the postrevolutionary period. Therefore, any observable changes between censuses of these periods may be viewed as a trend only with considerable caution.

The census data are disaggregated for the urban and rural areas and by age and gender. Economic activities are divided into agriculture, mining (including crude oil and natural gas production), manufacturing, public utilities (electricity, gas, and water), construction, services (including public administration and defense), and activities that are not adequately defined or are not reported. The classification of employment status in the Iranian census is based on the International Classification of Status in Employment adopted by

7. These three censuses will be referred to either as MAI, *Census 1976, Census 1986,* and *Census 1996* or as MAI 1980, 1988, and 1997 in the context of references/sources.

the International Labor Office (ILO 1996, 1104–5). This classification defines workers' status in employment on the basis of their contractual relationship, which is closely associated with the property relations in the production process (63). This is necessary information for any study of class structure, yet few countries provide the data on employment status, for practical or political reasons. Interestingly, such a classification was adopted by Markaz-e Amar-e Iran for the census of population during the Shah's regime, and the necessary data have been gathered quite consistently in the various censuses in the pre- and postrevolutionary periods.

The Iranian census defines employment status in six categories: employers, self-employed workers, wage and salary earners employed by the private sector, wage and salary earners employed by the state (including those employed by parastatal enterprises, *Bonyads*), unpaid family workers, and those individuals whose employment status is not specified or is not reported. In the past two censuses wage and salary workers of the cooperatives are specified as a separate category. In this study, we have added these workers to the number of private sector employees.[8]

The Iranian census relies on the ILO's International Classification of Occupations (ILO 1996, 1110–11; 1969) to differentiate major occupational groups according to their skills and expertise. Workers are classified based on their area and level of expertise ranging from high-level scientists and administrators to clerical and skilled production workers and the unskilled manual workers in various economic activities.

The Iranian censuses of population for 1976 and 1996 consider age ten as the threshold for entering the labor force. However, the minimum age for being included in the labor force in the census for 1986 is only six. Thus, the number of those children in the active labor force between ages six and nine (nearly all among family workers) must be subtracted from the total number of those children in the active labor force for 1986 to make the three sets of data comparable.

We rely on the cross-classification of occupational status, economic activities, and occupational groups to deduce the class nature of the Iranian workforce and construct the social hierarchy of work in Iran in the postrevolutionary years.

---

8. In 1996, the number of wage and salary earners of the cooperatives was only 56,715, compared with 3,270,472 who received their wages or salaries from the private sector (MAI, *Census 1996*, 190).

In the following chapters the data for any year are from the census of the corresponding year, unless otherwise indicated. That is, to avoid inserting identical references, we cite bibliographical references only for data from other sources. The only exception will be tables and figures, for which census sources are cited as well.

2

A Conceptual Framework
for Analysis of Social Classes

THERE ARE MUCH AMBIGUITY and many controversies in the study of social classes. Our intention is not to resolve all these debates. Yet in our study
of the class nature of the Iranian workforce, we need to reduce ambiguities in
the meaning of the terms that we use and to define our conceptualization of
social classes. Subsequently, we will operationalize our interpretation of class
structure in the case of Iran.

The Basic Elements of Class Structure

The general framework of our class analysis in this study is influenced by John
E. Roemer (1982, 1994), Rosemary Crompton (1993), Rosemary Crompton and Jon Gubbay (1977), and John Scott (1996), and is mostly consistent
with the views of Erik O. Wright (1997, 2001). A study of social class requires
an understanding of its structure and structural relations, as well as awareness
of how human actions shape these structural relations. Economic systems
bring individuals together in economic activities (or processes) of production
and distribution. These individuals have different rights and power over the
inputs used in the production of goods and services and over the distribution
of the output. The differential ownership of inputs that are used in economic
activities is the source of differential economic rights and power, which determine the social relationship between people and make up social relations in
economic activities.

Class relations are formed when the ownership of these means of economic activities gives rise to differential rights and power over the appropriation of the output of economic activities. The differentiated access to, and
control of, property in economic activities leads to inequality in the amount
of labor given and received. This process is known as appropriation, when the

advantage of one group causes the disadvantage of another (Roemer 1982, 21). In this sense, classes exist in relation to each other, and the concept of class reflects relations between people through the ownership of the means of economic activity. Such a social relationship constitutes a class structure, which is, more or less, a stable relationship between those who own the means of economic activities and those who don't.

Social relations that are formed in economic activities define class locations, which give rise to antagonistic class interests. Class interests may lead to class action when members of a class become aware of their common interests and the content of their antagonistic relations with other classes. The awareness of social relations is class consciousness.

Class in a Capitalist Society

A capitalist economy is a generalized commodity production system, based on differentiated private ownership of scarce economic resources. The differentiated ownership results in decentralized economic decisions by the owners of these resources. The market brings together the decentralized decisions of the participants in all economic activities. Differential ownership of economic resources leads to a gradational inequality of income or material conditions of the participants in economic activities, which in turn, gives rise to an essential distinction between those who own and those who do not own these resources. This unequal relation generates classes that exist only in relation to each other.

In a market economy, this relationship involves the appropriation of part of the value by those participants who control economic resources. However, it is within the work process that the appropriation of labor effort, or exploitation, takes place. Exploitation is "the control of a valuable . . . resource from which" one can "extract returns only by harnessing the efforts of others," whom one excludes "from the full value added by that effort" (Tilly 1998, 86–87).[1] Irrespective of the source of the ownership of economic resources (inheritance, purchase, chance, or coercion), differentiated rights and power explain the appropriation of labor effort, and, therefore, common interests in economic activity for those individuals who employ, on one side, and for those who are employed, on the other. Hence, the basis of any class structure is the relationship that is formed in economic activities within the

1. See Wright (1997, 10–11) on criteria of exploitation.

work process. These common interests result in a class location that has a relational content with the location of those who contributed to the creation of value. That is, paraphrasing Tilly (1998, 87), this relationship constitutes a class structure that is based on exploitative inequality: one location coexists with other unequal relations across that location; the location and the unequal relations reinforce each other. Thus, what people have (ownership of economic resources) and what people do with what they have (reflected in employment relations in the work processes) determines relations in economic activities (Wright 1997, 30–31).

Lifelong Opportunity and Class Analysis

Differentiated rights and powers over the utilization and disposition of economic resources in economic activities generate "strategic alternatives people face in pursuing their material well-being" (Wright 1997, 30). Thus, through work relations and in exchange relations in the market, those who own economic resources and those who don't receive differentiated lifelong income in the form of profit, interest, rent, and wages. This differential lifelong income (wealth, when accumulated) may change the command of people over resources, relatively or absolutely. The strategic interest of the individuals who acquire the upper hand in this process is to maintain the prevailing differentiated social relations, and their access to resources. This structural situation cannot be maintained if the owners-controllers of resources do not reproduce their lifelong opportunities in economic activities. Their lifelong opportunities are combinations of economic, social, and political circumstances that are favorable for the realization of their strategic objective.

In a capitalist economy, the advantageous position of capital can be maintained only if wealth could be accumulated. However, accumulation would be possible only if resources and labor power created value in work relations and value were realized through market exchange. Higher income is put into use for expanding the command over economic resources. Thus, in a market economy, differential control over resources is intimately related to, and is reinforced by, exchange activities. Hence, the distribution of resources that flow from relations in production takes place through the mediation of labor, and by means of markets for goods and services, and markets for financial and physical assets. State, family, and the educational system, each as an institution, contribute to accumulation of financial, physical, and human capital (including cultural assets). Understanding the role of these markets and institutions is crucial in class analysis. In direct interaction with work processes, market exchange generates market capacity for differential wealth distribution or economic life opportunities.[2]

The substance of life opportunity is the reproduction of the command over resources by the individual (and the family). Differentiated life opportunity is manifested in unequal distribution of wealth that is enjoyed by some and contested by others. The interest of those who own scarce resources is to maintain their position as owners and controllers of productive property. This requires production of goods and services and accumulation of capital through production and exchange activities based on differentiated property relations. Thus, life opportunities and disadvantages give rise to distributional conflicts, whereas employment (work or production relations) based on the appropriation of labor effort in economic activities generates production conflicts. Life opportunities are passed on in inter- and intragenerational movements, through family, marriages, kinship, clubs, associations, or inheritance. But they may also be disrupted or lost by factors such as political, social, and economic struggles; economic crises; or economic policies.

In the real world, with the given demographic, sociopolitical, and technological circumstances, the more distinct the life opportunities are, the more well defined and established the class structure becomes. In Iran, particular circumstances have destabilized, deformed, and weakened the relative rigidities and homogeneities of social classes and their corresponding life opportunities. Economic reforms and revolutionary changes are obvious factors in destabilizing the class structure. Significant rural-urban migrations in response to urban economic development, mass exodus of skilled and professional workers fleeing political oppression and economic crises, and protracted wars are circumstances and events that allow rapid and once-and-for-all movements of a large number of individuals between class locations. The abrupt changes among these class locations will have a distinct effect on the interclass movements.

Moreover, a bloated state economic sector, financed mainly by the oil rent, which provides relative autonomy for the state, permits the state to affect the interclass movements of the workforce vastly and directly. The interclass movements caused by any combination of these destabilizing forces take different forms. They may be manifested as career mobility, new differential ac-

---

2. Inequalities in life opportunities are also shaped by the interacting effect of class, status and political power. See Fulcher and Scott (1999, 608), and J. Scott (1996, 208–16).

cess to accumulation of capital (in primitive or nonprimitive forms) by political or other means, or a rent-seeking opportunity. For others, there may be engagement in petty economic activities as a means for survival or dejection and marginalization. In societies that go through political and economic transitions, such fluidities deform and slow down the formation of classes (that is, class in action) by frequent disruption of the process of development of class homogeneity and class awareness, and in the establishment of class associations. These disruptions will impair the realization of common class interests and the consequent action of its members.

In short, production and market relations are in constant interaction with each other, and reinforce one another in their effect on differential control over lifelong income and resources. This interaction solidifies the economic foundation of class relations by maintaining and reproducing the lifelong advantages and disadvantages. To paraphrase Wright (1997, 30–31; 2001, 20), class analysis is about what people have and what people do with what they have, reflected in interrelated social processes of production and exchange, enabling them to get what they want relative to others, and maintaining their advantaged situation, reflected in their life opportunities.

Class in a Capitalist Economy

Is Employer-Employee Bipolar Division Sufficient?

In a capitalist economy the differentiated ownership of alienable economic assets (machines and natural resources) results in the dichotomous relations between two class locations of capitalists (employers) and workers (employees) in economic activities. Yet, in the real world, because of the uneven and combined development of societies, different modes of economic activities or economic structures coexist and relate to each other under the domination of one economic structure.[3] In any capitalist society, the capitalist economy, as the dominant mode of production, is in constant interaction with the state and the petty economic activities in production and distribution of goods and services. These interrelated structures of economic relations are based on differentiated ownership of the means of economic activities, and, therefore, generate different class locations. The concrete composition of these class locations is the result of the historical specificities of the development of any so-

---

3. A mode of production or economic activity is a way of producing a set of relations that provide "a framework of power in which producing occurs" (Cohen 2001, 79).

ciety. However, in abstraction from concrete cases, in a capitalist economy the fundamental determinant of class division is the differential ownership of the means of economic activities that leads to two primary and bipolar classes, capitalists and workers.

Nonetheless, the conceptualization of a structured class location at this level of aggregation and abstraction cannot account for all the complexities of empirical class location. Thus, the definition of a polarized employer-employee class structure is not altogether useful because of the reality of uneven and dynamic development of capitalism. The complexities of actual socioeconomic development in capitalist systems require the recognition of location of the vast numbers of those individuals who are involved in various kinds of relations in their economic activities and within different modes of production. These complexities require decomposition of classes into different estates, to recognize formation of new classes in ambiguous relation with primary classes (Wright 1997, 19–21, 36–37; Crompton and Gubbay 1977, 171–73). The development of capitalism has given rise to pronounced class distinctions and increased similarities among workers within each class, which requires analytical scrutiny of three issues:

1. The definition of the working class. *Who is in the working class?*

2. The connection between employees' authority and employees' skill attributes to their class location, which raises the issue of ambiguous or contradictory class location of the "middle class." *Who is in the middle class?*

3. State employees within the middle class and the working-class locations. *What about state employees?*

Who Is in the Working Class? Development of capitalism has been associated with technological change, progressive socialization of the means of economic activities, and an increasing differentiation of the division of labor. These developments have obliterated some of the traditional distinctions in labor categories, such as "productive" versus "nonproductive" and "manual" versus "nonmanual" labor. Meanwhile, the proliferation of occupations and division of labor has reduced the homogeneity of a class in terms of skills and occupations. Nevertheless, clerks, salespersons, and assembly-line workers all share the economic location of the working class, because they are mere owners of their labor resource. This fact obliges them to enter into an employer-employee relation in work processes. They all share similar market situations in being subjected to the wage mechanism prevailing in the market, and to the instabilities of the labor market. They are engaged in a complex division of labor, in which each kind of labor is coordinated with others who possess differentiated abilities and skills. Yet their employee situation subjects them to the authority and control of employers and managers, and their location differentiates them from professional employees in terms of autonomy in work and receiving any part of the profit.

Despite the common class location of the clerks, salespersons, factory workers, and unskilled construction workers in terms of their lack of ownership of the means of economic activity, there are differences among them that empirical studies have to take into account. These differences are determined by variations in their working conditions and their income. Such variations reflect differentiated market capacities that lead to privileged strata within the working class.

Who Is in the Middle Class? The distinction between employers and employees in the capitalist mode of production and the recognition of self-employed workers with no employees in petty-commodity production and distributive activities are only the first instances of abstraction and analysis in the real world of class studies. Certain long-run structural developments, such as an increase in the complexity of the command structure of the modern firm, the development of high-tech services, and the integral role of scientific research as part of productive forces in relations of accumulation, require elaboration in conceptualization of new class locations.

Employees may differ from each other in terms of their skill and the extent of the authority delegated to them by the employer, for management of the firm, or the degree of autonomy that they enjoy in their work. These attributes of employees generate differential bargaining power in production relations and in the market, favoring employees who own skills or credentials and are in positions of exercising managerial power (organizational assets) and enjoy various degrees of autonomy. These differentiations give rise to gradational differences for economic and life opportunities of managerial and professional employees. Therefore, those individuals who neither own property nor have skills, credentials, or organizational assets and have little autonomy in their work process fall in the working class.

In modern market economies, capitalists do not merely own (and therefore control) means of economic activities. They also control their employees' labor effort in the process of creation, realization, and distribution of value in production and exchange processes. The control over the labor effort involves surveillance, positive-negative incentives, and different forms of hierarchies. Crompton and Gubbay state that "the functional distinction between control and coordinated labour tends to be realized correctly in disjunct role complexes, but this separation is not now complete nor is ever likely to be. Those who carry out both control and coordinated labour are in an objectively ambiguous position" (1977, 171). Thus, the employees who find themselves in objectively determined positions of controlling and coordinating labor functions would identify with the objective of both capital as well as the collective labor. However, this functional distinction between control and coordinated labor in the development of capitalism leads us to identify some of the employees in the contradictory class locations because of the dimensions of organizational assets/authority or skills/credentials of their class location.

In addition to the ownership of scarce economic resources, employers control strategic decisions. They hire employees, evaluate their work, and provide incentives for their performance within different forms of hierarchies. In short, the command (domination) or authority in economic relations follows property relations and could be implemented in different forms as the market system and division of labor develop, in the process of economic activities and in the labor market. Thus, managers and administrators in modern economic systems are delegated by employers to wield authority (power) in economic processes. In this capacity, managers who are hired by their employers (capitalists) and are, therefore, dominated by employers, in turn, exercise authority over other employees. The occupants of such strategic positions usually receive more income. This additional income is for their managerial labor power. It is a "loyalty rent" and is a part of the profit of owners of the means of production. This ability of managers results in a privileged appropriation location within the employee class (Wright 1997, 20–22).

According to Wright, the ownership of inalienable organizational and skill/credential assets by employees such as managers, administrators, and professionals that leads to rents levied on the property-owning class differentiates middle-class (contradictory or ambiguous class) locations from the working-class, capitalist, and petty-bourgeoisie locations.[4]

The possession of high skills, as enhanced and complex labor power and expertise, in its cognitive and physical forms, also signifies the potential ability for employees to enjoy a privileged appropriation location within a class structure in the form of "skill rent" in the labor market. The sources of this rent, aside from salaries for the reproduction of the enhanced labor power,

---

4. The exercise of organizational control and the autonomy associated with skills/credentials in these contradictory class locations are conceptualized as relational, even though Wright asserts that in reality they can also be gradational (1997, 20–23, 30–31).

could be different kinds of inequalities that exist in the society and give rise to a privileged position for skilled employees. This rent could be the result of differentiated access to "social capital" (such as access to high-quality education, networks, and information), "cultural capital" (for example, appearances, accent, and manners that could be different in different times and places), and even genetic endowments (Wright 1997, 22–23). The possession of special skills and control over knowledge also enables such employees to enjoy relative autonomy at work and relative freedom from control by owners and managers. Therefore, in order to encourage the cooperation of these employees, owners may create a "loyalty rent" by enabling the skilled workers to share in part of the profit (33).

Thus, within production relations, and in distributive activities, some of the employees have a contradictory position between labor and capital. For example, managers and administrators control workers and have access to part of the profits besides their salary, while at the same time they are controlled by owners of capital. Skilled employees enjoy relative autonomy at work and may have access to part of the profits, but they are also creating value or taking part in the realization of it (Wright 1997, 19–23).

It is also important to point out that differences in skills among the working class generate varied work capacities that result in slightly different work conditions and in wages. These differences will cause internal divisions among workers and may result in the movement from one occupational level to a higher one within the working class. Empirically, however, such gradational differences have not generated significant differences in the life opportunities and lifestyles of the workers.[5] Their children continue to go to the same type of schools, marry within the same class, and face the same probability of being unemployed. Nevertheless, either once-and-for-all jumps in individuals' class locations because of abrupt social changes, movements between classes because of interclass marriages, lottery winnings, or illicit market activities are possible for a few individuals in a class location. However, the delegated authority of managers and administrators, the educational credentials and intellectual skills of professionals, and the degree of autonomy that managers and professionals enjoy in their work situations enable them and their families to have a life opportunity of which the best-paid clerk or assembly worker would never dream. Managerial and professional workers, despite

5. See Savage (2000, 47, 51–68) and Saunders (1990, 77, 88) despite their difference with our class approach. See also Westergaard and Resler (1975, 31–51).

their employee status, claim part of the profits, besides their salaries. For all these reasons, professional, managerial, and skilled workers have an intermediary class location between the capitalist class and working class; hence, they may be called the *middle class*. In the past, most of these people, such as doctors, artists, and lawyers, were self-employed, and many still are. With the development of capitalism and the increase in the complexity of the corporate firm, and with the expansion of the role of the state, many of these professionals have become employees.[6]

In the past, typical employers were owner-managers of their firms. With the professionalization of management, as a result of increased complexity of the corporate structure, capitalists have increasingly delegated the power of running the affairs of the firm to professional managers. Moreover, in the past, the largest group of professional and technical workers was the self-employed petty bourgeoisie. These changes have affected the class location of those employees who possess skills and credentials. Now they have differential access to authority and enjoy relative autonomy in making decisions and shaping their work conditions. The impact of this change on differential life opportunities of these employees is both in production processes and in the labor markets.

Thus, in spite of the centrality of property relations in the definition of class, it is possible for a professional worker (for example, a lawyer or an engineer) to have a higher income and more advantageous life opportunities than some small capitalists. The individuals who occupy these locations may also enjoy differential prestige and social mobility that affect their life opportunities or even determine their strata within a given class. True, class structure is neither a simple cluster of occupations nor only a division of people according to levels of income, status, or education. Nevertheless, the interactions between class structure, occupational structure, and the level of education are important for the understanding of the degree of the workers' security, authority within a formal structure, and status. In reality, at the microlevel, such differential opportunities as the degree of workers' flexibility and ability to interact with others, and at the macrolevel, the dynamics of social and political change and economic development influence the life opportunities of employers and employees, their locations, and the stratification within the class. Yet in the final analysis and in the long run, it is the differential ownership of

---

6. Goldthorpe (1980, 39–40) identifies these people as a service class, as they exercise the delegated authority over other employees on behalf of the state and capital. See also Erikson and Goldthorpe (1992, 35–44), Savage (2000, 68–69, 155–56), and Saunders (1990, 93–97).

economic resources that makes a difference for life opportunities, no matter how differentiated a single class might be in the above attributes. Owning means of economic activities empowers one differently than owning only unskilled labor power or enjoying the fruits of one's education or charismatic personality. Remaining in the working class means having limited autonomy at work.

What about State Employees? Empirical class analysis is further complicated by the existence of the state. States that enjoy monopoly over a valuable source of income have the peculiar advantage of expanding and extending the apparatuses of the state without being fully constrained by their ability in extracting taxes from the citizens. The states in oil-exporting countries are in this peculiar position. In Iran, the state has benefited from a substantial source of income from oil revenues since the mid-1930s. From the early 1960s the state became increasingly more reliant on oil revenues, expanding its bureaucracy, military, and social and economic activities without any need for increased taxation. In the 1970s, with the huge increase in oil revenues, the Iranian state became fully an oil-based state, which was inherited by the Islamic Republic in the 1979 revolution. The Islamic Republic has a giant administration and bureaucracy, large military and paramilitary forces, and monopolistic power in many economic activities. In this situation, the state dominates and overshadows all other power relations and their associated conflicts in the society.

The class location of state employees should be examined within the context of a class analysis in a capitalist society. For the purpose of an empirical analysis we find Erik Wright's conceptualization of state employment relevant and useful (1997, 459–64). From Wright's perspective, the state is composed of internally divided apparatuses that have varied and nonunitary functional relationships to the dominant economic system in the society. In a capitalist society, the state has two internally divided apparatuses that have different functional relations to the economy. We recognize them as "political state" or "political functionaries" and "decommodified state services" or "social services" for brevity (462). The state may also, to varying degrees (especially in developing countries), take a direct part in the production of goods and services for the market, referred to as the state's "economic activities."

Many aspects of these activities of the state are influenced by market parameters, such as market wages and salaries, the price of scarce resources in the market, availability of foreign exchange, and interest rates on domestic or international borrowing or lending. These activities are also subject to management (control) of labor's effort, and require long-run strategic decisions based on expectation of future market conditions. In short, state activities should be cost-effective because of the constraint in the state's budget (from taxes or other revenues) in its effort to obtain resources from the market. Yet in the state's activities, economic ownership (that is, the ability to make long-run decisions) is at the disposal of top administrators and managers of the state. They possess the delegated control over labor, capital, and other resources at the disposal of the state (Crompton and Gubbay 1977, 175–76).

"The political state" consists of executive and administrative, legislative, and judiciary branches of the government. It also includes the coercive arms of the government—the police, military, and the paramilitary groups. The primary long-run function of these organs is to protect and facilitate the re-production of capitalist social relations. Because of its functions and the forms of its employment relations, particularly in coercive forces, we place those individuals who are engaged in the "political state" in an ambiguous class category and call them "political functionaries" of the state. Bauman (1974) calls them "political officialdom." Within the category of political functionaries, however, we distinguish among various major categories. The legislators, judges, and high-level government executives (ministers and their deputies, bureau chiefs, at the national and provincial high-level bureaucrats), high-level officers of the coercive forces, and professional and technical workers (accountants, financial analysts, lawyers, physicians, engineers) are grouped as "administrative and managerial" and "professional and technical" employees. These workers are, in many ways, similar in their characteristics to the middle-class workers.

The "lower-ranks" category is the rank and file of political functionaries. Some of these workers are the civilian rank-and-file workers of the various ministries and bureau offices. The rest are members of the armed forces. Whereas the first subgroup (civilian workers) may be, in many respects, close to the working class, the second is mostly ambiguous. Most peculiar among the members of the armed forces is the category of military draftees and temporary volunteers. Their "employment" relations have little to do with the labor market or wage labor, although once their period of compulsory or voluntary service is over, they, mostly, join the rank of the working class or the petty bourgeoisie.

The second apparatus of the state is engaged in production of decommodified (nonmarket) services, like public education, public health, and public recreation. These functions are carried out, principally, by skilled professionals and technical workers (for example, teachers, physicians, and nurses), administrators and managers (high-level bureaucrats), and a supportive staff of rank-and-file workers (such as custodians, secretaries, and clerks). Those employees in the decommodified social services of the government are essential in the reproduction of social relations. They receive market wages, are controlled and coordinated, and are subjected to the long-run strategic decisions of the state with respect to its revenues, budget constraints, and efficiency concerns.

In Iran, before and after the revolution, state-owned enterprises produced a long list of products and services, from petroleum, cigarettes, and cement to banking, communication, and transportation services. These endeavors are the "economic activities" of the state. Employment in these enterprises is composed of the same categories of wage- and salary-earning employees as in the private sector. They include laborers and managers in various occupational categories, from administration and management to production, sales, and services. They are in all major activities, including industries, construction, and services. Complete separation of state employees in the production of decommodified services and in economic activities is not always empirically possible. We will view administrators and managers and professional and technical workers as members of the middle class, and the rank-and-file workers as in the working class.

Thus, within the state apparatuses of the political state, decommodified services, and economic activities, we distinguish the state middle class from the working class (see Wright 1997, 659–70). In the middle class or working classes, we view state employees as "mediated" classes.[7] These employees are in mediated classes in the sense that their individual material interests are linked to economic relations within the dominant mode of production, and not through their personal jobs in the private sector. In such situations, the state provides the mechanism through which people in political and decommodified jobs and those individuals employed in the economic activities of the state are indirectly linked to the class structure. State ties constitute the important basis for mediated class locations and relations.

Occupations and Class

The empirical study of class locations and the operationalization of class typology require the elucidation of three interrelated issues. First, we should

---

7. See Wright (1997, 26–27) for the general meaning and significance of mediated class locations and relations.

justify the validity of the use of occupational data for the construction of empirical class structure. Second, our study should be clear on the class assignment of men-women and the gendered and ethnicity aspects of class. Finally, we should address the correspondence among class, occupation, gender, and the social hierarchy of work.

In modern societies work is related to "jobs." Individuals, men and women, fill these jobs or occupations with a formal or informal contract. Yet an occupation is not only the work one has to perform or a simple division of labor. It is also an indicator of marketable resources that one commands and controls, and the power and prestige associated with them (Fulcher and Scott 1999, 608).[8] Jobs are associated with formal and informal work contracts concerning the rights and obligations governing employers and employees relations.[9]

Occupations, like class locations, have characteristics that are independent of the holder of the occupations. Being agents of employers, employees are obliged to act according to the interests of employers in economic processes. In addition, employment contracts (formal or informal) are not complete in identifying all the details of employees' responsibilities for an efficient performance according to the profit motive of employers. To make sure that employees work consistently toward the profit object of the employer, some kind of control of employees by employers would be necessary. The kind of control varies by position of the employees. In addition, flexible or inflexible working hours, salary versus hourly wages, and formality of monitoring job performance associated with different major categories of occupations, such as blue collars versus white collars, are important discriminating attributes of employment relations for class locations within employee groups.[10] Therefore, the study of class as a relational concept, and differential

8. The use of occupational data for class analysis in different schools of thoughts has been scrutinized widely. See, for example, J. Scott 1996, Fulcher and Scott 1999, Giddens 1984, Marsh 1986, Marshall 1988, Reid 1981, and Hakim 1980. For a survey of debates on class analysis as well as a neo-Marxist critique of the use of occupations in empirical class analysis, see Hindess 1987; Crompton 1993, 1989; and Wright 1997.

9. For these reasons, in modern societies, "the background of the class structure, and indeed the entire reward system. . . , is the occupational order. Other sources of economic and symbolic advantage do coexist alongside the occupational order but for the great majority of the population, these tend to be secondary to those driving from the division of labor" (Parkin 1971, 18).

10. In this sense, our conceptualization relies partly on neo-Weberian studies like Erikson and Goldthorpe 1992; Goldthorpe and Hope 1974; Goldthorpe 1980; Levy and Joye 1994,

life opportunities are enhanced only by occupational data that can be controlled for class axes of ownership of the means of production, authority, and skills. Such regrouping of aggregate occupational statistics is a close proxy for class locations and class relations.[11]

In our empirical study, individuals' occupations are controlled for three explicit class dimensions. As such, the structure of occupations is a reliable proxy for the mapping of the class nature of the employer-employee relations in the workforce.[12] Therefore, it is possible to rely on occupational titles for approximating class structure, as long as the above analytical distinctions between class and occupation are respected. These analytical distinctions are not insurmountable in our study. First, the objective is an examination not of social classes in action (class for itself) but of the class nature of the employed workforce in Iran and its change in the period 1976–96. Second, in our study of class relations among the employed workforce in Iran the primary axis of class location is ownership of the means of economic activities, and, therefore, employer-employee relationship in production and exchange processes is the most significant factor of consideration. The closest indicator of this conceptualization of class location is occupational data that classify workforce in terms of those who employ others because they own the means of production, those who are hired by the owners of means of production because they themselves possess none, and those who work with their own means of production without hiring any paid employees. Therefore, no matter what the occupation of an employer, a self-employed worker, or an employee is in the census data, the individual occupies a capitalist, a petty bourgeois, or an em-

---

316–21; and Evans and Mills 1998, 87–90. However, neo-Weberians, despite their recognition of ownership criterion in the identification of class types, are mainly concerned with the distinctions in "class situations" among employees. They see these employment relations as attributes of a social structure. Therefore, they too see social classes as a relational phenomenon and not as just a hierarchical list of occupations.

11. Yet in spite of the use of occupational data by different theoretical approaches to class and stratification analysis, the empirical research on class structure has been challenged by the loose correspondence between class locations and occupational categories in census or survey data. Nevertheless, even the critics concede that "employment or occupational class will not cease to be a significant variable employed in a wide range of empirical investigations: it is simply too useful" (Crompton 1993, 190).

12. See Wright 1997, Wright and Singelmann 1982, Parkin 1971, Golthorpe 1980, Erikson and Goldthorpe 1992, and Savage 2000, among others, for empirical studies on class structures.

ployee location, respectively. However, if we disaggregate among the employees those workers whose occupations are managerial-professional from those who have a clerical, services, agricultural, or production job, we have close proxies for the middle class and working class.

In addition, Iranian decennial census data rely on comparable definitions and classifications of major categories of occupations in terms of employer and employee relationship and ownership of the means of production. This factor is indispensable for a study of changes in class-employment position of the workforce. Nevertheless, depending on our objectives, and at the same time because of the lack of comparable data in 1976–96 for certain aspects of our study, we might either introduce sublocations within fundamental class locations and contradictory locations or combine some of them in order to map a smaller-category typology.

Class, Gender, and Ethnicity

Gender and ethnicity, in an interplay with class structure, are sources of inequality of lifelong opportunities. They are embedded, overtly or covertly, in the social structures. They have persisted for a very long time, and have their own patterns of disadvantages. Gender, ethnic, and class inequality intersect and interact with each other and are difficult to separate. Gender and ethnic categories are not, however, class phenomena. As a structured inequality, class relations are independent of division and inequalities reflected in gender and ethnic relations (J. Scott 1996, 201–3; Wright 1997, 247–48). Yet a class typology that combines ownership, authority, and skill credentials with an occupational classification should allocate men and women, and people of different ethnicities, to relevant class locations.

Class assignment of women and the gendered aspect of class relations were neglected for a long time by major approaches to class analysis.[13] The sphere of economic activities, be it in work or market situations, is gendered. Occupational segregation by gender gives rise to inequality in wages and salaries for occupations that are considered "women's work," compared to

---

13. Some neo-Weberians assign class situations only to men (Goldthorpe 1983) or identify class position for the household by considering the individual with the highest income as the head of the household (Erikson and Goldthorpe 1988). Thus, it is not the individual but the family that is considered the unit of class analysis, and, therefore, the class position of the family is the position of the head of the household, who is usually a male.

others, and even within the same occupations (Crompton 1993, 93–97; and A. M. Scott 1986, 200–203). The gendered nature of the occupational structure, which is the manifestation of class relations, permits us to take occupations as proxies for gendered distinctions and class locations. In market economies, jobs (occupations) are held by individuals, and because jobs may reflect class locations, individuals, men and women, married or single, will be the appropriate unit of analysis. In Chapter 6 we will examine the nature of gendered class relations in Iran. Unfortunately, little data are available on ethnicity and occupations in Iran, so we are unable to pursue this important line of inquiry.

We need to point out that our study explores the changing pattern of the class structure of the Iranian workforce in the 1976–96 period. An examination of class formation, consciousness, and struggle is beyond the scope of this book.[14]

The Social Hierarchy of Work

The study of the class nature of gender and spatial divisions in the Iranian workforce requires the construction of a "social hierarchy of work." Lawson (1990), Faulkner and Lawson (1991), and Brown, Mandel, and Lawson (1997) have examined the social hierarchy of work by applying Wright's conceptualization of class to the case of Latin American countries.

The social hierarchy of work is a complex structure in which class, occupation-employment, and gender in rural and urban areas are brought together in a relational and hierarchical manner. The construction of such a structure enables us to focus on the nature of work and economic power relations in interaction with gender relations, ethnicity, and special divisions.

In our study, class is a relational concept based on three dimensions of the ownership of the means of production, organizational assets, and skill credentials. These class relations are reflected in the social hierarchy of work for men and women, as well as their spatial distribution in different types of occupational groups.

14. On the problem of class and consciousness, that is, the relationship between the objective and subjective conditions in class analysis, see Wright 1997, chaps. 13 and 16, and the neo-Weberian interpretation in J. Scott 1996, chaps. 3 and 8. Crompton views Wright's approach as "processual." She favors more "fluidity" and "contextual specificity" in class analysis (1989, 583).

Moreover, the concept of class as a principal attribute of power distribution is by nature a relational hierarchy. Production-distribution relations are founded on differential rights and power over scarce resources, and for this reason they result in domination and subordination in work relations. This means that social relations in economic activities, that is, class relations, are combined with hierarchies as boundaries separating individuals or groups of persons with a set of asymmetric social ties (Tilly 1998, 47; and Westergaard and Resler 1975). Thus, the relational character of class structure results in a hierarchical order that is observed with reasonable certainty in occupational orders and indexes of income and wealth. As such, occupations, income, and wealth become manifestations of the underlying class relations (Korpi 1978, 19–20).

Mapping Class Locations and Operationalization of Class Typology

We summarize our discussion in this chapter in a schematic view of class locations in a market economy in figure 2.1. This schematic presentation of our class typology is a slightly modified version of Wright's nonelaborate class taxonomy based on three axes: property relations, organizational assets/authority, and possession of scarce skills/credentials (Wright 1997, 24–25). In our theoretical analysis, and our empirical verification, we recognize the individual, rather than the family (household), as the unit of analysis within the class structure.[15] Our schematic view also reflects this theoretical and analytical vantage point. In this typology, we rely on "jobs" or occupations (employment) of the workforce for the analysis of the class location of individual women and men.

In general, the ownership of the means of economic activities defines the capitalists as employers, and the petty bourgeoisie as nonemployers. Similar to Wright's schema, we rely on four locations for nonowners of the means of production, and differentiate them from each other in terms of relations to authority and skill or expertise. However, because of the importance of the role of the state in employment in Iran, unlike Wright, we divide each of these locations into different estates or strata in terms of private and state employees, and the latter are further divided into political functionaries in social-economic activities. The middle class's contradictory locations (in private or

15. The only exception in our empirical study is examination of the income-expenditures inequality, for which only household data are available.

Figure 2.1
Class Typology

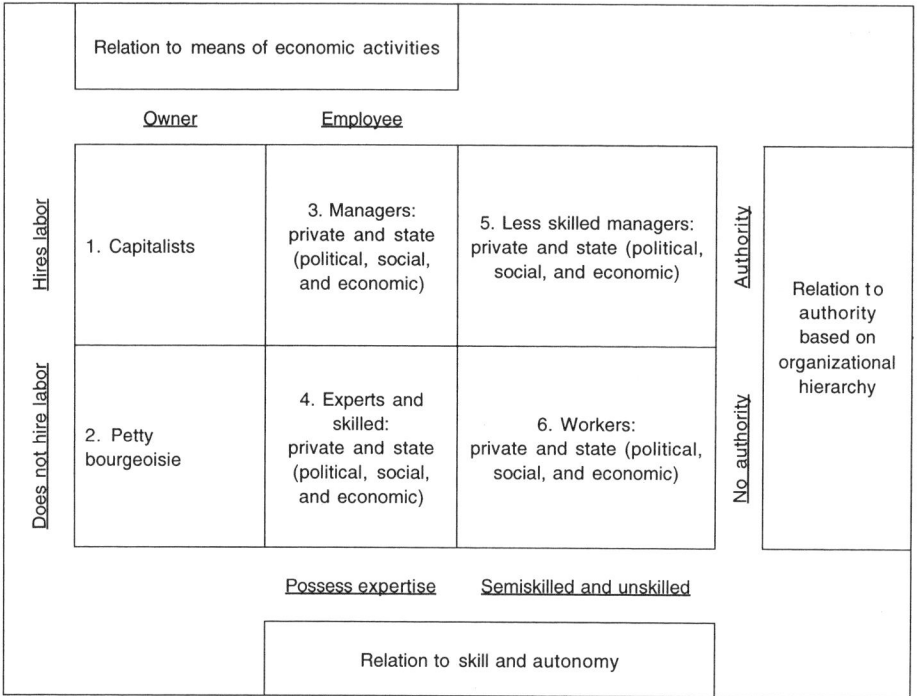

	Relation to means of economic activities			
	Owner	Employee		
Hires labor	1. Capitalists	3. Managers: private and state (political, social, and economic)	5. Less skilled managers: private and state (political, social, and economic)	**Authority** — Relation to authority based on organizational hierarchy
Does not hire labor	2. Petty bourgeoisie	4. Experts and skilled: private and state (political, social, and economic)	6. Workers: private and state (political, social, and economic)	**No authority**
		Possess expertise	Semiskilled and unskilled	
		Relation to skill and autonomy		

state employment) consist of managers and experts who control the labor effort or possess scarce skills and credentials.

Depending on our empirical-analytical objectives in other chapters, and the availability of data, we may introduce subgroups within primary class locations and contradictory locations presented in class typology in figure 2.1.

A serious challenge in our study is the discretionary aspect of the operationalization of abstract concepts in terms of concrete empirical data. At the outset we noted that our study is mostly consistent with Wright (1997).[16] In our interpretation of Wright's approach to class analysis, class locations can be defined by cross-classification of organizational assets/authority and

16. The three axes of ownership of resources, authority, and skills exercised in work relations was originally formulated by Erik O. Wright and his colleagues (1982) in an explicit manner in their empirical study of the class structure in the United States. Wright (1997) has applied this class conceptualization to the cases of advanced capitalist economies.

skills/credentials that generate differential life opportunities in economic activities. Class dimensions of property, organizational assets/authority, and skills have to be measured by indicators that are always underdetermined conceptually. These indicators must be brought together and represented by aggregate variables that operationalize our class typology. In the absence of a detailed and comprehensive survey we have relied on the detailed occupational censuses. By reclassifying occupational data in aggregate categories that approximate property-authority-skill axes we have constructed the class composition of the Iranian employed workforce in 1976, 1986, and 1996 (table A.1 in the Appendix). In a later chapter we will introduce operational definitions of major classes in Iran.

In order to relate the social hierarchy of work to the actual occupational data of the Iranian decennial censuses we modify Lawson's (1990) classification. Such modifications are partly conceptual and partly data driven.[17] Our work classification for the case of Iran differs from Lawson's scheme in several ways. First, we do not subdivide major occupational status categories into economic activities because a social hierarchy of work is more reflected in occupational status groups than in economic activities. Second, instead of Lawson's classification for the employees in terms of their level of skill, we assign these levels of skills to the conventional occupational groups, such as professionals, production workers, and so on. Thus, professionals and technical workers are more skilled than clerical, sales and services, agricultural, and production workers in our classification.

Tables A.3, A.4, A.5, and A.6 in the Appendix display the social hierarchy of work for the employed workforce in Iran. These tables have been constructed by cross-classifying census data in three types of matrices for the employed workforce. These matrices are occupational status–economic activities, occupational status–major occupational groups, and major occupational groups–economic activities, and their interlacing is based on the three axes of class locations.

In our depiction of the social hierarchy of work we classify work groups into upper and lower categories to note the many attributes of the workforce. The upper-level work group approximates the advantaged positions of the

---

17. Lawson's social hierarchy of work (1990) includes owners of productive resources who employ labor, the self-employed, managers, and skilled autonomous, semiskilled autonomous, unskilled, and unpaid workers. At the same time this structure classifies each category in major economic activities and, in the case of employees, in private and public sectors.

employed population in comparison to the disadvantaged groups in terms of economic property, authority, and skill/autonomy in economic activities in production and market situations. Thus, the upper-level work group includes capitalists and modern petty-bourgeoisie managerial, professional, and technical employees of the private and state sectors. The lower level brings together the traditional petty bourgeoisie: unpaid family workers, unspecified employees, and the private-state workers in clerical, sales, services, agriculture, and production occupations.

Final Words

We rely on the above conceptualization of social stratification for the empirical study of class nature of the Iranian workforce and its change in 1976–96 for the following reasons. First, our approach facilitates the structural analysis of class relationships. Second, this approach enhances the understanding of inequality in the ownership of the means of production, differential life opportunities, and the pattern of socioeconomic change in the long run. Third, the empirical application of this framework of class analysis that leads to the construction of the class structure of the Iranian employed workforce can explain the objective structural changes in the balance of economic power, the relative rise and fall of collectivities of people in relation to each other. Fourth, this class approach and its tools of analysis cast light on the relative contraction and expansion of private and state economic sectors and different modes of economic activities that reflect the developmental capacities of the economy in the 1976–96 period. Finally, our study of the sources of change in different aspects of the attributes and peculiarities of the class nature of the Iranian workforce informs us about the class capacities of those individuals who in the existing setup, in the postrevolutionary years, in terms of work situation, gender relations, employment and unemployment, and income, have acquired advantaged life opportunities and those who have not.

3

Postrevolutionary Economic Crisis

Structural Involution and Deinvolution

REVOLUTION IS A SOCIAL RUPTURE. It disrupts the "normal" functioning of social activities and disturbs the existing social relations, particularly in the domain of production. The intensity of disruptions in economic activities depends upon the potency of the social upheaval and the antagonism of the revolutionary movement toward the existing social relations of production. Revolutionary movements jeopardize the security of capital and undermine the sanctity of private property rights. Owners of capital and property are threatened. They take cover by minimizing their outward presence and their exposure to risks arising from social turmoil. They also search for maximizing their liquidity and mobility. These strategies imply decapitalization of industries, excessive borrowing, flight of capital to safe havens of foreign banks and currencies, and real or bogus bankruptcies.

In the revolutionary period, the state becomes paralyzed and its machinery dysfunctional. The inability of the state in fulfilling its functions in facilitating the accumulation process intensifies the crisis of production. Crisis continues in the postrevolutionary period, when the definition and establishment of a new economic order become the subject of an intense political struggle among contending social forces.

We argue that "postrevolutionary economic crisis" is a distinct economic phenomenon, resulting from a postrevolutionary structural crisis. Furthermore, we argue that in the past two decades Iran has been plagued by an economic crisis of the postrevolutionary type, the outcome of open social confrontation over the definition of a new social order.

In these circumstances, political instability and social turmoil, with a severe expression of antagonism toward capital and property relations, caused the retrenchment of capital, disrupted the accumulation process, and weak-

33

ened, and destroyed, many market institutions in the Iranian economy. The disturbances in international economic linkages accentuated the seriousness of the disruption in the accumulation process. Many capitalists fled the country, and many others curtailed, or even altogether stopped, their activities. Some enterprises were nationalized; many others became simply dysfunctional (A. Rahnema and Nomani 1990; Behdad 1995).

Structural Involution

The outcome of the postrevolutionary crisis is more than simply a decline in output or even an erosion of industries, that is, deindustrialization (see, for example, Amuzegar 1993). The changes in the economy, in these circumstances, are tantamount to the shriveling of capitalist relations of production, and expansion of petty-commodity production with a gargantuan increase in redundant service employment. This is a degenerative process, creating tangles within the existing economic structure, obstructing the accumulation process and aggravating the economic crisis. We call this "structural involution" (Behdad 1994b; Behdad and Nomani 2002).

The term *involution* has been used in political economy by Clifford Geertz (1963) and Andre Gunder Frank (1967), independent of one another, to imply two different, and even opposing, economic processes.[1] Geertz borrows the concept from Alexander Goldenweiser, a cultural anthropologist, who suggests that involution is the "progressive complication" of the existing social pattern without evolving into another (1936, 103). Geertz extends Goldenweiser's notion of involution to explain the development of agricultural production in Java under the Dutch domination in the nineteenth century. The profitable colonial plantation and mining activities could not absorb the high rate of population growth, because they were land and capital intensive. Consequently, the surplus population remained within the traditional wet-rice production, whereby elaboration of the existing system of production enabled everyone to eke out a subsistence existence. Yet the ability of this

1. *Oxford English Dictionary* defines *involution* as "enwrapping, infolding" in seventeenth-century usage. Lord Ernest Hamilton in a book titled *Involution* suggests the meaning of "folding in toward the center . . . [in] the form of an automatic convergence" (1912, preface). Freud uses involution as an equivalent for *Rückbildung,* meaning sexual "regression" (Brennan 1992, 158–60). The term has been used in mathematics (MacDuffee 1925; Olver 1995, 372–408) and graphic and architectural design. The use of the term in human pathology is closest to the conceptualization that we present here. See, for example, Dixon and Mansel 2000.

system to absorb the overflow of the population, albeit at a low level of subsistence, prevented it from either stabilizing or transforming "into a new pattern but rather continue[d] to develop by becoming internally more complicated" (Geertz 1963, 81).

Andre Gunder Frank employs the concept of involution as a corollary of the dependency theory in his study of Latin American economies. Frank argues that in 1930s, when international linkages of Brazil were weakened by the depression of its "metropolis," Brazil enjoyed a spurt of economic growth. Frank calls the growth experience "active capitalist involution" (1967, 174–90). He does not refer to either Goldenweiser or Geertz in using the term *involution*. It is unlikely that he would have been aware of the use of the term by Geertz, a proponent of the dualistic model of development, which Frank opposed vociferously.

We believe that the alternative conceptualization of involution in the work of Geertz and Frank explains different aspects of a complex phenomenon in the postrevolutionary economy of Iran. The withdrawal of large and oligopolistic capital, many with strong affiliations with foreign capital, and the interruptions in the international economic linkages of the economy, could have provided breathing room for smaller domestic-oriented firms within the Iranian economy (à la Frank). Yet the disruption in the functioning of the market, the inability of the state to facilitate the reproduction process, even its own initial antagonism toward the private enterprises, and the general atmosphere of insecurity of capital and private property caused the withdrawal of large foreign-affiliated capital. Yet in this process, the medium-size domestic capital was not spared from the damage. Moreover, soon the dysfunctional oligopolistic enterprises that had come under the ownership and control of the state or the parastatal foundations regained domination over the economy. Under these circumstances, the initial impetus for the expansion of small inward-oriented enterprises was decimated.

Hence, there was a retrenchment of capital and weakening of capitalist relations of production in the postrevolutionary period. The other side of the coin was an expansion of petty-commodity production. The flow of the large sums of oil revenue into the economy via the distributive mechanisms of the state prolonged this degenerative and characteristically unstable condition of "structural involution."

Structural involution is manifested in sectoral shifts in production and employment, increased peasantization of agriculture, deproletarianization of the labor force, and expansion of service activities in a myriad of occupations such as those jobs held by small retailers, street vendors, and moonlighting cabbies.

We use the term *involution* in Goldenweiser's sense because of the meaning that it has acquired in the literature, namely, a process of change involving elaboration and the entanglement in the existing pattern, without transformation of the pattern itself. We use the term in this general conceptual sense, without subscribing to Geertz's dualistic model and the peculiarities that he attributes to Java's development.[2]

In contrast, the reversal of the involutionary process would be transition of the economic structure toward reconstitution and revitalization of the capitalist relations of production and market institutions, restoration of the accumulation process, proletarianization of labor, and depeasantization of agriculture. We call this reversal process "deinvolution" of the economic structure.

We propose two periods in postrevolutionary Iran. The first period is the years of a fervent search for a populist-statist Islamic utopia, which began with the 1979 revolution and came to a dead end by 1988, when the burden of the war with Iraq and the glut in the world oil market made the populist project of the Islamic Republic of Iran practically defunct. The death of Ayatollah Khomeini in June 1989 was the beginning of the second period, characterized by a policy move toward "economic restructuring," à la the IMF and World Bank. It aimed for a general liberalization of economic activities, including foreign-exchange realignment, decontrolling of prices, reduction of subsidies, and privatization of nationalized enterprises.

In the first period social disturbances, political turmoil, and the open expression of antagonism toward capital and property rights disrupted the accumulation process. These circumstances led to the structural involution in the Iranian economy. In the second period, still in progress as this book goes to print, the Islamic Republic has struggled to reconstitute the institutions of the market and to reinvigorate capitalist relations of production through its economic liberalization policy. Although the state's liberalization policy has not proceeded consistently, it has made notable advances in the reconstruction of market institutions and capitalist relations. Thus, the years of 1989 to the present may be viewed as a period of reversing the transitional changes in the first postrevolutionary decade, or the deinvolution of the economic structure.

2. For a critique of Geertz's involution thesis, see Kahn 1985.

Economic Decline and Structural Involution

The postrevolutionary economic crisis in Iran has been examined extensively.[3] Here, briefly, we tell our story.[4] Economic disruptions began in the fall of 1978. Strikes in large enterprises were the prelude to the revolutionary disruption. Soon the newly formed workers' councils began taking over the enterprises whose owners had fled the country (Bayat 1987; S. Rahnema 1992). In the summer of 1979, banks, insurance companies, and many large manufacturing enterprises were nationalized and brought under the state's ownership.

Revolutionary Islamic Courts also confiscated the assets of those whom the Islamic judges found "corrupt on earth." These confiscations brought under the domain of "public ownership" a large collection of economic assets. Public ownership in Islamic jurisprudence is distinct from state ownership. "Public properties" are at the disposal of the Imam (religious authority), not the state, to be used in strengthening Islam and the society of Muslims. Although in an Islamic state, political and religious authority should conceptually be considered the same, Ayatollah Khomeini chose to keep the confiscated properties as "public" entities and not as state enterprises. As such, they were similar to religious endowments (*waqf*), not subject to state audit and control and only under the disposal of the Imam. Thus, they became quasi- or parastatal enterprises. Bonyad Mostazafan va Janbazan (Foundation for the Oppressed and Disabled) was formed in 1979, with the directive of Ayatollah Khomeini, to hold and manage "public" assets. Soon, other foundations, such as the Bonyad Shahid (Martyr's Foundation) and the Fifteenth Khordad Foundation,[5] were formed (Maloney 2000). We refer to the collection of these parastatal enterprises as *bonyads*, as they are known in Iran.[6]

Takeovers were extensive. The newly formed Islamic state, while defend-

3. See, among others, Coville 2002, Mazarei 1996, Karshenas and Pesaran 1995, Ghaffari 1995, Amuzegar 1993, and Ghasimi 1992.

4. We have told more elaborate versions of this story elsewhere previously. See A. Rahnema and Nomani 1990, Behdad 1995 and 2000, and Behdad and Nomani 2002. This chapter includes segments of the latter three studies.

5. Fifteenth of Khordad 1342 (June 5, 1963) was when Ayatollah Khomeini led widespread demonstrations in Tehran against the Shah. The demonstrations, which soon spread to other cities, were put down brutally by the armed forces. As a result, Khomeini was sent to exile, where he continued his opposition to the Shah.

6. For a review of activities of the *bonyads*, see Aqevli 2004; Khosrokhavar and Roy 1999, 134–36; and Ra'is-Dana 2004. On Bonyad Mostazafan, see Farzin 2004.

ing the principle of private ownership, endorsed, and at times even promoted, the wave of takeovers as a means for mass mobilization. The revolutionary ethos of the new state cast further doubt on the security of property. The Iranian Constitution asserts that "the Iranian Revolution . . . has been a movement aimed at the triumph of all oppressed and deprived persons over the oppressor," condemns "concentration and accumulation of wealth and maximization of profit," and diminishes the place of the private sector in the economy as the residual that will supplement the state and cooperative sectors (Article 44). Although the Constitution recognizes "legitimately acquired" private property (Article 47), the criteria (Article 49) are so vague that any property may be declared illegitimate.[7]

In this environment, production was severely disrupted. By 1981, the gross national product (in constant prices) was only 64 percent of what it was in 1977, before the revolutionary disturbances began. In the same year, value added in "industry and mining" amounted to 87 percent of the 1977 amount. All major economic activities had declined in real terms, except agriculture, which grew at an impressive rate. In 1981 value added in agriculture was 17 percent higher than in 1977.[8] In the same period, gross fixed capital formation (investment) declined drastically. In 1981, the private sector's investment was only 52 percent of the 1977 level (in constant prices), and the state's investment was only 61 percent of the 1977 level. Investment of the private sector in machinery and equipment is a more sensitive index of business outlook. That investment declined by 66 percent between 1977 and 1981.[9] When in 1979 the Provisionary Revolutionary Government provided eighty billion rials of easy credit (at 4 percent interest rate) for resumption of industrial activities, only twenty-five billion rials were borrowed by private enterprises, indicating the serious disruption in the accumulation process in the revolutionary turmoil (BMI 1984, 181).

Moreover, the disruptions in the international economic linkages of Iran, because of domestic disturbances and international antagonism toward the Iranian revolution, aggravated the postrevolutionary economic crisis. The Iranian economy is heavily dependent on imports. More than 80 percent of Iranian imports are intermediate and capital goods, most of which are used in the manufacturing sector. In 1983 more than one-half of the total value of

7. For the Constitution of the Islamic Republic, see Algar 1980.
8. Calculated from BMI (2003, 54–55) in 1997 prices.
9. Calculated from BMI (2003, 62–63) in 1997 prices.

primary and intermediate inputs into Iranian industries were imported. The interruptions in international economic linkages had made procurement of imports uncertain and more expensive, because frequently roundabout ways had to be established for obtaining the needed imports (Alerassool 1993; Alikhani 2000).

Procurement of imported industrial inputs and capital goods became even more seriously impaired when Iran confronted the international oil glut of 1986–88. The oil boom of the 1970s had brought the oil revenues of Iran to about twenty-one billion dollars. In the immediate postrevolutionary years, thanks to the sharp increase in the international oil price, Iran managed to receive oil revenues sufficiently high for paying its high import bill, in spite of some decline in its oil output because of the damages of the war with Iraq. In 1983 Iran received twenty-one billion dollars in revenue from oil exports. By 1985, after oil prices began to fall, this figure had declined to fourteen billion dollars, and in 1986 it dipped to less than six billion dollars. Iran's average import bill hovered around fourteen billion dollars. The war with Iraq, and the cost of obtaining military needs at high prices under economic sanctions in the black market, made the foreign-exchange shortage a more acute constraint for the Iranian economy.[10]

Above all, while the new regime had committed itself to restructuring the economy, it had no clear idea about the parameters of its ideal economic order. All that it could declare was that the new order would be Islamic. Thus, the pull and the push in the struggle of various factions in the Islamic Republic for defining the new economic order took place in the context of a discourse on Islamic jurisprudence. The range of Islamic economic ideals constituted a spectrum from the left of Proudhun to the right of Friedman, yet all toward construction of an Islamic utopia.[11]

Debates continued between different factions of the Islamic state as the economy declined, or at best stagnated (figure 3.1). All major economic activities exhibited a decline, except agriculture. In 1986 gross national income in constant prices was only 63 percent of what it was in 1977. The non-oil gross domestic product was only 5 percent more than in 1977, while the population of Iran had increased by 47 percent in the intervening decade. Industry and mining had remained stagnant in comparison to the prerevolutionary year. Value added in services had declined by 9 percent in comparison to 1977

10. Data from BMI (*Economic Report,* various issues).
11. See A. Rahnema and Nomani 1990 and Behdad 1994a.

(table 3.1), mainly because of the decline in the financial and banking services (by 85 percent), and in public services (by 25 percent). Meanwhile, in services, "trade, restaurant, and hotel" grew by 5 percent, and "real estate and professional services" (mainly because of the increase in the housing rental) increased by 55 percent in this period (BMI 2003, 54–55).

The impressive growth of agriculture, in comparison to other economic activities, in the midst of the revolutionary turmoil and economic disruptions is an interesting phenomenon and deserves an explanation. Most important, the divisibility of land and the Islamic jurisprudential view on land and crop ownership are relevant. In the first postrevolutionary years about eight hundred thousand hectares of fertile land (6 percent of arable land in Iran) was redistributed among landless or small landowning peasants by means of forceful appropriations. When land was appropriated, peasants immediately began cultivating their newly acquired parcels to prove their ownership. The divisibility of land and productive usage of it (in a contrast with manufacturing activities), even with the limited means of the small peasants, made cultivation of appropriated land possible. Moreover, according to Islamic jurisprudence, any land that is not cultivated for a specific period of time may be considered abandoned *(bayer),* and therefore, may be confiscated and redistributed by the

Figure 3.1

Index of Value Added in Major Economic Activities, 1977–2000 (in 1997 Prices)

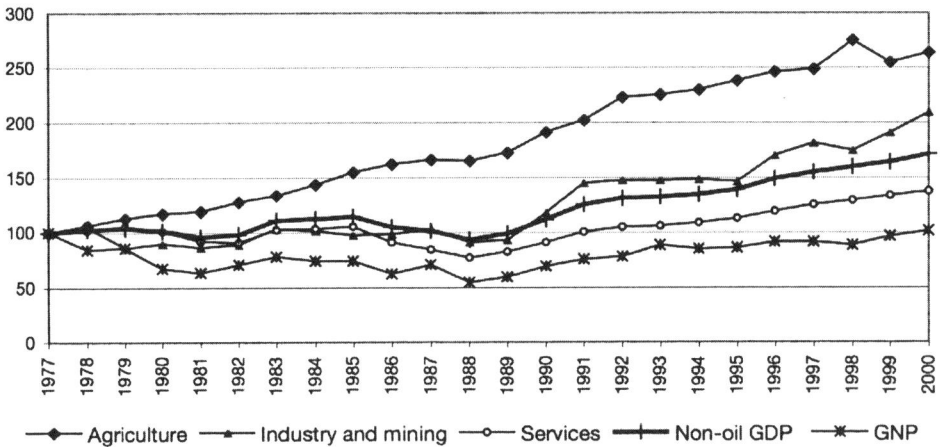

Source: BMI 2003.

Table 3.1

Growth of Value Added in Major Economic Activities in Selected Years, 1977–2000 (in 1997 prices)

	Value-added index				Value added % Δ*			Value added per capita % Δ*
	1977	1986	1996	2000	1977–86	1987–96	1997–2000	1977–2000
Agriculture	100	162	246	264	5.5	4.3	1.7	1.5
Industry and mining†	100	99	170	209	-0.2	5.6	5.2	0.5
Services	100	91	120	137	-1.0	2.7	3.5	-1.3
Non-oil GDP	100	105	149	171	0.5	3.6	3.6	-0.3
GNP	100	63	92	101	-5.1	3.9	2.5	-2.6

Source: BMI 2003.

*Average annual rate of growth.

†Includes construction, electricity, water, and gas.

Islamic state. At the time of the revolution, it was also widely believed, as a matter of Islamic law, that any crop grown on a land, even if illegally acquired, would be the rightful property of the cultivator. Hence, peasants would quickly cultivate the land that they had acquired in the de facto land redistribution of postrevolutionary Iran.

For these reasons, unlike the industrial sector, which became widely dysfunctional because of social upheaval and ownership contestations, the agricultural sector underwent even a more intensive cultivation than the prerevolutionary years. It turned out that what was adverse to urban industrial activities was favorable to agriculture, at least in the short run. In addition, with the disruptions in the international trade of Iran, and the decline in the foreign-exchange earnings of the country, higher reliance on domestic output of agriculture (which relied relatively less on imported inputs than the industrial activities) brought the state to favor this sector more than before in allocation of resources such as credit, infrastructural investment, and even foreign exchange.

The disruptions in economic activities were reflected in the serious decline in the rate of capital formation, in constant prices, in the economy (figure 3.2). Because of the general volatility of the rate of investment over the years we have constructed an index based on the average annual investment over the period of our consideration. We have taken 1977, the last "normal" year prior to the 1979 revolution, as the base year for our index. Over the 1979–86 period, in the depth of the postrevolutionary economic crisis, we note a severe decline in the rate of capital formation (table 3.2). This decline in the rate of capital formation is a manifestation and a source of the structural involution in the postrevolutionary economy of Iran.

The average annual value of investment in the 1979–86 period was only 64 percent of the rate of investment in 1977 (table 3.2). (All values are in 1997 prices). There was a substantial decline in investment by the private sector (to 62 percent of the 1977 rate) and by the state (to 68 percent), as well. Disaggregating the investment of the private sector and the state into construction, machinery, and equipment, we note a more clear picture of the involutionary situation. The decline of capital formation by the state is larger in its construction activities (to 56 percent of the 1977 level) than in machinery and equipment (to 88 percent). This analysis indicates the state abandoned many infrastructural activities of the ancien régime.

More significant from our perspective, with regard to the retardation of capitalist production relations in the involutionary period, is the disaggregated rate of investment by the private sector. In table 3.2 we show that between 1979 and 1986 the average annual rate of investment of the private sector in construction actually increased by 16 percent from the 1977 level.

Figure 3.2
Index of Gross Fixed Capital Formation, by State and Private Sectors, 1977–2000 (in 1997 Prices)

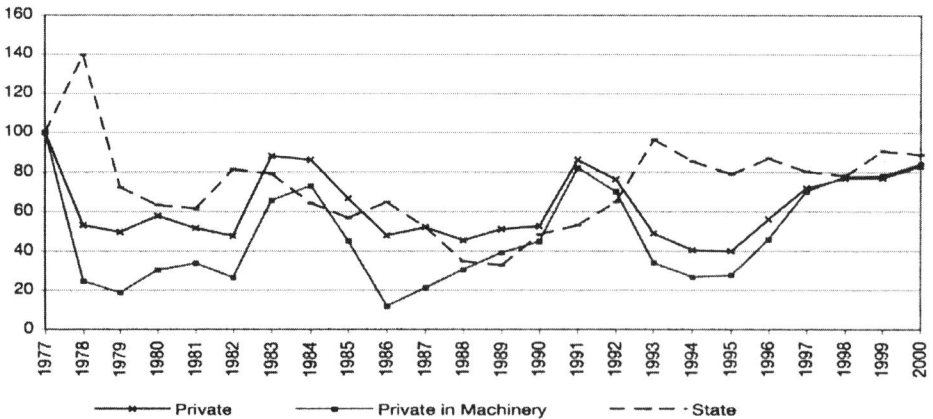

Source: BMI 2003.

Table 3.2
Index of Gross Fixed Capital Formation, 1977–2000 (in 1997 prices)

	1977	1979–86	1987–96	1997–2000	1979–2000
Total	100	64	58	80	64
Private	100	62	55	77	61
Machinery	100	38	42	77	47
Construction	100	116	84	76	94
State	100	68	63	84	69
Machinery	100	88	65	74	75
Construction	100	56	62	90	65
Machinery, total	100	49	47	77	53
Construction, total	100	85	71	84	78

Source: BMI 2003.
Note: Calculated as the average annual capital formation over the period of consideration.

The most significant component of private-sector investment in construction was residential housing. In the postrevolutionary years, residential construction increased in spite of economic disruptions. The liberal mortgage lending policy of the state-owned banks (all banks became state owned soon after the revolution), redistribution of urban land by the state, and the state's encouragement of the formation of housing cooperatives, particularly among state employees, contributed to the rapid rise in residential construction.

Investment of the private sector in machinery and equipment is a more reliable index of the rate of accumulation, or capitalist reproduction, in the economy. Between 1979 and 1986, the private sector's annual investment in machinery and equipment (in constant prices) was, on average, only 38 percent of the 1977 level. Such a sharp decline in investment of the private sector is indicative of the acute interruption in the accumulation process in the ongoing postrevolutionary crisis and its resulting structural involution.

As the economic crisis persisted, and in the midst of the debates on the nature of the ideal Islamic economic order, the day-to-day imperatives of public policy making led the Islamic state to implement ad hoc measures with two pivotal concerns: first, maintaining the requirements for the high rate of mobilization for a costly war with Iraq and, second, mitigating the downward pressure on the living standard of the population in a declining economy. These concerns gave the state a wide scope for intervention in the economy in a myriad of price controls and subsidies in the sphere of production and consumption.

These populist-statist policies provided rent-seeking opportunities for the officials of the regime, mostly the clerics, and their cronies. They congregated in various kinds of affiliation and business arrangements around the nationalized enterprises and, more important, the parastatal foundations, the *bonyads*. In this way, on the landscape of battered capitalism in Iran a small group of giant oligopolies was reconstructed. In the other extreme, the unemployed workers, the migrants to the cities, and the youth entering the labor market found refuge in the vast marshland of urban petty economic activities. Squeezed in between were the midsized capitalist enterprises, which were not only deprived of the scarce industrial input and foreign exchange but also constantly harassed by the official and vigilante protectors of the *mostazafan* (the oppressed) as "blood-sucking," "exploiting" capitalists.

Between 1976 and 1986, the number of "small" manufacturing enterprises (with fewer than 10 workers) increased by 100 percent, to about 330,000. In 1987, these enterprises made up about 97 percent of all manufacturing establishments. On the other hand, 10,000 medium-size firms (with 10–49 workers) and 1,300 "large" (with more than 50 workers) produced 61 percent of the manufacturing output and employed about 50 percent of manufacturing workers. Between 1976 and 1987, the average size of small establishments increased from 1.9 to 2.3 workers (21 percent increase), while the size of the large establishments increased from 294 to 407 workers (38 percent increase). In the same period, however, medium-size firms became smaller, on average, from 29 to 18 workers (37 percent decrease). Thus, in spite of an increase in the number of these firms, their share of employment in manufacturing decreased from 18.5 to 13.2 percent. As the share of all establishments with 10 and more workers in total manufacturing output fell from about 84 to 60–70 percent, the share of medium-size firms in the output of these establishments declined from 28 to 24 percent. Hence, as industrial output stagnated between 1976 and 1987, the medium-size enterprises were squeezed from both sides, by a mass of small workshops, on one side, and the huge state-owned enterprise, on the other.[12]

Economic Liberalism and Deinvolution

Structural involution is manifested in the retardation of the accumulation process and stagnation of the economy. In the first postrevolutionary decade,

12. Data from MAI 1981a, 1981b, 1990a, 1990b.

in the Khomeini era (1979–89), real national income per capita declined by 58 percent, the real non-oil gross domestic product per capita fell by 32 percent (BMI 2003), and fixed capital formation by the state and the private sector (in constant prices) remained significantly less than the prerevolutionary years (figure 3.2 and table 3.2). The decline in the oil revenues between 1986 and 1988, resulting from the glut in the world oil market and the destruction of Iranian oil facilities in the war with Iraq, placed the state's ad hoc economic policy in an untenable situation. In this stagnating economy, it could no longer try to maintain the standard of living of a population that had grown from 38 million to 53 million (by 40 percent) in one decade.[13] Nor could it pay for the high cost of the war with Iraq. It was in these circumstances that on July 20, 1988, Ayatollah Khomeini accepted the United Nations' cease-fire resolution 598 to end the hostilities between Iran and Iraq.

These circumstances revealed the futility of the Islamic utopian dream of the leaders of the Islamic state. Meanwhile, in the Khomeini era, corruption, clientalism, and the war economy had made ample opportunities for "primitive accumulation" for those individuals who had access to the power of the state. Bonyad Mostazafan alone owned four hundred companies with monopolistic power in production of many essential goods, from glass containers, tires, and motor oil to soft drinks, synthetic fibers, sugar, textiles, and dairy products. It had also become in possession of nearly one-half of the total hotel capacity of Iran and was Iran's largest real estate developer and construction company.[14] With assets amounting to about $12 billion (Maloney 2000, 153; Waldman 1992), it became the largest economic entity in the Middle East.[15]

The giant *bonyads* and the networks of their affiliated enterprises have benefited from special privileges and have reaped extremely attractive profits over the years. The foreign-exchange gap and the shortages that developed in the market accentuated the monopolistic position of these networks. Meanwhile, the "unaffiliated" enterprises were deprived of the essentials for keep-

13. Population estimates are from BMI (2003, 70–71). See Chapter 4 for a study of the population and its growth.

14. *Payam-e Emrouz* 4, Feb.–Mar. 1994), 23; *Payam-e Emrouz* 21, Dec.–Jan. 1997–98, 75.

15. Maloney (2000, 153) cites Kazemi (1996, 146) in reporting four hundred thousand workers employed in "thousands of enterprises and properties" under the control of the Mostazafan Foundation. We believe both numbers are exaggerated, if "control" means ownership or management. See Chapter 5 for the number of state employees in economic and service activities. "State employees" in the censuses includes also those individuals in "public enterprises," such as the Bonyad Mostazafan.

ing their businesses running. The battered and denigrated bourgeoisie that had survived the revolutionary turmoil was no match for state enterprises, the *bonyads*, or even the merchants who had close association with the regime. Realizing that the normalization process held little promise for its rejuvenation, the bourgeoisie took its battle to the political arena and raised the banner of economic liberalism, demanding denationalization (privatization) of industries and deregulation of the market.

Two other concurring developments helped to advance the cause of economic liberalism. First, the public had become disillusioned with revolutionary rhetoric and worn out by the prevailing state of siege. Its standard of living had been declining, and it had become the seemingly unlimited supply of martyrs for a war whose senselessness was becoming every day more apparent.[16] The foreign-exchange gap had intensified this state of public disenchantment. Faced with the shortage of foreign currency and the persisting need for war mobilization, imports of items of mass consumption, which were relied upon to mitigate domestic shortages, declined from $2.9 billion in 1983 to $1.5 billion in 1988 (BMI, *Economic Report* for 1983 and 1988). If these circumstances were not enough, the economic burden of the public increased as the government began raising indirect taxes and the price of services that it provided in order to ameliorate its budget deficit, which had increased by the declining oil income and the falling revenues from import taxes. As the economic burden increased, and the revolutionary fervor subsided, people's longing for a program of peace and prosperity intensified.

Second, the acute foreign-exchange crisis and the chronic deficiency in the level of domestic investment brought the Islamic state to abandon its cardinal revolutionary principle in rejecting foreign capital. Sometime in 1987–88 the state had begun borrowing from abroad. It was done secretly because public disclosure of borrowing would have added to the unpopularity of the war. In August 1991, explaining the situation for ending hostilities with Iraq, Hashemi-Rafsanjani, then the president of the Islamic Republic, revealed in a Friday prayer sermon that in 1988, "We had serious difficulties. We had reached the red line in the use of our economic resources and budget. We had gone even below the red line, we had $12 billion debts" *(Kayhan Hava'i* August 14, 1991).

However, external financing, whether borrowing or investment, had been viewed as deeply objectionable. Some Islamic leaders remained opposed

16. See Chapter 4 on casualties of the war.

to foreign borrowing and saw it as "rejuvenation of the dependent capitalist economy of Iran under the Shah." On August 30, 1988, *Kayhan,* a Tehran daily, editorialized, "Our borders must not be opened to dependent capitalism." Similarly, Ayatollah Montazeri viewed foreign borrowing as "selling our country to foreigners" *(Kayhan,* February 18, 1989). But the imperatives of economic reconstruction did not leave any room for revolutionary slogans. The Islamic state was confronted with a large foreign-exchange gap, and foreign borrowing was unavoidable. The First Economic Plan, approved by the Majles for implementation in the years 1989–93, had already projected $28 billion in external borrowing for the duration of the plan.[17] Hashemi-Rafsanjani confronted the issue directly in his Friday prayer sermon in Tehran on January 12, 1990. He stated that foreign capital is not inherently evil and may be used in productive endeavors for the benefit of the society *(Kayhan Hava'i,* January 17, 1990). This announcement marked a major official turnaround in the life of the postrevolutionary government in Iran. But the need for foreign borrowing and foreign investment was seen as so obvious, and already so much practiced, that the justification by Hashemi-Rafsanjani was no more than an official sanction or acknowledgment of the practice.

The move toward external financing had two important implications. First, it was an open admission of the failure of the state in constructing its utopian Islamic economy. Second, to attract foreign capital, the state had to demonstrate its commitment to reconstruction of the market institutions and to the promotion of a free-market economy. A symbolic follow-up to this move was Iran's reception of the IMF–World Bank mission in Tehran in June 1990. It was the first mission of these two international financial institutions to Iran since the 1979 revolution. The visit seems to have been fruitful. Upon its return, the summary report of the mission was published in *IMF Survey* of July 30, 1990, under the heading, "Islamic Republic of Iran Undergoes Profound Institutional, Structural Changes." The report added that Iran's officials "expressed their determination to move forward with broadly based macroeconomic adjustment, encompassing a strengthened role for the private sector and a step by step opening up of the economy." It was the beginning of the move toward economic liberalization in postrevolutionary Iran and the beginning of the deinvolutionary process.

The 1990 invasion of Kuwait by Iraq, and the subsequent Persian Gulf War, was a blessing for the Islamic state at a critical point in its postrevolution-

17. For a study of the First Five-Year Plan, see Ghasimi 1992.

ary transformation. It accelerated the move toward reconstitution of capital-ism ("a strengthened role for the private sector," as viewed by the IMF–World Bank). Disruption in production and export of oil by Iraq and Kuwait caused oil prices to increase. Hence, Iran's oil revenues increased when Iran was in a serious need of acquiring foreign exchange to carry on its reconstruction pro-gram and to pull the economy out of its most serious postrevolutionary de-cline.[18] The oil production of Iran in 1990 increased to 3.2 million barrels a day, from 2.2 million barrels a day in 1986. The price of Iranian light crude oil in the spot market increased from thirteen dollars in 1986 to around twenty dollars per barrel in 1990 (BMI, *Economic Report* for 1986 and 1990). The oil revenues of Iran in 1990 and 1991 increased to eighteen billion dollars and sixteen billion dollars, respectively, in spite of some decline in the price of oil in 1991, and remained above sixteen billion dollars in 1992. This substantial increase in oil revenues generated the growth of the oil-dependent economy of Iran. Imports increased from eleven billion dollars in 1988 to twenty-four billion dollars in 1991. Meanwhile, the non-oil gross domestic product grew by 8.5 percent in 1990, 10.4 percent in 1991, and 7.0 percent in 1992. The increase in the oil revenues and the resulting economic growth created an aura of optimism and enabled the Islamic Republic to muster support for the wis-dom of its policy of economic liberalization, and to further weaken the pop-ulist-statist tendency within the regime.[19]

The liberalization policy of Iran included unification of exchange rates and adoption of a floating exchange-rate system, privatization of nationalized enterprises, decontrolling of prices, and elimination of subsidies. The main-stream view on this standard IMF–World Bank prescription is that by opening the economy to the forces of competition in the marketplace and by mak-ing prices a true indicator of scarcity of resources, productivity and profitabil-ity will increase, production will expand, consumption growth will be con-tained, imports will decrease, exports will increase, and as a result the economy will grow, employment will increase, and, not the least, the foreign-exchange gap will be eliminated. To reach this state of economic fitness the economy needs to undergo a painful period of adjustment, which may metaphorically be similar to "sweating out" the fever after the patient takes the healing medicine. However, if the case has become overly complicated, a high

18. For an account of the reconstruction program in these years, see Amirahmadi 1990, chap. 4.

19. Data from BMI *(Economic Report,* various issues).

dose of the medicine may cause such a convulsion that either the patient dies or the dosage has to be reduced, in which case the relapse of the illness is unavoidable. Such is the story of Iran's experience with the standard liberalization policy.

Iran's multiple exchange-rate policy was an instrument of the Islamic Republic's industrial and social policy. It served two aims: first, to run an industrial structure highly dependent on imports and, second, to minimize the erosion of the standard of living of the mass of the population in a stagnating economy with a high rate of population growth. The artificially low foreign-exchange price provided Iranian industries with low-cost imported inputs. Iranian industries were mostly established between the mid-1960s and the mid-1970s, when "cheap" foreign exchange was becoming ever more abundant, thanks to the increase in the volume and price of Iranian oil exports. Since the largest portion of Iranian imports are industrial inputs and there are few domestic substitutes for them, Iran's demand for imports (thus for foreign exchange) has a relatively low elasticity. That is, only a large devaluation results in a significant decrease in imports.

On the other hand, a devaluation will have only a small effect on export earnings because the export of oil is not affected by exchange-rate changes.[20] The non-oil exports constitute a small fraction of the total value of exports. Only a major increase in their earnings can have an appreciable effect on Iran's total exchange earnings. The issue is accentuated by the fact that non-oil exports have a large import content. Putting together foreign-exchange demand and supply, overcoming even a small foreign-exchange gap needs a large devaluation. This is not to say that a devaluation does not have a positive impact on the size of the foreign-exchange gap. It does, but because of low elasticities on the in-payment and out-payment sides, the foreign-exchange market has a low degree of responsiveness to exchange-rate changes.[21] But a devaluation large enough to overcome the foreign-exchange gap will have drastic effects on an economy so dependent on imports. For example, a 200 percent revaluation of foreign exchange may increase by as much as 100 percent the input

20. It will have only a small effect because oil prices are in dollars and the volume of Iran's exports of oil depends on its international market considerations (mainly OPEC) but not on the rial cost of production of oil.

21. The so-called stability condition is not the issue. The reactions of the foreign-exchange market to the recent changes in the exchange rate of Iran shows that the stability condition is met. See Pesaran 1992, Behdad 1988a, and Lautenschlager 1986 for elaborate discussions of the issue.

cost of an establishment that imports half of its inputs.[22] With little substitution of domestic inputs possible, it is highly improbable that such a large increase in cost could be absorbed by the increase in the efficiency in production, which may result, for example, from privatization of these enterprises. Simply put, many enterprises depending on imported inputs will have to raise their output prices correspondingly or shut down if they cannot because of the state's price control. The widespread price effect of such a devaluation shocks the economy.

The political implications of a devaluation policy in these circumstances are clear. Most directly, the privileged industrialists and merchants who received cheap foreign-exchange quotas and the wide array of consumers who received goods at official prices would be most seriously affected. The first group (including, among others, the *bonyads* and the cronies of the regime) cannot openly defend its privileged position and may easily negotiate with the state for other privileges in the economy. The second group, "the consumers," will be the losers. They will end up paying for the promise of having a better job (or just a job) somewhere in the economy, when it will, they hope, expand, by enduring the devastatingly high rate of inflation. Other policies to reduce domestic absorption by measures such as cutting direct government subsidies for essential food items and increasing the cost of services provided by the government would have a positive impact on reduction of the foreign-exchange gap by squeezing "the consumer," many of whom constituted the popular base of the Islamic state.

The Islamic state began a gradual liberalization of the foreign-exchange market in 1990. In 1991 the cabinet issued a communiqué declaring its decision to privatize nearly four hundred nationalized enterprises.[23] Meanwhile, the government abandoned much of its control over prices of goods produced by the private sector. These liberalization measures were implemented at the opportune time of increasing oil revenues. With confidence in the favorable conditions of the world oil market, in March 1993, the Islamic Republic moved to unify the exchange rates by floating the rial from $1=IR 70 (mostly used for government orders) and $1=IR 600 (for favored enterprises that received exchange quotas) to a "float" of $1=IR 1,542. As prices began to in-

---

22. That is with the assumption that the cost of domestic inputs does not change as the result of the devaluation of the rial. For data on import dependence of various manufacturing activities, see Behdad 1988a.

23. For the details of the communiqué, see Sherkat-e Sarmayehgozari 1992, 34.

crease in response to the sharp devaluation, the oil revenue began to decline. At the same time, a loan crisis, resulting from the overdue letters of credits used to finance the large value of imports, which surfaced in January 1993, became a crucial factor constraining the Islamic Republic's foreign-exchange credit. With a foreign-exchange crunch, the value of the rial continued to fall in the free market. By late May 1994, the exchange rate had increased to $1=IR 2,850, and consequently Bank Markazi resumed its control over the foreign-exchange market (*Kayhan*, May 28, 1994).

Meanwhile, price increases (60 percent in the consumer price index; see table 3.3) generated strong opposition. In the parliament this opposition was directed toward the government for increasing, or intending to increase, the price of goods and services it provided, such as water, electricity, telephone, mail, airline and train tickets, and, most important, petroleum products. In January 1994, the Majles deputies rejected the government's proposed increases in the price of petroleum products. Soon after, the minister of commerce announced a moratorium on the increase in the price of goods provided by the government. In April 1994 some deputies introduced a bill to the Majles requiring that any future price increase for goods and services provided by the government be approved by the Majles (*Kayhan*, Jan. 31, Mar. 9, Apr. 27, and May 3, 1994). Thus, as exchange control was restored, a cap on price movements was also restored. Moreover, many subsidies were promised to continue.

Devaluation has an inflationary impact on the economy. The price of imports increases, and so would the price of those goods with import content. If the devaluation has any notable impact on the international demand for exports, the domestic price of the exportables would increase, too, especially when capacity expansion is limited because of various internal economic constraints. Nearly all prices change to accommodate the changes in price of tradable goods. In the two years (1993 and 1994) following the devaluation, the wholesale price index increased by 78 percent and the consumer price index by 96 percent. As expected, products with a higher import content had a higher rate of increase in their prices.

The price effect is expected to remedy the foreign-exchange gap from two avenues. First, with the price increase for imported goods and goods with a high import content, domestic demand would shift toward the domestic alternatives, provided that the price of these products does not increase in step with the increase in the price of imports and those products with high import content. Second, if the rate of inflation in consumer prices is not matched

Table 3.3

Consumer Price and Wage-Rate Indexes and Inflation Rate, 1990–2000

	1990	1991	1992	1993	1994	1995	1996	1997	1998	1999	2000
Prices and inflation											
Consumer price index	100	121	150	184	294	372	459	538	646	777	904
Consumer price inflation rate (%)	9	21	24	23	60	27	23	17	20	20	16
Indexes of wage rates											
Minimum wage rate	100	167	227	299	389	533	691	848	990	1,206	1,527
Unskilled construction workers	100	121	151	184	218	292	392	452	498	569	627
Workers in large manufacturing establishments★†	100	137	179	247	310	428	584	763	943	1,197	1,834

Source: BMI, *Economic Report,* various years.

★Establishments with 50+ workers until 1996, those with 100+ workers from 1997.

†Includes fringe benefits.

with an increase in nominal wages, real income of the wage earners declines, and consequently the demand for domestic and imported products decreases. The lagging wage-rate effect appeals to the policy makers because it is anti-inflationary and would, at least partially, compensate the increase in the demand for imports owing to the rising domestic prices, and would help to promote exports by containing the labor cost of production.

It is in this context that one may view the emphasis of the proponents of the liberalization policy on cutting subsidies and raising the price of products of mass consumption offered by the government. These policy measures not only would divert some resources from producing these products, whose cost of production is higher than their subsidized market price, but would also help to reduce the real income of a large mass of population and thereby reduce the demand for other products, many of which are imported, have high import content, or are exportable.

All these goals are achievable at the cost of reducing the standard of living of the general population, which, as the proponents of liberalization policy see, is in itself a blessing for the economy, because the inflationary trend, and subsequently the decline in real wages and the standard of living, reduces the distributive share of labor and augments the share of capital (profit) in the economy. Consequently, as the argument goes, private consumption would decrease and the possibility for investment would increase, which would potentially increase productive capacity, employment, and output. As attractive as these possibilities seem, it is the mass of population that must pay the cost of the increased investment today, in return for uncertain benefits for the wage earners of tomorrow. Hence, the opposition to the liberalization mounted, and the state retreated for fear of widespread mass opposition.

Following the retreat, the state began a zigzag strategy to pursue economic liberalization. It pushed forward where it could, mainly in the arenas that were inconspicuous, and gave in when public discontent mounted. As riots and demonstrations in opposition to government policies (for example, in Mashhad, Qazvin, Arak, Akbarabad, and Islamshar) became elements of political negotiation, the parameters of public tolerance gained higher importance in the equation of political stability. Demand for wage increases was accommodated under pressure and ignored otherwise. Thus, salaries of government workers were increased occasionally to partially catch up with the inflation. The official minimum wage rate was also increased periodically to compensate for the rising prices. Ironically, the main beneficiaries of the increase in the minimum wage rate are workers in state enterprises and other large corporations, who generally receive higher wages, and in addition are entitled to a series of fringe benefits, which are calculated based on the official minimum wage rate. On the low end of the wage scale, little is gained because the minimum wage rate is substantially lower than the prevailing rate for un-skilled workers. The wage rate of unskilled construction workers is the benchmark wage rate for unskilled and low skilled workers in most economic activities in Iran. Their wage rate clearly lagged behind the increase in the consumer price index.

Figure 3.3 and table 3.3 demonstrate that from 1994, the minimum wage rate increased significantly faster than the rate of inflation. It may be a reflec-tion of the Central Bank's downward bias in estimating the inflation rate, or an indication of the state's sensitivity to political pressure. The data, however, show that the workers in the large enterprises were beneficiaries of the wage policy of the government. The wage rate of unskilled construction workers did not keep up with the inflation in the years of our observation. This fact, too, indicates that it is concentrated political power (which the workers in large establishments possess and the unskilled workers do not) that matters most in determination of wages. Also, in several steps the state increased the wages and salaries of its employees. However, because we do not have access to the statistics on average wage and salary of state employees we cannot make any assessment about the income of these employees (although we should note many of the workers in large enterprises are employees of state-owned establishments and as such are state employees). Nevertheless, our study of household income distribution in Chapter 8 indicates that the relative posi-tion of state employees improved in these years.

With the oil revenues averaging more than nineteen billion dollars in the years 1990–96, Iran had some of its more fortunate times. The IMF, which re-gards this situation as an ideal condition for pursing a liberalization policy, ex-pressed its displeasure about the zigzag strategy of the Iranian government and its limited success in opening the market to the private sector.[24] After seven years of pursuing a privatization policy, in 1996, the state (including the *bonyads*) remained the dominant actor in the economy. Between 1986 and 1996, the number of government employees, instead of declining, increased by almost a quarter (see Chapter 5). Public current expenditures remained nearly constant at about 14 percent of the gross national expenditures, even though the cease-fire with Iraq had reduced the war-mobilization budget. At

24. "Iran: IMF Points to Lost Opportunity," *MEED* (Jan. 30, 1998).

Figure 3.3
Consumer Price and Wage-Rate Indexes, 1990–2000

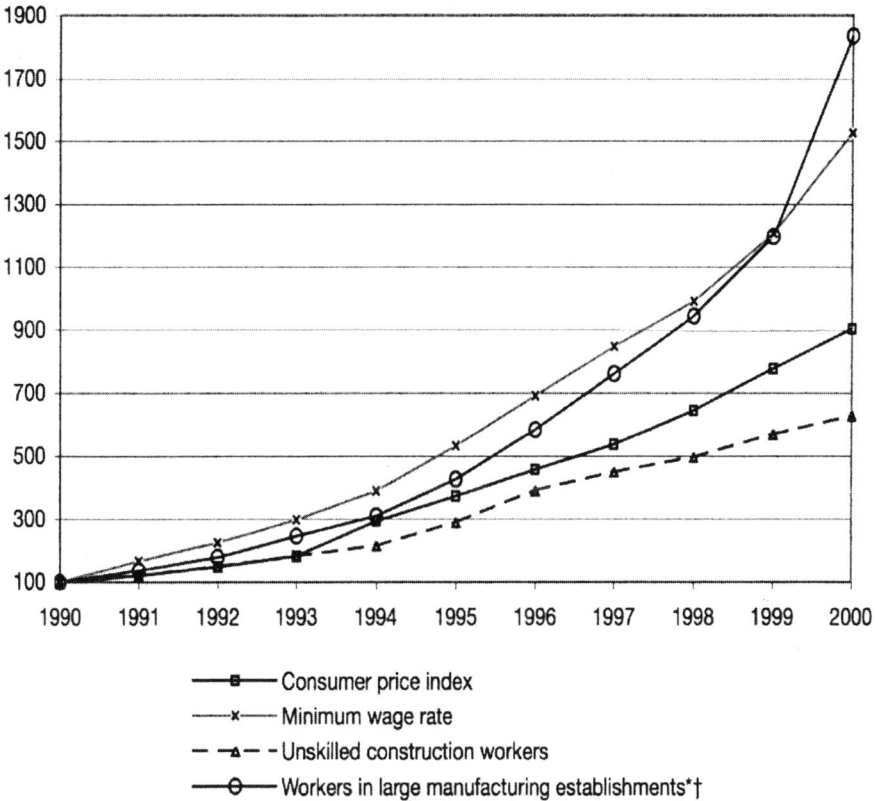

Source: Table 3.3.
*Establishments with 50+ workers until 1996, those with 100+ workers from 1997.
†Includes fringe benefits.

the same time, in 1990, public-sector investment accounted for 32 percent of total capital formation in the country. In 1996 public investment accounted for no less than 43 percent of the total (BMI 2003, 11–12), a trend contrary to the objectives of privatization policy.

One of the objectives of the liberalization policy is to increase the level of investments in the national economy, generally by reducing the share of private consumption and government current expenditures in the gross national expenditures. In the early 1990s, total investment (in constant prices) increased in pace with the economic expansion, brought about by increasing oil prices. The share of gross domestic investment in gross national expenditures in the initial years of liberalization also increased as the result of two concurrent changes: first, a decline in the share of private-consumption expenditures and, second, an increase in imports. The share of private-consumption expenditures in the gross national expenditures declined from about 51 percent in 1990, 1991, and 1992, to a range of 46 percent to 49 percent between 1993 and 1997, as the impact of economic liberalization was felt in the economy. However, with the retreat on the liberalization policy, this share rose to 53 percent in 1998 and 1999, and 51 percent in 2000 (table 3.4; BMI 2003, 63–64).

Overall, in the first decade of economic liberalization the Iranian economy exhibited some economic growth, accompanied with, and benefiting from, the increase in oil revenues. This growth and the more open political space for the private sector facilitated the capitalist accumulation process as reflected in the growth of private investment, particularly in machinery and equipment. The economic liberalization policy, however, had only a minimal effect on this process, because it was intermittent and did not result in any significant reduction in the share of state economic activities in the market. Nevertheless, the increase in the rate of private capital accumulation led to increased proletarianization of labor, the main characteristics of the process of deinvolution.

Whither the Economy?

By 1996, the non-oil gross domestic product had increased by 49 percent since 1976 (see table 3.1), whereas the population had nearly doubled. In the same period, national income per capita had declined by more than half (see table 3.4). The result would be even more disheartening if one were to consider the bias of the price deflator, which underestimates the extent of inflation. By 1996, the official consumer price index had reached 459, from 100 in 1990. This is hardly a success story. Contrary to the aims of the liberalization policy, the state still dominated the economy. Prices were controlled, government bureaucracy had grown, and privatization had been limited. To pursue the path of liberalization the state had to implement a tight austerity policy, which would entail abandonment of its populist stature and loss of the political base that it still claims to represent.

On the other hand, promoting economic liberalism requires providing security and high-profit potentials for capital. To do so the state must commit

Table 3.4
Vital Statistics, 1966–2000

	1966	1972	1976	1986	1996	2000
Population (millions)	26	30	34	49	60	64
Urban (%)	38	43	47	54	61	64
Rural (%)	59	57	53	46	39	36
Oil revenue per capita (current US$)	28	81	621	127	321	323
Non-oil GDP/capita (IR1,000s)*	1,808	2,901	4,773	3,434	4,009	4,342
National income/capita (IR1,000s)*	2,076	3,804	8,847	3,064	4,111	4,269
Private consumption expenditures/capita (IR1,000s)*	1,157	1,549	2,528	2,263	2,247	2,598
Shares in gross national expenditures (%)*						
Private consumption expenditures	46	34	26	56	46	51
Gross fixed capital formation	31	36	40	30	25	29
By private sector	24	27	26	18	14	19
By private sector in machinery	15	19	18	3	8	13
Unemployment, urban (%)	5.7	3.5	5.1	18.9	8.9	
Unemployment, rural (%)	11.8	NA	14.2	9.2	9.4	16.1†

Sources: BMI 2003 and *Economic Report*, various years; MAI 1968, 1980, 1988, 1997.

*1997 prices.

†16.1 is the total percentage of both urban and rural unemployment.

itself to pursuing, consistently and unequivocally, a policy to protect the domain and freedom of activity of capital by its own withdrawal from the market, both as a producer and as a regulator. It also requires the state to reformulate the rules of the market to facilitate capital accumulation. The constitutional limitation on the domain of activity of the private sector (Article 44) and the Labor Law of 1990 are the main areas of legal contention.

The presence of the parastatal foundations, *bonyads,* and their huge conglomerates is another major obstacle of the state promoting economic liberalism. While the *bonyads* have been a source of monopolistic rent and the mainspring of much "primitive accumulation" for some privileged few, they are a cause for concern, caution, and even hostility for the majority of players in the market. They are too powerful for any competitor to withstand. The issue is more complicated by the formal and informal political and economic ties between the *bonyads* and the Islamic Revolutionary Guards and the other "revolutionary institutions," which together serve as the coercive force of the Islamic state.

In a different sphere, the intensification of the cultural confrontation in Iranian society led to a different realignment among the forces within the regime. After two decades of cultural oppression, the Islamic state could not succeed in bringing the population to submit to its traditionalist Islamic norms of personal and public conduct and to accept its idealized traditional Islamic cultural mores. The landslide victory of Mohammad Khatami in the May 1997 presidential election was a definite achievement for the Iranian people in expressing their opposition to the imposition of the traditionalist cultural norms. Khatami, however, came to the forefront of the battle for the leadership of the Islamic state by the alliance of two hitherto opposing factions within the regime, namely, a liberal coalition promoting economic liberalism and the hard-core remainders of the populist-statist tendency. These two factions are known in Iranian politics as the "modern Right" and "modern Left," respectively. Their "modernity" comes from being viewed as being more moderate on imposition of the traditional Islamic values than the hardliners, who are also distinguished as the "traditional Right" and "traditional Left."

The cultural confrontation aside, Khatami had to chart the course of economic development of the state. The sharp decline in oil prices in 1998 brought urgency to the issue. In 1998, in fact, oil revenues amounted to $9.9 billion. Khatami was approaching an economic crisis. Prices began rising sharply since the spring of 1998 as foreign exchange had become more scarce and a decline in the flow of imports was expected. In May 1998 *Payam-e Em-rouz* declared the condition of the industries "shocking" and listed four hundred factories that had just closed and warned that "several hundred are at the verge of closure."[25] It took Khatami more than a year after his election to the presidency of Iran to enumerate his economic plan. His plan was an eclectic composition of the views of the two factions supporting him (Behdad 2001a). On the one hand, he stressed that the key to the economic recovery of Iran is mobilization of domestic capital and attraction of foreign investment, which may be possible, he noted, only if security of capital is guaranteed and constraints imposed on the private sector are eliminated. On the other hand, to satisfy the populist-statist faction of his alliance, which finds this liberal proposition unpalatable, he made a pledge that his administration "will do its best to maintain social justice and a more equitable distribution of income."[26] Yet the structure of his proposed budgets does not indicate a major departure from the policies of the previous years. Therefore, the debate over the free market and state intervention continued. The economic crisis was coming once again to the center of the political stage, while factional disputes and political assassinations intensified the crisis of the regime.

Miraculously, the international oil market came to Khatami'a rescue. International oil prices and Iran's oil revenues began to rise in 1999. Iran's oil revenues nearly doubled to $17 billion, reached $24 billion in 2000, remained $19 billion in 2001, and increased to $23 billion in 2002 (BMI, *Economic Trends,* nos. 30–34). The increase in the oil revenues reduced the economic pressure on Khatami's presidency, and the zigzag strategy of economic liberalization continued in the midst of the push and pull between the "cultural reformist" backers of Khatami and their "cultural conservative" opposition. Meanwhile, the quiet push and pull between the free-marketeer and statist factions of the Islamic state continued. Yet so far as the statistical data exist, the evidence suggests little was accomplished in accelerating the capitalist accumulation in the Khatami years.

The "vital statistics" of the Iranian economy for the past four decades (table 3.4) reveal the predicaments of the Islamic state. In the postrevolution-

25. "Doshvariha-ye Eqtesad: Besyar Beham Pichideh, Moqe'iyat-e San'at: Besyar Tekan Dahandeh" and "400 Karkhaneh Ta'til Shod; Chand Sad Karkhaneh dar Astaneh-ye Ta'til," *Payam-e Emrouz,* May 23, 1998, 116–19.

26. *Hamshahri,* Nov. 30, 1990, electronic ed., http://www.neda.net/hamshahri.

ary years the population of Iran increased from thirty-four million in 1976 to sixty-four million in 2000 (by 88 percent). This high rate of population growth was because of a boom in the fertility rate in the 1976–86 decade, as discussed later. The population boom of the first postrevolutionary decade has had important economic implications. The baby boomers first confronted tight bottlenecks in the public services necessary for babies and youth (health care and education) in the 1980s and the early 1990s, and then in the present decade are faced with the anxiety and frustration of joblessness. Throughout the postrevolutionary years, however, the rural-urban migration continued persistently. By the year 2000 about 64 percent of the Iranian population lived in urban areas, and only 36 percent were still rural. In 1966 the shares were 39 percent and 61 percent, respectively, and at the time of the revolution in 1979 it was almost 50–50.

There is no doubt that economic growth and prosperity in Iran ride on oil revenues. From mid-1960s to the years prior to the 1979 revolution per capita oil revenues of Iran increased from a mere $28 to $621. Thus, national income per capita more than quadrupled and private-consumption expenditures more than doubled in these years. The growth in private-consumption expenditures in the prerevolutionary years was slower than the increase in national income, which explains the falling share of private-consumption expenditures in gross national expenditures from 46 percent in 1966 to 26 percent in 1979. Consequently, the share of fixed capital formation continued to increase in the prerevolutionary years, from 31 percent in 1966 to 40 percent in 1976. A very large portion of this increase was attributed to various infrastructural investments of the state. Nevertheless, the private sector managed to invest a growing share of the gross national expenditures in machinery and equipment while the economy was growing in a rapid pace. In 1976, 18 percent of gross national expenditure was allocated by the private sector for investment in machinery and equipment; in 1966 it was 15 percent (see table 3.4).

The postrevolutionary period is characterized most acutely by the low rate of capital accumulation, as a smaller proportion of the gross national expenditures is allocated to capital accumulation. In the entire postrevolutionary period the proportion of annual national output allocated for fixed capital formation is less than what it was even in the mid-1960s before the oil boom of the 1970s. The shortfall is dramatically more acute for investment of the private sector in machinery and equipment. In 1986 it was 3 percent of the gross national expenditures, and in 1996, after seven years of economic liberalization, it was only 8 percent of that amount (see table 3.4). By 2000, investment of the private sector in machinery and equipment and total gross fixed capital formation (by the state and the private sector in construction and machinery) were approaching the 1966 level.

Meanwhile, as the population of Iran has rapidly grown, private consumption per capita has been kept relatively stable. Private consumption per capita in 1986 (in constant prices) was 45 percent more than in 1972 in spite of a 20 percent decline in the national income per capita in these years. In other words, in the postrevolutionary years, the share of private-consumption expenditures in gross national expenditures rose significantly to maintain a standard of living close to the last prerevolutionary level in a declining economy with a growing population. It is true that the state's policies in the postrevolutionary years have been directed toward maintaining the standard of living for political considerations, but the situation also reflects the docility of the private sector and its timid presence in the national economy.

The objective of the economic liberalization policy, in plain language, is to change the functional distribution of income by increasing the share of capital accumulation (profit) and reducing "absorption," that is, most important, private consumption. But that policy is obviously unpopular, as it brings pain and suffering now for the majority of the population (mainly wage earners) with the promise of better days in the future. Any rational human being would be hesitant in accepting the certainty of pain in the present time only for the promise of an uncertain improvement in some distant future. The stronger and the more widespread the undemocratic image of the state and of the corruption, nepotism, and rent-seeking activities in the economy, the stronger will be the hesitation in public acceptance of the liberalization policies. Khatami and his reformist supporters, in two terms of his presidency, had only marginal success in pursuing the economic liberalization policy. Thus, the deinvolutionary process advanced only very slowly and timidly.

The election of Mahmud Ahmadinejad to the presidency in June 2005 has further complicated the deinvolutionary process. He came to power by the mobilizing effort of the Basij and Revolutionary Guards and the allure of his populist platform to those who had lost in the process of economic liberalization. Ahmadinejad campaigned against Hashemi-Rafsanjani, his opponent in the second round of the presidential election and the champion of the economic-liberalization policy.

Ahmadinejad's populist rhetoric and his close alliance with the *bonyads* have created a gloomy horizon over the economic landscape. His amateurish and hardheaded political stance, underscored by a cultural conservatism based in his allegiance to Islamic fundamentalism, has generated a specter of uncertainty and instability in the political economy of Iran. If the postelection performance of the Tehran stock market is any indication, capital accumulation could be thwarted. Capitalists who are not affiliated with the *bonyads,* or connected to the political core of the Islamic Republic, are once again fearful and intimidated, while the unemployed, the low-income households, and the rank of traditional petty bourgeoisie are hanging onto Ahmadinejad's slogans in despair.

Almost three decades after the revolution, Iran has not fully overcome its postrevolutionary economic crisis.

4

Population Growth and the Supply of Labor

THE STUDY OF THE CLASS NATURE of the workforce requires the analysis of the trends in population growth and the rate of participation of the population in the workforce. In this chapter we will identify the major demographic trends between 1976 and 1996 and their impacts on the supply of labor. This analysis will help us to identify major sources of change in the size and composition of the workforce, and will point to the implications of these trends for the future rate of growth in the workforce and the changes in its class configuration.

Demographic factors determine the maximum bounds of the size of the economically active population, within the context of the existing economic relations, level of socioeconomic development, and cultural norms (including observed religious codes of conduct). In this context, demographic factors influence the rate of participation of adult men and women, young and old, in the workforce. The definition of adulthood is itself a socioeconomic issue, determined in the specific conditions of a society. Generally, the more economically advanced societies choose a higher age for definition of labor (ILO 1996), simply because young adults enter the labor market after a long course of education and internship. In most developing countries, however, children of age ten, and often even younger, enter the labor force. In the 1986 census of Iran the working-age population includes anyone six years or older. In the previous and subsequent censuses ten is the age for counting the working-age population.

Demographic factors leave their trace on the class nature of the workforce. Differential birthrates in different social classes or among different ethnic populations influence the future pattern of class configuration. Changes in the size and age composition of the population within working-class families and other disadvantaged classes, who constitute the majority of the population, are bound to affect the quantitative composition of classes in future. Coming of age of population in a society where employment opportunities do not grow in step with its labor force inevitably results in a chronic high rate of unemployment for the less-advantaged classes. This situation leads to increased polarization of life opportunities of the participants in economic activities.

Supply of labor, "economically active population," or "workforce" is the sum of all those persons willing and able to participate in economic activities. It includes all individuals who are employed or are unemployed (but seeking work). The number of persons in the workforce in a given period of time is only a rough approximation for the supply of labor. A more refined measure would specify part-time and seasonal workers, average hours of work of workers per unit of time (day, week, or month), and the turnover of people in the workforce in a given period. Survey and census data, however, generally measure the quantity of labor supplied for employment and self-employment in the labor market by the simple count of people in a short period of time, irrespective of the extent of their participation in the labor market.

The employed category includes the civilian and noncivilian labor force (including those individuals attending military school or in military service), trainees, unpaid family workers, and part-time and seasonal workers. Those in the working age population who are not employed and are not seeking employment make up the "economically inactive population." In this segment of the working-age population, the most significant categories are homemakers, students, and income recipients without employment (retired persons, rentiers, and absentee owners). The ratio of "economically active population" to the working-age population measures the activity rate or labor force participation rate.

Demographic factors, such as population size, age, and sex distribution of the population, and secular trends in fertility and mortality have long-run effects on the size and structure of the workforce and the activity rates. Activity rates are also affected by the rate and patterns of migration and by socioeconomic variables that influence the attractiveness of the labor market for the working-age population. The participation rate of the male population in the prime age (midtwenties to midfifties) is relatively stable, but the participation rates for youths, women, and the elderly are affected by a myriad of factors. They are factors such as socioeconomic conditions and public policy measures that affect the work environment, employment practices (gender or ethnic discrimination), and availability of alternatives (like access to education for youths and pension programs for the older workers). Activity rates are also influenced by cultural norms such as the dominant societal view about the presence of women in the public arena, value of education and training, attitudes toward child rearing and division of domestic labor, the growth in urban population, and patterns of marriage and fertility (Bauer 1990, 615–17). Changes in activity rates (particularly in the number of employed workforce) is simultaneously determined by the structure and change in economic activities and employment opportunities on the demand side of the labor market.

Population Growth and Its Components

Between 1976 and 1996, Iran's population increased 2.9 percent a year, from 33.7 million to 60.1 million (table 4.1). The average annual growth of population in Iran between the 1976 census and the 1996 census has gone trough a dramatic rise and fall. There is a concern about the possible overcounting of the population in the 1986 census, which reports a 3.9 percent average annual growth since 1976, compared with a 2.7 percent growth rate in the previous decade and only a 2.0 percent growth in the subsequent (1986–96) period. Such a sharp fluctuation in the rate of growth of population is rather unusual and may raise concerns about the degree of accuracy of the census.[1] The issues related to the accuracy of the census gathering notwithstanding, we are certain that there was a large increase in the rate of population growth in the early postrevolutionary period and a swift decline in that rate in the decade that followed. The question is why there was a sharp swing in the population growth of Iran.

First, there is the question of migration. Population growth reflects the net flow of migration. In the 1976–86 period, there was a large inflow of refugees from Afghanistan (following the Soviet invasion of Afghanistan in December 1979 and the ensuing war in that country) and Iraq (following the start of the Iran-Iraq War in September 1980). The Iranian census puts the number of nonnationals at 927,000 in 1986 and 1.10 million in 1996. The number of refugees, however, is significantly larger, according to the United Nations High Commission for Refugees (UNHCR). By UNHCR's account, in 1986 there were 2.6 million refugees in Iran. In 1996 their number was 2.0 million (2000, 311–12).[2] Without the refugee population, the rate of

---

1. The concern was first raised by Naser Pakdaman (1987).
2. The number of refugees in Iran peaked at 4.4 million in 1991 (UNHCR 2000, 311).

Table 4.1
Population Profile: Decennial Statistics, 1966–1996

	1966	1976	1986	1996
Total population (1,000s)	25,789	33,709	49,445	60,055
Growth rate (average annual, %)	3.1	2.7	3.9	2.0
Refugees*	–	179	2,590	2,030
Total population excluding refugees	25,789	33,530	46,855	58,025
Growth rate (average annual, %)	3.1	2.7	3.4	2.2
Urban population (1,000s)	9,794	15,855	26,845	36,818
Growth rate (average annual, %)	5.1	4.9	5.4	3.2
Rural population (1,000s)	15,994	17,854	22,349	23,028
Growth rate (average annual, %)	2.1	1.1	2.3	0.3
Median age of population	16.9	17.4	17.0	19.0
Female-to-male ratio				
Total	0.93	0.94	0.96	0.97
Urban	0.92	0.91	0.95	0.96
Rural	0.94	0.97	0.96	0.98
Average age of women at first marriage				
Total	18.4	19.7	19.8	22.4
Urban	19.0	20.2	20.0	22.5
Rural	17.9	19.1	19.6	22.3
Married women 10 years or older (%)				
Total	61.00	58.50	53.22	53.22
Less than 20 years old	20.14	15.79	17.46	8.34
20 years and older	79.59	80.64	70.73	78.16

Sources: MAI 1968, 1980, 1988, 1997; UNHCR 2000.
*Except for 1976, which is the number of those born abroad (MAI 1980).

population growth in the past two decades would have been 3.4 percent and 2.2 percent, respectively (see table 4.1).

Thus, the inflow of refugees into Iran in the postrevolutionary years could partially account for the upswing of the population in the 1976–86 period. Yet we should note that in the same years an unknown number of Iranians migrated abroad to avoid revolutionary turmoil and the destruction of the war, to escape political repression and religious persecution, or simply to search for a better job or to follow their capital for better investment opportunities. Kazemi (1996) estimates that between 1979 and 1984 close to 2 million Iranians left Iran for Western countries. Torbat (2002, 277) reports that between 1980 and 1998, more than 213,000 Iranian immigrants were admitted to the United States.

The population growth would have been even larger if the emigrants had not emigrated. We do not have any reliable measure of how many Iranians emigrated, but if a number between 1 million and 1.5 million is near reality, then the impact of Afghan and Iraqi refugees on the population growth is nearly offset by the emigration of the Iranians.

However, it is not clear to what extent the emigrants, in their absence, were excluded from the censuses of 1986 and 1996. Many emigrants, at least initially, view their absence as temporary. So do their relatives remaining Iran. This situation was especially the case at the time of the 1986 census, when the system of rationing many essential goods provided an incentive for the remaining relatives to pretend that the emigrant family members were still present.

Aside from the sheer numbers of the Iraqi and Afghan refugees to Iran, and Iranian refugees and emigrants abroad, the two populations were characteristically different. The refugees into Iran were nearly all unskilled and semi-skilled rural laborers (particularly the ones from Afghanistan), whereas Iranian emigrants were mostly skilled and professional workers, and nearly all urban. Torbat (2002, 282) reports, based on statistics of the U.S. Immigration and Naturalization Service, that 41.9 percent of Iranian immigrants into the United States were in managerial, professional, and specialized occupational categories. Most of the rest were skilled workers. Bozorgmehr and Sabagh (1988) also provide similar evidence about the characteristics of Iranians in the United States.[3]

The migration flows notwithstanding, there was a population swing in postrevolutionary Iran. The population boom of 1976–86 and the subsequent bust in 1986–96 challenges researchers of Iranian demography for explanation. A population boom could result from a fall in mortality rates or a rise in fertility rates or a combination of both. There is no reason to believe that in the postrevolutionary years mortality declined. In fact, the general deterioration of the standard of living in the postrevolutionary years would suggest, if anything, a rise in the mortality rate (Aghajanian 1991, 711). Moreover, the

3. For a study of brain drain from Iran and sixty other developing countries, see Carrington and Detragiache 1998.

war with Iraq claimed the lives of many Iranians and resulted in many injuries. The Martyr's Foundation estimates the number of war casualties at 205,000 and the number of wounded, including by chemical weapons, at about 400,000.[4]

Therefore, any rise in the rate of population growth must be explained by the increase in fertility rate, which had declined in the prerevolutionary decade (1966–76), as women delayed their age of marriage, fewer women of child-bearing age became married, and age-specific fertility rates declined. These changes were the results of enhancement of the legal and social status of women, increase in education, and urbanization (Aghajanian 1991).[5] Although this decline in the fertility rate coincided with the promotion of a family-planning policy by the state, there is doubt if this policy accelerated the rate of decline in fertility in any significant way (Raftery, Lewis, and Aghajanian 1995). The fertility boom of 1976–86 is clearly an aberration since the transition toward fertility decline continued in the 1986–96 period. Hence, the question remains, what did contribute to the increase in the fertility rate between 1976 and 1986?

In a study that relies on decomposition technique (Horiuchi 1995), Hakimian (2001) finds that structural factors (or population momentum), embedded in the age and gender composition of population, had some partial impact on the rapid increase of fertility between 1976 and 1986. Hakimian (13, 35) notes that the large increase in the number of women in the reproductive ages, and within this category, the increase in the proportion of those in their prime reproductive ages, had a combined structural effect toward increasing the fertility rate in the first postrevolutionary decade (fertility boom). This momentum subsided in the subsequent decade (fertility bust). Yet the more significant factor contributing to the fertility boom, according to Hakimian (15), was the rise in marital fertility, particularly among older women.[6] The change in marital fertility rate is a behavioral factor, which is influenced by cultural, socioeconomic, or environmental conditions or by state policies.

Neither Hakimian nor other investigators of population swing point to the precise variables determining the behavioral factor of fertility in this pe-

4. Among the casualties, 188,000 were military. The rest were civilians (Islamic Republic News Agency, Sept. 23, 2000). See also *Independent* (June 25, 1995). We are thankful to Gary Sick and Gulf2000 for these references. Cordesman and Wagner (1990, 3) put the number of casualties between 1.1 million and 1.9 million. These numbers are obviously too high. Amirahmadi (1990, 63, 330) reports 300,000 casualties, including 61,000 missing in action.

5. See Sanasarian 1982, Paidar 1995, and Kian-Thiébaut 1998 on the impact of these changes on the status of women.

6. Raftery, Lewis and Aghajanian (1995, 179) note the same.

riod.[7] Although some researchers note in passing legal changes and the state's ideological propaganda aiming to reinstitute the traditional role of women, or policies like rationing of essential items of consumption, as possible factors contributing to the increase in fertility in the boom period (Aghajanian 1991, 1992a, 1992b), they do not scrutinize the impact of these conditions on fertility.[8] It is not revealed, for example, why these environmental changes caused a sharp increase in the marital fertility of older women, and not the younger (noted above), or why the total fertility rate for urban women increased much faster (16 percent) than for rural women (8 percent) (Aghajanian 1991).

Similarly, it remains a puzzle why at the same time that age-specific marital fertility and total fertility increased, there was "a general and sustained decline in the proportion of married women among the total female population" (Hakimian 2001, 14). Questions remain to be explored about the fertility boom, the suddenness of the fertility bust, and the specific behavioral response of different social classes or regional (urban or rural), ethnic, or religious groups to specific environmental or policy measures. Nevertheless, the existing demographic studies provide us with many valuable findings, particularly in presenting the concrete changes observed in the situation of women.

Changes in Demographic Characteristics:
Religion, Language, and Ethnicity

The Islamic Republic, in practice, moved Iran toward religious homogeneity. In 1976, Jews, Christians, Zoroastrians, and "others" numbered 312,000 and accounted for almost 1 percent of the country's population. By 1996, they were 267,000 in number and only 0.44 percent of the country's population (table 4.2). The number of Baha'is is not known from the census. Given their high rate of emigration, the degree of religious cleansing in the Islamic Republic was in fact higher than the data suggest. Unfortunately, we do not have access to data relating religious affiliation and occupational status or position. Therefore, we cannot make any inferences with respect to the class location of the population based on religion-ethnicity.

7. See, among others, Aghajanian 1991, 1992b; Aghajanian, Agha, and Gross 1996; Hakimian 2000, 2001; and Salehi-Isfahani 2001.

8. Interestingly, Raftery, Lewis, and Aghajanian (1995), in an elaborate statistical model, conclude, as we noted above, that the state's effort in family planning (that is, ideation) had little impact on the fertility decline in Iran in the prerevolutionary decade.

Table 4.2
Population Growth by Religious Affiliation, 1976 and 1996

	Population (1,000s)		Percentage of population		% Δ	Growth shortfall (1,000s)
	1976	1996	1976	1996	1976–1996	
Muslim	33,396.9	59,788.8	99.07	99.56	79.0	0.0
Non-Muslim	311.8	266.7	0.93	0.44	-14.5	291.6
Jewish	62.3	12.7	0.18	0.02	-79.5	98.7
Zoroastrian	21.4	27.9	0.06	0.05	30.5	10.4
Christian	168.6	78.7	0.50	0.13	-53.3	223.0
Other	59.6	57.6	0.18	0.10	-3.4	49.1
Undeclared	0.0	89.7	0.00	0.15	undefined	-89.7
Total	33,708.7	60,055.5	100.00	100.00	78.2	291.6

Sources: MAI 1980, 1997.

Table 4.2 shows that between 1976 and 1996 the Jewish population of Iran decreased by 80 percent and the number of Christians fell by 53 percent, when the total population increased by 78 percent. In this period, however, the population of the Zoroastrians increased by 31 percent, and the new category of "undeclared" entered the census. In the 1966 and 1976 censuses the Baha'is were the largest group in the "other" category. In the Islamic Republic, the Baha'i religion is officially declared illegal as a "heretical sect," and among all religious minorities, they have been persecuted most severely. Many have emigrated. The relatively small decline in the "other" category, and the large increase in the number of "undeclared" indicate that some others, including Muslims, may have placed themselves in these two categories. If we add the two groups of "other" and "undeclared," their total number increased by 147 percent between 1976 and 1996. It is, perhaps, an expression of defiance by Muslims and non-Muslims against the religious state in Iran.

If we assume the same rate of population growth for all religious groups in Iran, then we can calculate what the size of each religious group would have been if they had not emigrated.[9] Subtracting the existing population in 1996 from the potential of the population growth for each population group, we find out by how much the existing population of a group is short of what it

9. The number of conversions from other religions to Islam is not reported anywhere, but cannot be significant demographically. According to Islamic law, conversion from Islam to other religions by anyone born a Muslim can be punishable by death!

would have been if there were no increase in its rate of emigration. That is, "growth shortfall," or Gi, measures the upper bound of number of emigrants for each population group:

$$Gi=[Pi76\ (1+R)]-Pi96$$

where Pi96 and Pi76 are the population of the religious group i in the respective years, and R is the rate of growth of Iran's population between 1976 and 1996. Table 4.2 shows that the population of religious minorities (except Baha'is) in Iran in 1996 was 292,000 less than what it would have been if the rate of emigration of minorities had not increased under the Islamic regime.[10] In effect, the Islamic Republic put into motion a process of "religious cleansing." Baha'is, Jews, Christians (mainly Armenians and Assyrians), and some "free-thinking" Muslims who had the means (financial or human capital), and felt they were severely persecuted, or could not tolerate a religious state, left the country.

The other dimension of diversity among Iranians is national ethnicity. After some flare-up of tensions in Turkman and Kurdish regions of Iran in the early postrevolutionary months, the Islamic Republic began to appease the ethnic minorities by recognizing some very limited rights for some non-Persian ethnic populations (Mojab and Hassanpour 1996). One of these moves, albeit preliminary, but essential, was the recognition of the existence of languages other than Persian. In 1986, for the first time, the Iranian census took count of non-Persian speakers by categorizing the population if they "Speak Persian," "Understand Persian," or "Do Not Understand Persian." Thus, the 1986 census reveals some measure of ethnic diversity, at least to the extent that knowing or understanding the dominant language is a criterion. Unfortunately, similar data are not available for the years previous to 1986, nor are they available in the 1996 census, to measure the extent of change in domination of the Persian language over the years.

Table 4.3 reveals the language divide among Iranians. In 1986, 7 percent of the urban population and 23 percent of the rural population did not understand Persian. If we add the category that could understand but could not speak Persian, the percentage of those individuals who were not fluent Persian

10. This measure is rough for two reasons. First, we assumed the rate of population growth among religious minorities would have been the same as the growth for the whole population. And second, the number of actual emigrants is smaller than the population shortfall because any emigration in the early years of the period reduces the growth of the population group in the later years. The two numbers would have been the same if all the emigrants had left in 1996.

speakers approaches 9 percent in the urban areas and surpasses 26 percent in the rural areas. That is, in 1986, out of 49 million Iranians, 8.5 million, or 17 percent of the population, was not fluent in or did not speak Persian. In Iran the official language of the state and the language of business, except in the enclaves of minorities, is Persian.

Even in these enclaves, the written language of business (for contracts, invoices, deeds, and so on) is Persian. Thus, being active in the national labor market, taking a managerial or professional position, or being an entrepreneur or self-employed proprietor, even in ethnic enclaves, presupposes knowledge of Persian. Not being able to speak or understand the dominant language of the market limits one's opportunities in the labor market. Conversely, not being able to speak or understand Persian is an indication of limited experience in the labor market. This point is revealed by the significantly smaller proportion of urban and rural women who can speak or understand Persian in comparison to men. Moreover, because ethnic languages are not taught in the school system, in effect, not knowing Persian implies illiteracy.[11]

Table 4.4 depicts the percentage of population that speaks Persian and the percentage that does not understand Persian in different provinces of Iran. In eight provinces less than 1 percent of the population did not understand Persian. In ten provinces between 1 and 25 percent of the population did not understand Persian. In the remaining six provinces more than a quarter of the population did not understand Persian. In East and West Azerbaijan and Kurdistan, more than one-half of the population did not understand Persian. Together, more than seven million (84 percent) of those individuals who did not understand Persian resided in these three provinces. In these three provinces the literacy rate was among the lowest in the country (the only exception is Sistan va Baluchestan). The correlation between literacy and ability to speak Persian in these Azari- and Kurdish-speaking provinces is in two directions. The low literacy rates indicate that few people have received instruction on how to speak or understand Persian. On the other hand, however, everything

11. Prior to the 1979 revolution, Armenians were allowed to have their schools, teach their language, and print their own publications. After the revolution, in the 1980s, Armenian schools were prevented from teaching Armenian. After some negotiations they are now allowed to teach Armenian, but must use Persian textbooks for teaching the basic curriculum. Currently books can be published in Armenian, Azari, and Kurdish, but there is a dispute about publishing popular books in Arabic in Khuzestan, where the Arab-Iranians reside. (This information is based on communication with Mohammad Ghaed, editor of *Lawh*). There has never been any limitation on publication of scholarly religious books in Arabic.

Table 4.3
Speaking and Understanding Persian in Urban and Rural Areas, 1986

	Speak Persian	Understand Persian	Do not understand Persian	Total*
Urban				
All (1,000s)	24,405	408	1,956	26,845
Percentage	90.9	1.5	7.3	100.0
Men (%)	92.8	1.2	5.8	13,760
Women (%)	89.1	1.9	8.9	13,065
Rural				
All (1,000s)	16,500	916	5,127	22,601
Percentage	73.0	4.1	22.7	100.0
Men (%)	77.9	3.6	18.3	11,511
Women (%)	68.0	4.5	27.2	11,078

Source: MAI 1988.
*Includes those undeclared, mute, or deaf.

else being equal, if the language of instruction is different from the native tongue, the rate of literacy declines.

Thus, the inability to understand and be fluent in the dominant language places the lowest categories of workers in a disadvantageous position, even in their own ethnic enclaves, for being illiterate and unskilled. When these workers migrate to the industrial centers, they are in an especially disadvantageous position. They constitute the most marginalized workers, many of whom are employed seasonally as construction workers. We are not aware of any studies examining the class position of ethnic minorities in Iran. Unfortunately, the absence of census data on minorities makes such studies rather impossible.

Age and Sex

Age and sex composition of the population and household–marital characteristics affect the supply of labor in general, and the supply of various groups of workers, depending on the differential growth rate of various social groups. They are also influential in determining the demand for certain products or

Table 4.4
Population, Understanding of Persian, and Literacy Rate
by Province, 1986

Province	Population (1,000s)	Speak Persian (%)	Do not understand Persian (%)	Literacy rate (%)
Yazd	574	99.1	0.17	69.6
Semnan	417	99.3	0.24	70.5
Fars	3,194	99.0	0.47	65.1
Kerman	1,623	99.1	0.49	58.0
Esfahan	3,295	99.1	0.58	70.9
Chahar Mehal va Bakhtiyari	631	98.4	0.79	56.9
Boshehr	612	98.4	0.82	60.9
Tehran	8,712	98.1	0.95	78.2
Hormozgan	762	97.0	1.44	51.6
Khorasan	5,281	96.5	2.76	56.4
Markazi	1,082	94.8	4.34	62.4
Mazandaran	3,419	87.4	8.54	63.4
Gilan	2,081	84.1	9.42	66.0
Khuzestan	2,682	81.7	12.64	59.0
Kohkiloyeh va Boyerahmad	412	57.3	15.78	53.0
Hamedan	1,506	80.7	16.53	56.8
Lurestan	1,367	71.8	16.83	52.6
Bakhtaran	1,463	68.4	24.40	55.6
Sistan va Baluchestan	1,197	66.7	28.32	35.9
Zanjan	1,589	64.2	31.28	57.8
Ilam	382	52.6	38.74	52.1
East Azerbaijan	4,114	40.7	54.57	52.2
Kurdestan	1,078	39.0	54.92	39.2
West Azerbaijan	1,972	39.0	57.35	47.0

Source: MAI 1988.

services (for example, housing and education) now and in the future. These demographic factors will have an impact on different aspects of the social, political, and cultural life (the preferences and demands of a young population versus an older population), and the dynamics of population shifts and move-ment (rural-urban migration).[12]

The Iranian population is young because of the high fertility rate, but is getting older as the fertility rate has declined in the past decade (see table 4.1). In 1966 the median age of Iranians was 16.9. By 1976, it increased to 17.4 years as the fertility rate declined, then it fell to 17.0 as the fertility rate in-creased in the postrevolutionary decade. But by 1996, with the resumption of the decline in the fertility rate, the median age increased to 19.4. The recent aging of the population indicates that the wave of baby boomers of the 1980s is now entering adulthood and the labor market. By 2006, more than eight-een million Iranians in the 15–24 age group will be joining the working-age population. They will be replacing four million older Iranians who will pre-sumably exit the potential labor force between 1996 and 2006 at the age of sixty. The resulting pressure for job creation is presently obvious in Iran. With the decline in the fertility rate since the late 1980s, a decrease in the rate of entry to the labor market will be expected toward the end of the current decade. Once the new wave of the children of the baby-boom generation hits the labor market in the subsequent decade, the rate of entry to the labor mar-ket will rise again, unless the fertility rate of the baby boomers (those persons between 9 and 19 in 1996) declines substantially.

Fertility, however, depends on structural and behavioral factors. The pro-portion of women in the population, their age composition, the proportion who get married, and their age at their first marriage are among the impor-tant variables to consider. Since the first systematic census in Iran in 1956, the male population has been larger than the female population (see table 4.1). However, from 1966, the censuses indicate a decline in the sex differential in the population, from ninety-three women per one hundred men in 1966, to ninety-four in 1976, ninety-six in 1986, and ninety-seven in 1996. This trend indicates that either the health and nutritional gap between men and women has continued to narrow or women are being counted less inaccurately than in the past censuses (at least at the aggregate level).[13] It is possible that both trends have been at work.

Moreover, whereas the ratio of women to men in the urban and rural

12. See Khosrokhavar and Roy 1999, chaps. 5 and 7, on the frustration and bitterness of the Iranian youth.

13. It is puzzling that there were ninety-seven women per one hundred men in the 1956 census, before dropping to ninety-three in the 1966 census (MAI, *Statistical Yearbook, 1999,* 61).

areas mirrors the change that we noted above, every census shows that there were more women per men in the rural areas than in urban areas. In 1956 there were four more women per one hundred men in the rural areas than in the cities. This difference increased to six in 1976, and then declined to one in 1986 and to two in 1996. The difference in the ratio of women to men in the rural and urban areas confirms the pattern of rural-urban migration, that male workers lead women in migration to the cities. If there were any undercounting of women in the censuses, it would have been likely to be more significant in the rural areas, which would then make the rural-urban differential even larger than observed by the data.

The increase in the ratio of women over men from 1976 to 1996 in itself will have a tendency to increase the fertility rate. The aging of the baby boomers to adulthood will also increase the potential fertility rate, as more women will be reaching child-bearing age. A countertendency would be, however, the decline in the proportion of married women in the population of adult women, and the increase in the age of women at their first marriage.

Since 1966, the average age of women at their first marriage has been increasing (see table 4.1). In 1966, an average Iranian woman would have had her first marriage at the age of 18.4. By 1976 her age at first marriage increased to 19.7, where it practically remained in 1986. By 1996, however, her age at first marriage increased to 22.5 for urban women and to 22.3 for rural women. The interesting phenomenon is the more rapid increase in the age of marriage of rural women, in comparison to the urban women, in the past decades. In 1966 the age at the first marriage for rural women was 17.9, and for urban women 19.0. Thirty years later, they were both getting married almost at the same age. It is also interesting that the age of women at the first marriage remained nearly constant between 1976 and 1986 in spite of the ideological propaganda of the Islamic Republic, celebrating women's domestic role, and reducing the legal age of marriage for women to 9. Nevertheless, according to the census, in 1986 there were seventy-two thousand female children, 10 to 14 years old, who had a husband.

The secular tendency toward increasing the age of women at the first marriage would reduce the proportion of married women in the population. The proportion of women who were married in the population of 10 years or older declined from 61.0 percent in 1966 to 53.2 percent in 1986 (see table 4.1). The decline continued even between 1976 and 1986 against the Islamic Republic's female-domesticity propaganda. It is, however, most significant that the proportion of younger than 20-year-old women who were married declined from about 20 percent in 1966 to just over 8 percent in 1996, with an aberration in 1986. In the decade between 1986 and 1996, the proportion of married women younger than 20 declined by more than 50 percent (table 4.1).

Thus, the change in the fertility rate would be the compound effect of the impact of various factors, namely, the age composition of the population, the proportion of women in the population, the age of marriage, and the proportion of married women in the women population. The first two are structural variables and easily predictable for the next decade. The latter two are manifestations of the behavioral factors. Moreover, there are other variables that affect men's and women's attitudes toward child bearing and child raising, and thus toward fertility. The overall effect is not predictable, although it is reasonable to expect a long-term decline in the fertility rate (influenced by behavioral factors), while we can expect a countertendency toward increasing fertility as the children of the baby boomers reach the marriage and childbearing age (a structural factor).

Urban-Rural Population Flows

Throughout the postrevolutionary period the flow of rural migrants to the cities continued its prerevolutionary trend.[14] In 1966 38 percent of Iran's population was urban. By 1996 only 38 percent of the population had remained in rural areas. Not all of the increase in the urban-rural population proportion may be attributed to rural-urban migration. The expansion of urban life into the rural areas, especially to the villages surrounding the big cities, and the increase in the population of villages, which causes a change in their classification from rural to urban, have also increased the rate of urbanization.[15]

Table 4.5 depicts a snapshot of the flow of migration at the time of the 1986 and 1996 censuses. In these two censuses respondents were asked if they had moved in the past ten years, prior to the time of the census. In the decade ending in 1986 about 6.5 million, or 13 percent of the population of Iran, moved. Clearly, a significant portion of the migration depicted in the 1986

14. For the prerevolutionary years, see Karshenas 1990, Hakimian 1990, Hooglund 1982, and Lieberman 1979. See also Kazemi and Wolfe 1997 for the postrevolutionary period.

15. The number of population centers classified as "city" increased from 452 in 1976 to 496 in 1986 and 614 in 1996. The number of populated rural "settlements" remained at about 65,000 in 1976 and 1986 and increased to 68,000 in 1996 (MAI, *Statistical Yearbook, 1987*, 35; *Statistical Yearbook, 1998*, 68).

and 1996 censuses must be attributed to the displacement of population because of the Iran-Iraq War. The absence of comparable data in the 1976 census prevents us from making even a rough estimate of the effect of the war on
displacement of the population. We know that in the 1986 census, 23 percent
of migrants were from provinces bordering Iraq, and 12 percent of the total
only from the Khuzestan province. Before the war, according to the 1976
census, 6.4 percent of Iran's population resided in Khuzestan.

According to the 1986 census, the largest group of migrants, 32.2 percent, moved from urban to urban areas. The move was mainly from smaller
towns to larger cities (table 4.5). However, 27.9 percent of the migrants
moved from rural to urban areas. The decade preceding 1986 included, in addition to the Iran-Iraq War, the last years of the Shah's oil bonanza and the
early postrevolutionary years. These situations attracted a large flow of population from rural to urban areas and from small to large cities, where there
seemed to be more opportunities for access to more amenities and jobs. The
relatively large figure of migrants from abroad (726,000 in 1986 census) reflects the displacement of the population across the border because of the turmoil in the neighboring countries, Iraq and Afghanistan. Nearly one-half of
these migrants resided in the rural areas of Iran at the time of the census.

Compared to the 1976–86 decade, in the decade ending in 1996 the flow
of internal migrants increased both absolutely (to 8.7 million) and relatively
(to 14.5 percent of population). The 1996 census reveals that the flow of
rural-urban migration slowed down substantially in comparison to the previous decade. This pattern is expected—as the rural population becomes
smaller, the absolute and relative flow of rural-urban migration would de-

Table 4.5
Migrating Population, 1986 and 1996

	Total	Rural-urban	Rural-rural	Urban-urban	Urban-rural	From abroad	Unknown
1986 (1,000s)	6,451	1,803	763	2,078	747	726	334
Percentage	100.0	27.9	11.8	32.2	11.6	11.3	5.2
1996 (1,000s)	8,719	1,890	943	4,062	1,541	238	44
Percentage	100.0	21.7	10.8	46.6	17.7	2.7	0.5

Sources: MAI 1988, 1997.

Notes: Numbers include those who had migrated in the past ten years at the time of the
censuses in 1986 and 1996. Census 1976 does not provide similar statistics.

crease. Instead, the urban–urban migration became a more important flow of population. Big cities grew at astonishing rates. Tehran's population increased from 4.5 million in 1976 to 6.8 million in 1996. Mashhad's population almost tripled to 1.8 million, and Isfahan, Shiraz, and Tabriz each doubled in size and surpassed the 1 million mark. Karaj, a small rural town near Tehran, grew from 15,000 people in 1956 to 138,000 in 1976, and to 941,000 in 1996. By 1996 20 million Iranians lived in twenty-three cities with more than 250,000 in population. Rapid urbanization and concentration of population have serious urban infrastructural implications, with a rapidly increasing demand for allocating large budgetary sums for their upkeep and growth. At the same time, these growing cities are becoming vibrant labor markets with a high degree of geographical mobility for many of its participants.

Moreover, there appears to be a notable flow of urban–rural migration in the 1986–96 decade. The reason and sources of this "upstream" migration are not known to us. In the absence of any definitive studies, it may be speculated that the large urban–rural flow of population in the decade preceding the 1996 census was a reflection of the return of the war-displaced population to their home villages in the postwar years, following the 1988 cease-fire with Iraq.

Population and the Workforce

Between 1976 and 1996, Iran's population increased by 78.2 percent (from 33.7 million to 60.1 million). In the same period the working-age population (ten years or older) increased by 97.4 percent. However, the active population (the workforce) increased from 9.8 million to 16.0 million, that is, by only 63.2 percent (table 4.6). Active population, according to the International Labor Office, consists of "all persons of either sex who furnish the supply of labour for the production of economic goods and services" (ILO 2000, 1). It includes all persons in paid or unpaid employment, as well as those individuals who are unemployed and are seeking a job. The activity rate (AR), or labor force participation rate, measures the proportion of active population (PAC) in the working-age population (PWA). Hence,

$$AR = (PAC/PWA) \star 100$$

If the working-age population grows faster than the active population, the activity rate would decline. In the involutionary years, the activity rate fell from 42.6 percent in 1976 to 39.0 percent in 1986. The activity rate contin-

Table 4.6

Workforce Characteristics, 1976, 1986, and 1996

	1976	1986	1996
Population 10 years or older (millions)	23.0	32.9	45.4
Active population (workforce)	9.8	12.8	16.0
Activity rate (%)	42.6	39.0	35.3
Dependency ratio	2.4	2.9	2.7
Employed (millions)	8.8	11.0	14.6
Unemployment rate (%), urban	4.4	6.5	12.6
Unemployment rate (%), rural	3.0	12.9	13.2
Students★ (millions)	4.4	6.5	12.6
Students per 1,000 population★	191.3	197.7	277.5
Homemakers (millions)	7.7	11.2	13.2
Homemakers per 1,000 population★	334.8	226.5	219.8

Sources: MAI 1980, 1988, 1997.
★Population 10 years or older.

ued to fall even in the deinvolutionary years. In 1996 it was 35.3 percent. The activity rate in Iran is significantly lower than in some other developing countries. For example, in Brazil in 1992 and Indonesia in 1994 it was 58 percent, and in Turkey in 1995 it was 51 percent (ILO 1996, 11–35).

The decline in the activity rates in Iran in these years was partly because of the considerable number of working people who exited the labor market, giving up their job search in the midst of a persistent and high unemployment condition. Also, many women left the labor market in response to gender discrimination, or found fewer job opportunities because of gender segregation (see Chapter 6). Nevertheless, the number of homemakers per 1,000 population (older than ten years) declined substantially, from 335 in 1976 to 220 in 1996 (see table 4.6). This outcome is consistent with the data indicating an increase in the average age of women at first marriage and a decline in the proportion of married women in the female population (see table 4.1). The decline in the proportion of homemakers is generally an indication of the increase in the activity rate of women. Interestingly, in postrevolutionary Iran, an "average women" would be less likely to consider herself a homemaker, even though she was less likely to be an active member of the labor force in comparison to the conditions depicted by the 1976 census.

It may be argued that the decline in the activity rate is the result of the increase in the number of students. This contention is partially true. The number in the ten-to-fourteen age group increased as the baby-boom children were growing up and a larger proportion of the working-age population was of school age. The number of students in the working-age population continued to increase in these years, from 4.4 million in 1976 to 12.6 million in 1996.

To understand better the changes in the activity rates in the postrevolutionary decades we disaggregate the activity rates from the decennial census data of 1966 to 1996 by gender and the urban-rural division. Moreover, to account for the increase in the number of students in the working-age population we adjust the activity rates by subtracting students from the working-age population.[16] Figures 4.1 and 4.2 depict the changes in the student-adjusted activity rates for male and female populations of Iran in urban and rural areas between 1966 and 1996. Although there is a large gap between activity rates of men and women (both in urban and in rural areas), the pattern of change for all the four categories of our working population is similar. The data show that between 1966 and 1976, prior to the revolution, female and male activity rates increased mildly in the urban areas, and more sharply in the rural areas. In 1986, however, the activity rate for all groups had declined substantially, but more sharply for female workers. The activity rates of urban and rural male workers decreased by 21.6 percent and 19.6 percent, respectively. Similar rates for urban and rural women decreased by 26.4 percent and 52.5 percent, respectively. Between 1986 and 1996 the activity rates for all four categories of workers increased sharply. This result is in contrast to the unadjusted activity rate reported in table 4.6, showing a decline in the 1986–96 period.

Nevertheless, even after adjusting for the increase in the number of students, by 1996 the activity rates for urban and rural male workers and for rural female workers were less than what they were in 1966, and much less than in

16. We measured student-adjusted activity rates (AR_S) by dividing the active population by working-age population minus students in the working-age population (PS10+), that is,

$$AR_s = (PAC/[PWA-PS10]) \star 100$$

Alternatively, we can calculate the student-adjusted activity rate à la Gregory (1986, 24) directly from the unadjusted activity rates by the following relationship:

$$AR_s = (AR/[100-\%S]) \star 100$$

where %S depicts the percentage of students in the working-age population.

Figure 4.1
Student-Adjusted Activity Rates for Rural and Urban Male Workers,
1966–1996

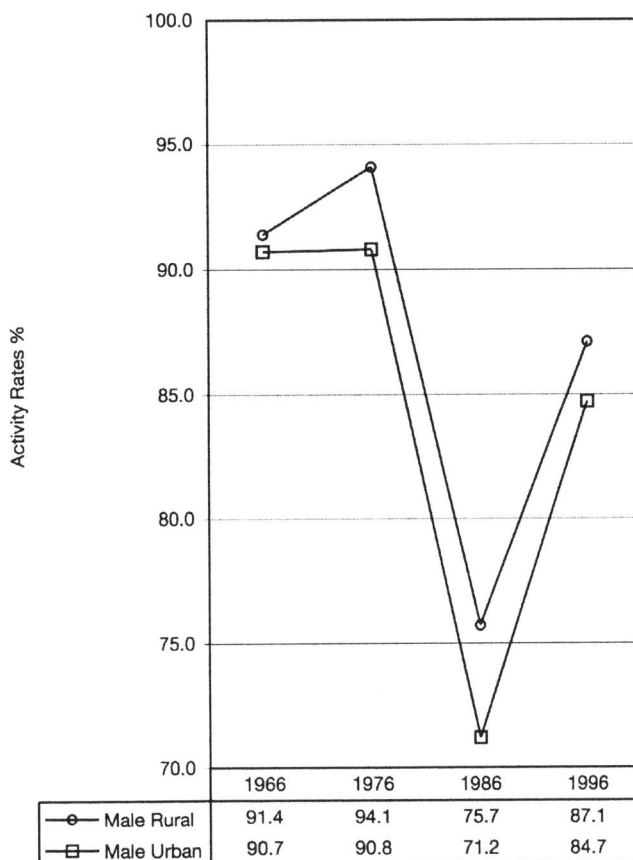

	1966	1976	1986	1996
Male Rural	91.4	94.1	75.7	87.1
Male Urban	90.7	90.8	71.2	84.7

Sources: MAI 1977, 1980, 1988, 1997.

1976, right before the revolution. The student-adjusted activity rate for urban female workers in 1996 was just about what it was in 1966 and less than what it was in 1976. We will examine the activity rates and marginalization of women's labor in Chapter 6. Here we will consider the changes in the age composition of the working-age population in the past decades (figure 4.3).

In examining the activity rate for different age groups we have adjusted the rates for the increase in the number of students by the method explained above. Therefore, here, for each age group we calculate the activity rate for

Figure 4.2

Student-Adjusted Activity Rates for Rural and Urban Female Workers, 1966–1996

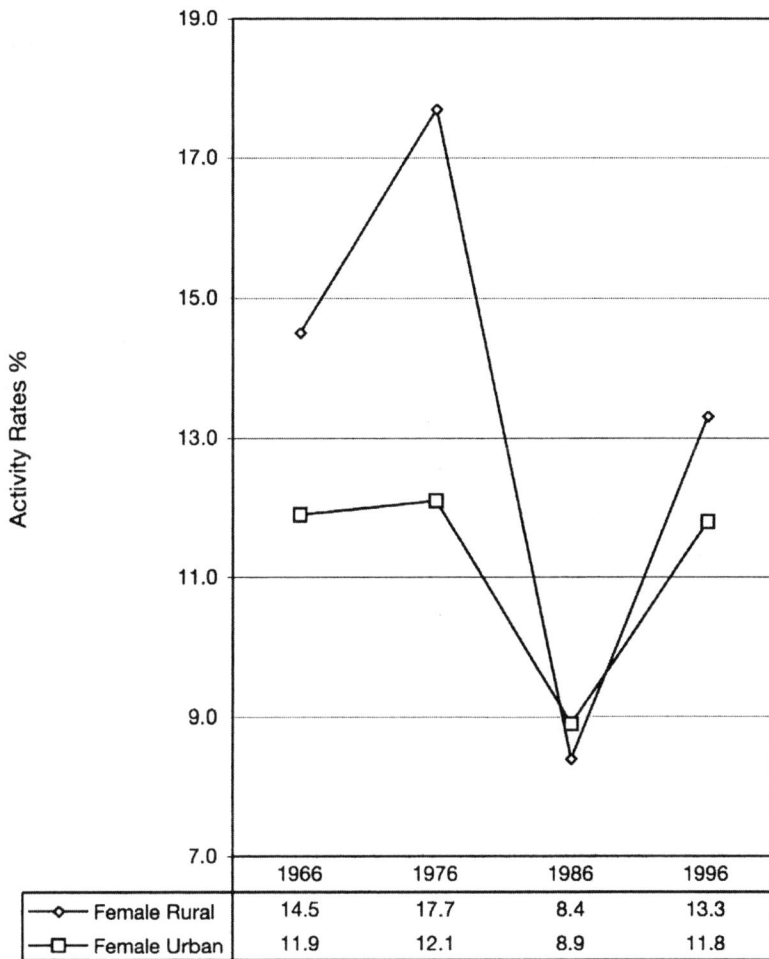

	1966	1976	1986	1996
—◇— Female Rural	14.5	17.7	8.4	13.3
—□— Female Urban	11.9	12.1	8.9	11.8

Sources: MAI 1977, 1980, 1988, 1997.

the nonstudent working-age population. This adjustment affects activity rates for the ten-to-nineteen age groups significantly.

Figure 4.3 reveals that in 1976 the student-adjusted activity rates had a double-humped curve. The first hump was for those individuals in the age group fifteen to nineteen, and the second hump was for those ages forty to

Figure 4.3
Student-Adjusted Activity Rates by Age Groups, 1976–1996

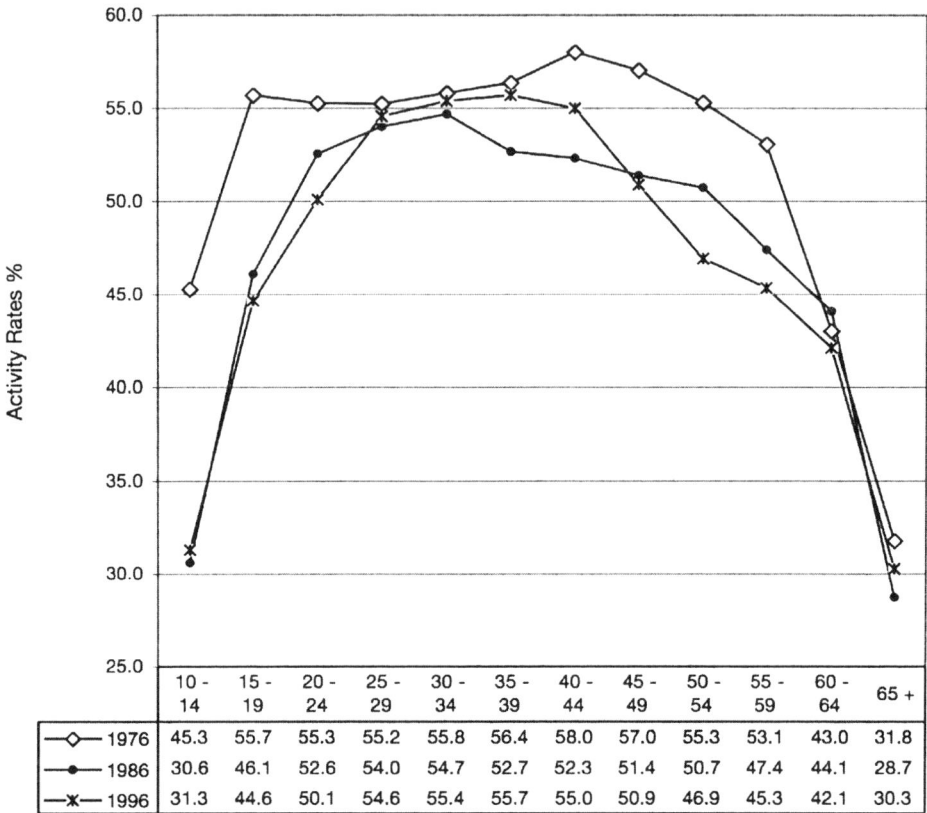

	10 - 14	15 - 19	20 - 24	25 - 29	30 - 34	35 - 39	40 - 44	45 - 49	50 - 54	55 - 59	60 - 64	65 +
1976	45.3	55.7	55.3	55.2	55.8	56.4	58.0	57.0	55.3	53.1	43.0	31.8
1986	30.6	46.1	52.6	54.0	54.7	52.7	52.3	51.4	50.7	47.4	44.1	28.7
1996	31.3	44.6	50.1	54.6	55.4	55.7	55.0	50.9	46.9	45.3	42.1	30.3

Sources: MAI 1980, 1988, 1997.

forty-four. Activity rates fell sharply for the sixty and older age groups. In 1986, activity rates decreased, in comparison to 1976, for every age group, except those persons sixty to sixty-four years old. Moreover, activity rates fell more significantly for the ten-to-nineteen age groups and forty-to-sixty age groups than in the twenty-five-to-thirty-four groups. The wide disparity in the activity rates in the ten-to-nineteen age groups between 1976 and 1986 reflects the difficulty of entry of the young workers into the labor market while the economy was suffering from the involutionary disruptions. We should note that these activity rates have already accounted for any increase in the number of students. Therefore, the decline in the activity rates is only with respect to the nonstudent population. Those individuals in the twenty-five-to-thirty-four age group represent the workers who entered the labor market just about the time of the revolution, or only a few years earlier. These young workers were more resilient toward the changes not only in the economic structure but also in the culture of the workplace, which had become overwhelmingly religious. Many of these workers became employed in the new state bureaucracies and state and parastatal enterprises and agencies. Therefore, for this age group, the activity rate remained relatively unchanged in comparison to 1976. In contrast, the middle-aged and older workers, in the ages forty to fifty-nine, were least resilient in the face of the changes in the economic structure and less accommodating toward the changes in the culture of the workplace. The majority of those workers who became the subjects of ideological cleansing *(paksazi)* and mandatory early retirement were in these age groups.

By 1996, entry into the labor market became even more difficult than in 1986 for the young workers in the fifteen-to-twenty-four age groups in spite of the increase in the level of economic activities in the deinvolutionary decade. The baby boomers of 1980s had reached the working age, though the economy did not have the capacity to absorb them. In comparison to 1986, the hump of the activity-rates curve for 1996 shifted to a higher age group (thirty-five to thirty-nine). However, the activity rates for all age groups older than forty-five (except those over sixty-five) and younger than twenty-five (except those younger than fifteen) were lower in 1996 than 1986.

More striking is the comparison of 1996 and 1976. In every age group, the student-adjusted activity rate was lower in 1996 than what it was in 1976. The youths reaching working age were less able to enter the labor market in 1996 than in 1976. The fifteen- to twenty-four-year-old nonstudents who were not active in the labor force were most likely sons and daughters of the working class or the poor traditional petty bourgeoisie, who are not attending school yet do not find any opportunities in entering the labor market. At the same time, a considerably smaller percent of the middle-aged and older population was in the labor market in 1996 than in 1976. The latter group remembers the more vibrant labor market of the mid- and late 1970s.

With the decline in activity rates, the dependency ratio would increase. The dependency ratio is the number of nonactive population divided by the number of active population (workforce). It shows how many individuals, on average, must rely on output (income) of one working (employed or unemployed) individual. In 1976, the dependency ratio in Iran was 2.4. It increased by 21 percent by 1986 and reached 2.9. It declined only slightly in the subsequent decade and became equal to 2.7 by 1996. The decline in the dependency ratio between 1986 and 1996, when the activity rate declined in the same period, is because of the decrease in the fertility rate in this period and the consequent decline of the proportion of children under ten in the total population. There were only a few countries, comparable to Iran, that had dependency ratios higher than Iran. Among those countries were Egypt (3.2 for 1994) and Pakistan (3.6 for 1994). The dependency ratio for Brazil was 2.1 (in 1992), for Indonesia 2.2 (in 1994), and for Mexico 2.5 (in 1995) (ILO 1996).

Conclusion

The social and political turmoil in the postrevolutionary decade had some notable impacts on the rate of growth, the composition of the population, and on the activity rates. These impacts in the involutionary decade were mainly an aberration from the secular trend that had been set in motion the previous decades, and subsided in the subsequent decade in the deinvolutionary period.

5

Revolution and
Reconfiguration of Classes

THE 1979 REVOLUTION stormed through Iranian society, giving rise to an economic crisis of the postrevolutionary type. We noted in our examination of the economic crisis existence of two distinct periods: structural involution in the first postrevolutionary decade and its reversal, deinvolution, in the subsequent decade. We expect that these opposite tendencies have had remarkable effects on the class nature of employment in Iran. Here we will examine these effects empirically and in the context of our analysis of class structure in Chapter 2.

Based on three dimensions of (1) property relations, (2) possession of scarce skills/credentials, and (3) organizational assets/authority and autonomy, we use the following class typology in our empirical study of the postrevolutionary Iran and recognize four class categories:

• *Capitalists* are the owners of physical and financial means of economic activities and employ workers.

• *Petty bourgeoisie* are self-employed persons who do not hire any paid workers but may rely on the work of unpaid family labor.

• *The middle class* are employees of the state or the private sector, in administrative-managerial and professional-technical positions. They exercise some authority and enjoy relative autonomy. In this category are those individuals employed in economic activities and social services of the state. Those employed in the political apparatus of the state are in an ambiguous class location that we call "political functionaries," and we do not include them in the middle class.

• *The working class* are those workers who do not own the means of economic activity and do not benefit from the authority and autonomy of those in the "middle class." They are employees of the state or the private sector. Those who work in the political apparatus of the state but have little autonomy or expertise constitute the rank and file of "political functionaries." We do not include them in the working class.

Revolution and the Class Structure

For the half century prior to the 1979 revolution, Iran had pursued a capitalist path of development, albeit one with many obstacles and "irregularities," giving rise to the specificities of the development of its capitalist economy in relation to other modes of production. In particular, we note the persistence of large petty economic activities, the presence of a gargantuan state in economic activities, and its accelerated integration in the world economy. The combined and uneven capitalist development of Iran was especially accelerated in the prerevolutionary decade by the immense increase in the Iranian oil revenues. The pattern of capitalist development of Iran in the prerevolutionary period has been examined extensively from different perspectives.[1] Here we are concerned mainly with the existing class structure at the dawn of the 1979 revolution.[2]

A summary of the class configuration of Iran at three points in time during the past two decades is shown in table 5.1. A more detailed presentation of class configuration is in table A.1 in the Appendix.

The Capitalist Class

In 1976 there were 182,000 capitalists in Iran. The capitalist class in Iran is small and fragmented. By that, we mean that despite fundamental common characteristics of members within the class, there are systemic differences among them in the size of their enterprise, their economic activities and occupational characteristics, and their market power. Some of these divisions are rather enduring and influence their life opportunities, such as access to loans, government contracts, and the ability to hold on to their market share, and even to penetrate into their competitors' market share. We divide the capitalists (and the petty bourgeoisie) into modern and traditional occupational categories. By modern subcategories of occupations, managerial-administrative and professional-technical, we mean capitalists (and petty bourgeoisie) whose

1. See, for example, Foran 1993, Karshenas 1990, Soudagar 1990, Nomani 1987, Razzaqi 1989, Pesaran 1982, Looney 1982, Katouzian 1981, Jazani 1980, Halliday 1979, and Amuzegar and Fekrat 1971.
2. For qualitative analyses of classes in Iran see, among others, Gabriel 2002; Kian-Thiébaut 1998; Abrahamian 1982, 1993; Moaddel 1993; Parsa 1989; and Ashraf 1969, 1981.

Table 5.1
Class Composition, 1976, 1986, and 1996

	1976		1986		1996	
	Total (1,000s)	%	Total (1,000s)	%	Total (1,000s)	%
Capitalists	182	2.1	341	3.1	528	3.6
Modern	23	12.8	22	6.5	75	14.1
Traditional	159	87.2	319	93.5	453	85.9
Middle class	477	5.4	774	7.0	1,493	10.2
Private-sector employees	102	21.3	64	8.3	219	14.6
State employees: economic and social	376	78.7	710	91.7	1,274	85.4
Petty bourgeoisie	2,810	31.9	4,390	39.9	5,199	35.7
Modern	34	1.2	48	1.1	164	3.2
Traditional	2,776	98.8	4,343	98.9	5,035	96.8
Unpaid family workers	1,021	11.6	484	4.4	797	5.5
Working class	3,536	40.2	2,702	24.6	4,533	31.1
Private-sector employees	2,970	84.0	1,810	67.0	3,109	68.6
State employees: economic and social	566	16.0	892	33.0	1,424	31.4
Political functionaries	731	8.3	1,851	16.8	1,560	10.7
Rank and file	672	91.9	1,647	89.0	1,315	84.3
Military and paramilitary forces★	386	52.7	1,197	64.7	881	56.5
Unspecified	41	0.5	458	4.2	463	3.2
Total	8,799	100.0	11,002	100.0	14,572	100.0

Source: Table A.1 in the Appendix.
★Includes rank and file and officers.

occupations are similar to those jobs associated with industrial market economies. Complexities in the hierarchical structure of command in the modern corporation requires active capitalists (in contrast to absentee owners) to have a strong professional management background and occupational position (Chandler 1962, 1990; Prechel 2000). Traditional capitalists are those individuals whose occupational category is in clerical, sales and services, agricultural, or production.

Only 12.8 percent of Iranian capitalists in 1976 had a modern occupational classification. The other 87.2 percent were traditional (in sales, services, production, or agriculture). The majority of the capitalists (142,000, or 78.6 percent) were active in the urban economy.

A rough estimate of the concentration of capital is the average number of wage earners per employer in the economy. In 1976 this ratio was 16.9.[3] Most of the capitalists were located in small- and medium-size enterprises, many employing only one or two wage earners. About 97 percent (164,000) of all manufacturing firms in Iran had fewer than 10 workers (table 5.2). Each one of these establishments, on average, had 1.9 workers and only 0.63 wage earners per establishment. These numbers indicate the predominance of one- or two-person workshops, composed of a working owner, with or without an employee, or an unpaid family worker. The number of "large" manufacturing establishments, with 50 or more workers, was no more than 923. In the same year, there were about 4,500 manufacturing establishments with 10–49 workers (medium-size firms). The total number of capitalists in manufacturing in 1976 was 49,900. Once we subtract 4,500 medium-size firms and about 900 large firms from the total, we are left with about 44,500 small capitalists (in our definition of the term) in firms with 1–9 workers. That is, almost 90 percent of capitalists in manufacturing activities in Iran were "small," many of whom had only one or two wage-earning employees.[4] Thus, we observe the predominance of small capitalists (alongside the petty bourgeoisie) in the manufacturing sector. We will see a similar pattern in rural agriculture in Chapter 7.

Unfortunately, we do not have access to similar data for construction and various activities in the service sector. It is not, however, far-fetched to claim that construction, wholesale and retail trade, restaurant, and transportation are also characterized by a similar pattern, that is, a large number of very small establishments on one side, a small number of large enterprises on the other, and a relatively small number of medium-size firms in the middle.

Even with our rough estimates, it is apparent that among those whom we count as capitalist, a large majority are the small bourgeoisie who own busi-

3. The ratio was calculated by dividing the number of working-class plus middle-class employees of the private sector by the number of capitalists.

4. Wright (1997, 48) regards small capitalists as working owners who have two to nine employees. He counts working owners who employ one or no workers as petty bourgeoisie. If we had the relevant data and applied Wright's definition we would have lost about one-half of our capitalists to the petty bourgeoisie!

Table 5.2

Size Distribution of Manufacturing Establishments, 1976, 1987, and 1996

	Total	Small	Medium	Large
1976				
Number of establishments	169,251	163,819	4,509	923
%	100.0	96.8	2.7	0.5
Output (in billion 1990 rials)	9,031	1,494	2,072	5,463
%	100.0	16.5	22.9	60.5
Number of workers (1,000s)	719	315	133	271
%	100.0	43.8	18.5	37.7
Number of wage earners (1,000s)	498	103	124	271
%	100.0	20.7	24.9	54.4
Workers per establishment	4.2	1.9	29	294
1987				
Number of establishments	339,334	327,715	10,367	1,252
%	100.0	96.6	3.1	0.4
Output (in billion 1990 rials)	7,185	2,805	1,061	3,322
%	100.0	39.0	14.8	46.2
Number of workers (1,000s)	1,441	741	190	509
%	99.9	51.4	13.2	35.3
Number of wage earners	1,019	338	172	509
%	100.0	33.2	16.9	50.0
Workers per establishment	4.2	2.3	18	407
1996				
Number of establishments	321,326	307,955	10,938	2,433
%	100.0	95.8	3.4	0.8
Output (in billion 1990 rials)	20,749	3,979	2,485	14,285
%	100.0	19.2	12.0	68.8
Number of workers (1,000s)	1,612	766	198	648
%	100.0	47.5	12.3	40.2
Number of wage earners	1,209	377	185	647
%	100.0	31.2	15.3	53.5
Workers per establishment	5.0	2.5	18	266

Sources: MAI 1981a, 1981b, 1990a, 1999a–c.

Notes: Small: establishments with fewer than 10 workers; medium: 10–49 workers; large: 50+ workers.

nesses such as bakeries, mechanic shops, brick-making plants, apparel work-shops, groceries, barbershops, and many other workshops, retail stores, and other service enterprises with one or two wage-earning employees.

Thus, in 1976, the largest group of those persons who are counted as cap-italists were those whose positions and life opportunities were not all that much different from the petty bourgeoisie. Our study of household income distribution for various social classes in Chapter 8 indicates that, in fact, some capitalists did no better than the petty bourgeoisie or some wage earners. A considerable number of capitalists were in the lower 40 percent income groups. Some were even among the very poor!

Forty-one percent of the bourgeoisie (50 percent in urban areas) was lo-cated in service activities. Almost a quarter (23.1 percent) of the urban bour-geoisie was engaged in retail services, where firms often employ less than ten workers. In the rural economy 67 percent of the bourgeoisie was involved in agriculture.

The occupational position of 66,000 (36.5 percent) of all capitalists was classified as production (see table A.1 in the Appendix). They were engaged mainly in industrial activities, such as textile, apparel, leather, construction material, carpentry, and machine and toolmaking. Fifty-three thousand (29.0 percent) of capitalists were in sales and service occupational classifications, en-gaged in any of the various activities, including retail and wholesale. The ma-jority (75 percent) of the 36,000 capitalists with an agriculture classification were rural.

Only a small number of very large enterprises were owned by a group of supersuccessful capitalists.[5] Many of the supersuccessful capitalists had bene-fited from state financing and support, or in many cases were partners with the state, its high-level officialdom, or multinational corporations. For example, the Pahlavi Foundation held 30 percent of stocks of Iranit Company, owned principally by Abdolaziz Farmanfarmaian, Ahmad Ali Ebtehaj, and Abdul-majid Aalam, 10 percent in Jafar Akhavan's General Motors Iran, and 9.5 per-cent in Khalil Taleqani's B. F. Goodrich Iran (Graham 1979, 256). It was mainly these capitalists who were swept away by the revolutionary wave, and whose enterprises were taken over (nationalized, or confiscated). Nearly all of these supersuccessful capitalists and some of the capitalists in the medium-size firms who managed their own firms were in the modern category.

5. See Vaghefi 1975 on the background and activities of supersuccessful capitalists in the prerevolutionary period.

Like the early days of modern capitalism in the West, in Iran, in 1976, after two decades of rapid growth of urbanization and industrialization, the division of ownership and control was still limited. The majority of Iranian capitalists relied on their own capital for financing their investments. Sales of shares were very limited and, at most, minority shareholding was the practice of the land, and only very few firms were owned by a range of different shareholders.[6] Thus, ownership of large private capital was direct and not dispersed, ownership and control were not divided between owners and managers, and the ownership of the great majority of firms in different economic sectors and activities was in the hands of individuals or families, some of whom managed to hold on to their property ownership after the 1979 revolution.

This class was still in the process of becoming when it received blows by the revolution and the heavy hand of the Islamic state and its parastatal foundations, the *bonyads*. These capitalists never had a cohesive class formation to become the ruling class of Iran. It never was any more than a class "by itself." They had their Chamber of Commerce and the Guilds of Trades (Otaq-e Asnaf), yet they never managed to form any genuine organizations or other means for expression of their class interests. The weakness of the bourgeoisie in defending and promoting its class interests was apparent in the final years of the Shah's regime, when he began to repress capitalists in his populist moves for handling the economic crisis resulting from the oil bonanza of the mid-1970s. The bourgeoisie found itself defenseless when its property, its modus operandi, and even its existence came under attack in the revolutionary process.

The Petty Bourgeoisie

We define petty bourgeoisie as self-employed workers who do not employ any paid labor. The term *khordehpa*, used commonly in Persian, is a reference mainly to members of this class engaged in traditional petty commodity activities (but also including small capitalists). Petty bourgeoisie, particularly those in the traditional category, frequently rely on the work of unpaid family workers. The Iranian census defines unpaid family workers as those who

---

6. For industrial financing in these years, see Benedict 1964, Salehi-Isfahani 1989, and Imam-Jomeh 1985. Imam-Jomeh examines the role of the state in providing financing for large private enterprises in its joint venture with foreign capital, through the Industrial and Mining Development Bank of Iran (217–98).

work for one of their family members without receiving a wage or a salary *(Census 1976,* panj).

We do not consider unpaid family labor as a distinctive class location because of its very ambiguous situation. It is a category reflecting different social and occupational relations, based on gender and age. Some family workers are young adults working for their family "business." Many among them (particularly males) are potential working-class employees or self-employed workers. However, some of those individuals who are considered unpaid family workers may be adult partners in the family business (farm, workshop, or retail store). The latter is more characteristic of women, whose husbands are counted in the census as the head of the household and the owner of the family business. It would be unrealistic to assume that only "the head of the household" is self-employed and that the other family members are unpaid workers. For this reason, unpaid family workers should be considered as part of the self-employed petty bourgeoisie. Yet because of the importance of the unpaid family workers and the significant changes in its size, our empirical study presents it as a separate, but highly related, category to the petty bourgeoisie.

In 1976, 2.8 million self-employed workers accounted for 31.9 percent of the employed workforce (see table 5.1 and table A.1 in the Appendix). There were also 1 million unpaid family workers. Together, the two groups added up to 43.6 percent of the employed workforce. Only 1.2 percent of the petty bourgeoisie was "modern," mainly in professional and technical occupational positions. The largest group among the traditional petty bourgeoisie was of those who had agriculture as their occupational position (60.7 percent of the class). The rest were classified mainly in production and transportation (21.1 percent) and sales and services (16.7 percent). The petty bourgeoisie in production was concentrated in rug making, textiles and apparels, wood products (carpentry), and metal works. This group also included drivers of motor vehicles. In 1976, there were 147,000 self-employed drivers, including cabbies of various sorts and truck owner-drivers. In sales and services, the largest concentration of the petty bourgeoisie was in retailing. The number of self-employed retailers in 1976 was 398,000.

The largest group of unpaid family workers (57.5 percent) was in agriculture, and nearly all of the rest (40.9 percent) were in production. Among the unpaid family workers who were occupied in production activities, 97.5 percent were in rug weaving and textile work, and of them, 85.9 percent were in the rural area. Similarly, 97.9 percent of all unpaid family workers in agriculture were in the rural area. Thus, unpaid family work in 1976 in Iran was primarily a rural phenomenon.

The concentration of nearly one-half (43.5 percent) of the labor force outside of the labor market and within petty economic activities continues to be a clear indication of the undeveloped state of the Iranian capitalist economy.[7] The self-employed in the traditional occupational categories and the unpaid family workers generally have very low productivity and, therefore, low income, as peasant farmers, small retailers, vendors, carpenters, metalworkers, repair persons, and taxi and truck drivers.

The Middle Class

The contradictory middle-class location includes those employees who wield delegated authority in their work (organizational assets/authority dimension of class location) or have scarce skills and expertise (skills/credential dimension). As employees of the private or state sectors, they enjoy relative autonomy at work and may receive a rent above their salary. On the contrary, workers who have limited skills and therefore do not receive a material return (rent) above their wages would not be considered in this location. They would be counted as a member of the working class. Those workers who are at the high level of managerial and administrative occupational categories, as well as those identified as professional and technical workers (we cannot differentiate professionals from technical workers in our class typology in the census data), are considered as proxies for the enumeration of contradictory class location within the class structure. We noted in Chapter 2 that employees who are in this contradictory class location are viewed as "the middle class."

A large proportion of the wage earners in Iran are employees of the state. In Chapter 2 we recognized various apparatuses of the state in a capitalist society. We categorized these apparatuses of the state as ones that function as the political state, provide decommodified state services, or are engaged in economic activities.

The political state consists of executive and administrators of the main branches of the government. It also includes the military and paramilitary arms of the state. The primary function of these organs is to protect and facilitate the reproduction of capitalist social relations. Because of its functions and the forms of its employment relations, particularly in the military and paramilitary organizations, we place those individuals who are engaged in them as

7. The number of self-employed in the employed population of the North American and European countries (including unpaid labor) in 1980s varied between 6 and 14 percent (Wright 1997, 46–52).

an ambiguous class category and call them "political functionaries of the state" or just "political functionaries."

Within the classification of political functionaries, however, we distinguish various major categories. The legislators, judges, and high-level executives (ministers and their deputies, bureau chiefs at the national and provincial levels—in short, high-level bureaucrats), high-level officers of the coercive forces, and professional and technical workers (accountants, financial analysts, lawyers, physicians, engineers) are grouped as "administrative and managerial" and "professional and technical" employees. They are the political officialdom. They numbered 60,000 in 1976.[8] They are, in many ways, similar in their characteristics to the middle-class workers.

The "lower-ranks" category, that is, the rank and file of political functionaries, numbered 672,000 in 1976. About one-half of these workers were the civilian rank-and-file workers of the various ministries and bureau offices, from custodians to clerks and typists. The rest (386,000) were members of the armed forces. Whereas the first subgroup (civilian workers) may be, in many respects, close to the working class, the second is mostly ambiguous (see table 5.1). Most peculiar among the members of the armed forces is the category of military draftees and the temporary volunteers (of Basij and *komiteh*s in the postrevolutionary period). Their "employment" relations have little to do with the labor market or wage labor, although once their period of compulsory or voluntary service is over, they, mostly, join the rank of the working class or the petty bourgeoisie.

The second apparatus of the state is engaged in production of decommodified services, like public education, public health, and other public services. These functions are carried out, principally, by skilled professionals and technical workers (for instance, teachers, physicians, and nurses), administrators and managers (high-level bureaucrats), and a supportive staff of rank-and-file workers (as in janitors, secretaries, and clerks). Those individuals employed in the decommodified social services of the government are essential in the reproduction of the social relations. They are obliged to follow market wages, and are controlled, coordinated, and subjected to the long-run strategic decisions of the state with respect to its revenues, overall budget constraints, and efficiency concerns.

In addition to these activities, states, to varying degrees, may take a direct

---

8. It is the difference between the number of political functionaries and "rank-and-file" workers of political functionaries in table 5.1.

part in economic activities by producing goods and services for the market. In Iran, before and after the revolution, state-owned enterprises produced a long list of products and services, from petroleum and cement to banking, transportation, and communication services. In the Islamic Republic, state employment includes the large number of employees of the parastatal enterprises, such as the Bonyad Mostazafan and Bonyad Shahid, which own and operate their own conglomerate of large enterprises (see Chapter 3). The censuses of 1986 and 1996 include the employees of the revolutionary foundations together with the employees of the state as "public employees." Therefore, in our study, they are included in categories of state employees in the social services and economic activities. Employment in *bonyads* is composed of the same categories of wage-earning workers as those in the private sectors, that is, laborers and managers in various occupational categories, from administration and management to production, sales, and services, in all major activities, including industries, construction, and services. Complete separation of state employees in production of decommodified services and in economic activities is not possible. Therefore, we consider these two functions of the state together. We will view administrators, managers, and professional and technical workers as members of the middle class, and the rank and file workers in the working class.

In 1976, only 102,000 high-level administrators and managers, professionals, and scientific and technical workers were employed by private enterprises. Professionals and scientific and technical workers composed 85 percent of this group. The small size of the middle class of the private sector is a clear indication of the low level of concentration of capital in the private sector of the Iranian economy. High-level managers and professional and technical employees are generally employed in the large and advanced enterprises. As noted above, there were only a few such enterprises in Iran in 1976.

In contrast to the relative small size of the middle class of the private sector, the state nurtured a rising middle class. In 1976, the number of people employed by the state was 1.67 million. Among the state employees, 376,000 were high-level managerial, administrative, professional, scientific, and technical workers employed in the state's decommmodified social services and economic activities (see table A.1 in the Appendix). In the 1960s and 1970s, the state entered the labor market, hiring most of the university graduates in scientific, technical, and managerial fields to run its expanding manufacturing and service activities, from the national oil company to the airlines.

In 1976, only 477,000 (5.4 percent) of the employed workforce could be considered in the middle class, and no less than 78.7 percent of this small middle class were employees of the state. They were employed, especially in the 1970s, with terms and conditions (including salaries and benefits) comparable with those received by the professional and technical employees in the private sector. A shortage of skilled workers had made the market quite competitive in those years. The competition for attracting scientific and technical workers eliminated much of the gap between state and private enterprises. The shortage of skilled labor was not limited only to professional and scientific workers. The problem was widespread. Truck drivers, bricklayers, nurse's assistants, and machine operators where also hard to find, and the competition in the labor market was quite intense (Johnson 1980). These conditions brought the middle class, with little difference between those persons who were employed by the state and those who were in the private sector, to a privileged position in a relative and absolute sense.

The Working Class

In 1976, as Iran was approaching its revolution, 3.5 million (40.2 percent) of its employed labor force was a fragmented working class, not unlike its corresponding capitalist class. About 84 percent (2.97 million) of these workers were employees of the private sector. The other 16 percent (566,000) were rank-and-file employees of the state in social services and economic activities (see table 5.1).

Production workers of the private sector constituted 1.9 million, 54.3 percent of the working class and 21.8 percent of the employed workforce (see table A.1 in the Appendix). Adding the 309,000 production workers employed by the state, the number of production workers in the working class becomes 2.23 million, or 63.1 percent of the working class. We should note, however, that about 1 million of these workers in the "production" class location were construction workers, most of whom had limited skills, worked as simple day laborers, with no job stability, contract, or fringe benefits, and with few legal labor rights.

In 1976, agricultural workers (614,000), constitutes the next significant segment of the working class of the private sector (table A.1 in the Appendix). Most of the agricultural laborers (86 percent) were employed in the rural areas, whereas the production workers were more evenly divided between urban (56 percent) and rural (44 percent) areas. (We will address the urban-rural dichotomy in Chapter 7.) Employees of the private sector in sales and services (294,000) and in clerical activities (132,000) together constituted about 12 percent of the working class. Overall, 31 percent of the employees of the private sector and no less than 56 percent of those employed by the private sector in production (including manufacturing, mining, construction and transportation) were unskilled in 1996 (see table 5.4). The situation could have not been any better in 1976 (for which such data are not available). These workers were in a disadvantaged position in the market with little to have, and even less to look forward to. Moreover, many of them were the displaced rural migrants trying to eke out a living to supplement their family income in the rural area. On the other hand, one could point to a more privileged segment of the working class, employed by the large modern enterprises owned by the private sector or the state.[9]

The existence of a large number of unskilled workers and an overwhelming number of small enterprises in the private sector of the economy leads one to conclude the existence of a highly fragmented working class, with a small "core of the industrial working class" (S. Rahnema 1992, 75). Although this contention is not untrue, it has never been carefully quantified. The ratio of all those who are identified as working-class employees of the private sector by the number of capitalist employers is a measure of the overall concentration of labor in the economy. In 1976 this ratio was 16.3. Although this ratio is a revealing measure in terms of relative changes in subsequent years, it is not a true reflection of the existing working-class concentration, because any average obfuscates the distribution. The size distribution for Iranian manufacturing establishments in 1976 is informative.

The analysis of the distribution of the wage and salary earners in Iran (see table 5.2) reveals that in 1976, of the 315,000 workers in manufacturing establishments of 1–9 workers, only 103 workers were wage and salary earners, whereas the rest were working owners or unpaid family workers. Once we adjust the figures by excluding the working owners and unpaid workers, we see that wage and salary earners in manufacturing were more concentrated in the medium-size and large factories. Only 20.7 percent of wage and salary earners in manufacturing were employed in small (1–9 worker) plants. However, more than one-half (54.4 percent) of the wage and salary earners in manufacturing were engaged in large establishments with 50 or more workers. The average size of these firms in 1976 was 294 workers. About one quarter (24.9 percent) of the manufacturing wage and salary earners were engaged

9. See Bayat 1987 and S. Rahnema 1992.

in medium-size enterprises with the average of 29 wage and salary earners per plant. Thus, 80 percent of the wage and salary earners in manufacturing were in medium-size and large enterprises. From table 5.1 we can estimate the ratio of managers, administrators, professionals, and technical employees in the private sector to the working-class employees. It is 3.4 percent. If the ratio of "managers" to "workers" is about roughly the same in state enterprises,[10] and if we take this figure to be the ratio for the manufacturing sector as well, about 75 to 76 percent of manufacturing working class was engaged in plants with 10 or more employees and about 50 percent in plants with 50 or more employees. True, the size of the manufacturing working class was only about 480,000 workers;[11] nevertheless, about 240,000 worked in firms with more than 50 employees.

In 1976, the state employed 1.67 million workers (19 percent of employed labor force). Among them, 566,000 were rank-and-file employees in economic and social service activities. In Iran, before and after the revolution, state-owned enterprises have produced petroleum, steel, tobacco products, tractors, and cement; operated banks, hotels, airlines, and railroads; and provided electricity, water, gas, and post and telephone services.

Some of the very large manufacturing establishments were state owned. In 1976 there were 130 state-owned manufacturing enterprises and 55 state-private joint ventures (MAI, *Statistical Yearbook, 1979,* 747). We do not have the data for the number of state employees in these establishments for this year, but we know that the number of state employees in the industrial sector was 264,500. This number includes those who were employed in manufacturing establishments, as well as the employees of gas, electricity, and petroleum extraction and refining. To them we must add the number of those workers in communication (post and telephone) and transportation (railroad

10. We do not have the necessary disaggregated data for the state sector. The comparable data for the state sector combine all those employed in the social service and economic activities. Social services include the very large number of administrative and professional, scientific, and technical employees (most important, teachers and physicians). It is not characteristic of economic activities. Nevertheless, we can expect the ratio of "managers" to workers in the state sectors to be somewhat higher than in the private sector. This situation could be the result of the possible lower efficiency of the state enterprises, and also the nature of the more advanced and large scale of these enterprises.

11. The total number of wage and salary earners in manufacturing, according to table 5.2, was 498,000; subtracting 3.5 percent from this figure as middle class (management and professional employees), we will come close to 480,000.

and airlines were state monopolies).[12] In addition, the working class in state banking and insurance (clerks, custodians, and salespersons) and social services (mainly health and education, noted above) is in this category. All in all, the state had 566,000 working-class employees engaged in providing social (decommodified) services and in production of market-related goods and services. Most of these workers were employed in large manufacturing and service enterprises, public utilities, and the oil industry.

Thus, we can conclude that while a large proportion of the working class was unskilled and was widely dispersed in small capitalist enterprises, at the same time there was a significant portion of the working class that was skilled and concentrated in large enterprises of the private sector and particularly the state sector. The first group of workers received low wages and had no labor contract, no job stability, no fringe benefits, and subsequently no more than a bleak life opportunity. The second group generally had many of the benefits and protections of the labor law, and many advantages that the first group did not.

Period 1: Deproletarianization, Peasantization, and Retraditionalization of Labor

We noted that social turmoil, antagonism toward capital, and the erosion of sanctity of property rights, with a dysfunctional and factionalized state machinery, results in structural involution, that is, shriveling of capitalist production and expansion of petty-commodity production. We expect that this condition would lead to deproletarianization of labor, peasantization of agriculture, and an increase in petty economic activities, especially in redundant services activities. We expect to witness a decrease in the size of the working class and a substantial increase in the size of the petty bourgeoisie in the postrevolutionary decade. This process was accompanied by a substantial expansion of social and economic activities of the state and a huge increase in the size of the political state, mainly for the Iran-Iraq War mobilization and

12. The total number of state employees in some major activities in 1976 were 37,000 in communication; 53,000 in electricity, gas, and water; 74,000 in transportation; 39,000 in production of crude oil; 23,000 in coal mining; 42,000 in banking and insurance; 42,000 in basic metals; 25,000 in machines and tools; and 27,000 in tobacco and food. The distribution of administrative and professional workers (middle class) and clerical, sales, and production workers (working class) at the aggregated level is not available to us for these activities.

domestic surveillance. Therefore, we would also expect a substantial increase in the number of political functionaries of the state, bureaucrats and soldiers, in addition to factory and service workers in the employment of the government. The question is if the decline in the number of working-class and middle-class workers employed by the private sector was offset by the increase in the number of those employed by the state in these classes.

The census data, in table 5.1 and table A.1 in the Appendix, reveal the changes in the class configuration in the immediate postrevolutionary years. We will examine them here.

The Shrinking Working Class

There was a dramatic absolute decline in the size of the working class in Iran in the first postrevolutionary decade, most severely reflected in the size of the working class employed by the private sector. It declined by 1.16 million (39.1 percent), while the size of the employed workforce increased from 8.8 million to 11 million (25.0 percent). Thus, the working class, which accounted for 40.2 percent of the employed workforce in 1975, shrank to 24.6 percent in 1986. There was absolute decline in all occupational categories of the working class employed by the private sector, from agriculture to services (except an increase in the "unclassified" category). The number of production workers in the private sector declined by 648,000 (33.8 percent).

However, the number of working-class employees of the state increased by 326,000 (57.6 percent). This increase was partly a result of the transfer of ownership of some large private enterprises to the state by nationalization decrees of the government, and confiscation by the Revolutionary Islamic Courts in the early postrevolutionary years.[13] This condition was particularly true in the industrial sector where state employment increased by 226,000, accounting for 13 percent of the increase in the number of state employees. In that sector, the number of private employees decreased by 346,000 (Behdad and Nomani 2002). Hence, some of the decline in the number of the working class employed in the private sector was the result of the move from the private sector to the state sector. Yet the increase in the number of working-class employees of the state was 834,000 short in offsetting the decline of the working class in the private sector.

13. See A. Rahnema and Nomani 1990, 239–44; Rashidi 1994, 46–52; and Khalatbari 1994, 185–90.

The Larger Class of Smaller Traditional Capitalists

At the same time that the working class declined in number, the size of the capitalist class increased by 87.4 percent. Almost all of this increase was in the number of traditional capitalists, and mostly (93.7 percent) attributable to the increase in number of those in agriculture and production. By 1986, the occupation of one-third of all capitalists in Iran was in agriculture, and 40.5 percent in production (19.5 percent and 36.5 percent, respectively, in 1976). Both groups increased faster than the increase in the employed labor force. The de facto confiscation and redistribution of land increased the number of agricultural capitalists. However, the absolute number and the share of capitalists in modern occupations, and in sales and services within traditional occupations, decreased.

Although the methodology and coverage of the survey of manufacturing establishments in 1976 and 1987 are somewhat different, we may make a rough comparison of size distribution of these enterprises with extreme caution (see table 5.2). Between 1976 and 1986, the relative importance of small firms (1–9 workers) increased in terms of number, value of output, number of workers per establishments, and output per worker. We see a significant decline in the medium-size firms in all the above accounts, except in their number. This trend is predictable in the involutionary process.

At one extreme, limited employment opportunities for wage and salary earners, particularly for those who were purged for being "un-Islamic" or "antirevolutionary," compelled some with special skills, or financial means, to pursue the "survival strategy" of organizing their own businesses. The disruption in productive activity of large capitalist enterprises also provided market opportunities for these small enterprises. A study reveals a countercyclical trend between output fluctuation of the large and small enterprises (Behdad 1994b). At the other extreme, state-owned enterprises with special privileges in having access to scarce foreign exchange and industrial inputs managed to keep their share in the market.

Squeezed between these two were the medium-size enterprises. The number of workers in their employment, and in their output per plant and per worker, declined. The average number of wage earners (managers and working-class employees) per capitalist in the private sector declined from 16.9 in 1976 to 5.5 in 1986. That is, in the Iranian economy in 1986, each capitalist employed only one-third as many employees as in 1976. Table 5.3 shows that the number of wage earners per employer declined in all major economic ac-

Table 5.3
Concentration Index, 1976, 1986, and 1996

	1976	1986	1996
Total	16.9	5.5	6.3
Agriculture	17.4	2.7	3.4
Industry	15.6	6.5	7.6
Construction	56.0	15.5	11.7
Services	7.7	4.6	5.0

Sources: MAI 1980, 1988, 1997.
Note: The Concentration Index is the ratio of working- and middle-class employees of the private sector to the number of capitalists.

tivities. These figures are all reflections of, as well as an explanation for, the decline in the rate of capital accumulation, which had its most serious long-run economic manifestations in the following decade.

The Growing Petty Bourgeoisie

By 1986 the petty bourgeoisie replaced the working class as the largest social class in Iran. Between 1976 and 1986, the employed labor force increased by 2.20 million. More than two-thirds (1.58 million) of this increase were added to the petty bourgeoisie. Their rank increased to 4.39 million, or 39.9 percent of the working population. By including unpaid family workers, together they constituted 44.3 percent of the employed labor force. Similar to 1976, only a very small proportion (1.1 percent) of the petty bourgeoisie was in the "modern" category. That is, only 48,000 were self-employed physicians, dentists, lawyers, accountants, engineers, and so on. The rest were in traditional categories of sales and services (14.1 percent), production (29.8 percent, including construction), and agriculture (53.1 percent). In 1986, there were 490,000 self-employed retailers and 336,000 self-employed cabbies and truck drivers, which adds up to 826,000 and 7.5 percent of the entire employed workforce, a 52 percent increase since 1976.

In agriculture, land redistribution increased the number of small landholders working as self-employed farmers with their unpaid family workers, or employing one or two workers. It is this phenomenon that led to a substantial decline in the number of wage-earning agricultural laborers from 614,000 in 1976 to 294,000 in 1986. This is the process of peasantization of agriculture, to which we will return in Chapter 7.

When petty-commodity relations in economic activities are rekindled, an increase in the number of unpaid family workers is expected. Instead, between 1976 and 1986, the number of unpaid family workers declined by 537,000 (52.5 percent). The number of rural unpaid family workers (constituting 92 percent of the total in 1976) declined from 936 in 1976 to 429 in 1986. Nevertheless, unpaid family work remained a rural phenomenon, still 89 percent of the total.

Various factors might have caused this seemingly contradictory situation. *Census 1986* shows more than a tenfold increase in the number of those individuals whose occupational status is "unspecified," from 41,000 to 458,000. Unpaid family workers are most likely to be undercounted, or counted as unspecified. As much as four-fifths of the decline in the number of unpaid family workers could be the result of reclassifying them as "unspecified" workers in the 1986 census.[14] Yet, in addition to reclassification, some real factors were also at work. The fall in the market for handwoven carpets reduced the need for female family workers. Revolutionary and war mobilization attracted many rural men. At the same time, increase in school enrollment, particularly among rural women, took away some children from family labor. Examining the ratio of young (under twenty) unpaid family workers to those older (twenty and older), we note that between 1976 and 1986 the ratio declined most dramatically for women. That is, the young-old ratio of female unpaid family workers in the rural area fell from 0.9 to 0.5, whereas for the rural men the ratio remained 1.9 for both censuses. Thus, though contrary to expectation, the number of unpaid family workers declined, the number of young women (under age twenty) unpaid family workers declined more sharply than any other groups. Most likely, this circumstance is not all a statistical deficiency. Revolutionary conditions have pulled many out of family work, some to war, some to school, some to start their own self-employment businesses, and others to the rank of unemployed.

14. The number of "unspecified" workers increased by 417,000 between 1976 and 1986. In the same period, the number of unpaid family workers declined by 537,000. If we assume the number of these two groups of worker had remained constant in the decade between the two censuses, then the possible change in classification could account for as much as 78 percent of the decline in the number of unpaid family workers. However, with a more realistic assumption, expecting both categories increasing at the rate that the number of the employed workforce changed in this period, then the possible change in classification could account for 51 percent of the decline in the number of unpaid family workers.

The Growing State Middle Class: Bureaucratic and Professional

The middle class grew in a peculiar way in the postrevolutionary decade. The middle-class employees of the private sector declined by 37.2 percent, and the number of those employed by the state increased by 88.8 percent. Obviously, as large private enterprises became bankrupt or were dissolved, so too were gone their managers and their technical workers. Capital crossed borders to seek refuge in more secure lands. Managers and professionals, too, crossed borders to seek security and better life opportunities.[15] Some managers, administrators, and scientific and technical employees of the private sector (and some of the state employees as well) migrated abroad for political and nonpolitical reasons. Among those persons who stayed, some became entrepreneurs, and many of those individuals whose enterprises had become nationalized or confiscated became state employees.

Thus, the number of middle-class employees of the private sector declined from 102,000 to 64,000, while the number of those in the employment of the state increased from 376,000 to 710,000. The largest increase in the latter group was an 88 percent increase in the number of professionals and technical workers in the employment of the state. These workers were mostly teachers and health-care employees, whose number increased from 371,000 in 1976 to 698,000 in 1986. It was the growth of this group of middle-class employees that contributed to the increase in the size of the middle class, from 477,000 in 1976 to 774,000 in 1986. The 62 percent increase in the size of this class between these years is larger than the rate of increase in the number of employed workforce. Thus, the relative size of the middle class increased from 5.4 percent in 1976, to 7 percent in 1986. This increase in size was wholly because of the increase in the number of state professional and technical employees. They accounted for 90 percent of all the middle class in 1986.

Takeover of Political Functionaries

Between 1976 and 1986, 1.12 million were added to the number of political functionaries of the Islamic state, a 153 percent increase in their number. No

---

15. The minister of science, research, and technology of the Islamic Republic has stated that in the year 2000, more than 200,000 leading academics and industrialists left Iran for the Western countries (Islamic Republic News Agency [IRNA], May 1, 2001). The head of the Foreign Ministry's Center for Expatriates Affairs claimed that "of 100 thousand Iranians in New York, 19.5 percent have Ph.D.'s, 9 percent have MDs and 8 percent have Masters degrees" (IRNA, Mar. 13, 2002). On emigration of Iranians, see Torbat 2002.

less than 811,000 of this increase was the addition to the number of the military and domestic coercive forces. Sepah-e Pasdaran-e Enqelab-e Eslami (Islamic Revolutionary Guards), formed immediately after the revolution, accounts for most of this increase. The category of "political functionaries" also includes the other segments of the "political state," namely, the administrative apparatus of the state, including the executive, legislative, and judiciary branches of the government. This group, as a whole, including civil and military employment, was 89 percent composed of the rank and file. The other 11 percent were administrative and managerial employees of the state (only 0.62 percent) and professional and technical employees (10.4 percent). These two subcategories constitute the officialdom of the Islamic state. All in all, in 1986, 16.8 percent of the employed labor force in Iran was engaged as "political functionaries" of the Islamic state, in the legislative, executive, and judiciary branches of the government, including, most important, the military and paramilitary forces. In 1976, in the Pahlavi regime, which was considered a highly militarized and bureaucratized state, this group constituted 8.3 percent of the employed workforce. The increase in the number of political functionaries of the Islamic state was in addition to the increase in the number of state employees who were engaged in social and economic activities.

Period 2: Economic Liberalization and Deinvolution

In the post-Khomeini period, beginning with the death of Ayatollah Khomeini in June 1989, the liberalization policy of the Islamic Republic, as indecisive and incoherent as it was, helped to rejuvenate the capitalist relations of production. Although the state continued its omnipotent presence in the market, the political and social environment provided a more hospitable condition for capital activities.[16] The increase in the oil revenues of 1990–96 was an added blessing, facilitating capital accumulation and a deepening of capitalist reproduction. If we called recoiling of capitalist relations of production in the previous period structural involution, what we observe in the second period is called structural deinvolution. Structural deinvolution, in contrast to the conditions of the previous decade, is expected to lead to acceleration of capital accumulation, proletarianization of labor, and depeasantization of agriculture. Although the process of deinvolution was not complete by 1996, when the last census was taken, its manifestations are amply present in the structure of social classes in that census. In spite of its important features, the

16. See A. Rahnema and Nomani 1990 and Khalatbari 1994.

Figure 5.1
Class Composition, 1976, 1986, and 1996

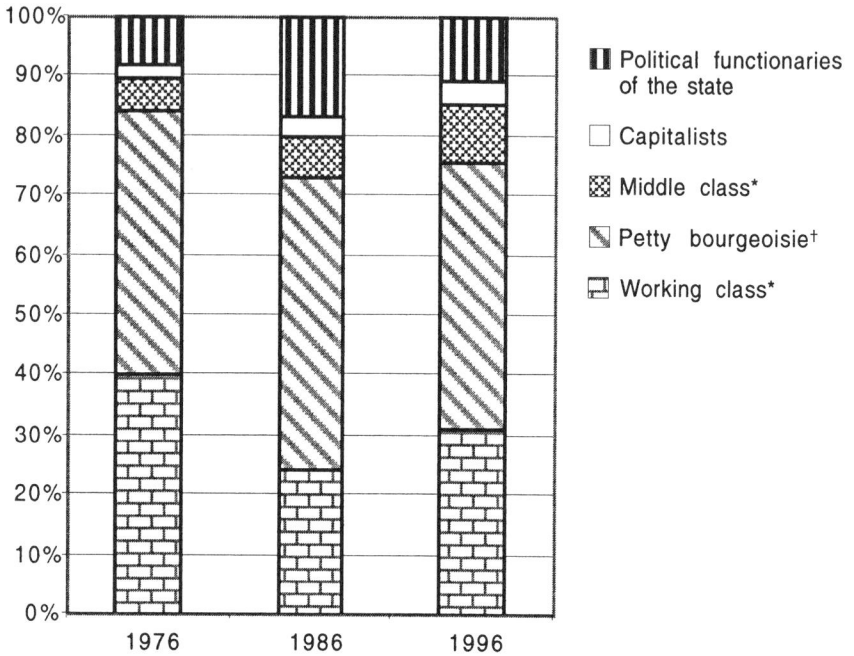

Source: Table A.1 in the Appendix.
*Includes employees of the private sector and the state.
†Includes unpaid family workers and those "unspecified."

class structure of the employed workforce in 1996, in stark contrast to that in 1986, reflects a change toward resembling the prerevolutionary class structure (figure 5.1).

Between 1986 and 1996, total employment in Iran increased by 32.5 percent (3.6 million), compared to 38.1 percent increase in the population of those ten years and older, indicating the limits of employment creation and the potential for increasing the number of unemployed. No less than 79.7 percent (2.8 million) of the increase in the number of the employed workforce was in the urban economy, which increased by 47.8 percent in this decade. Rural employment in this period increased only by 14.5 percent (724,000).

The State and the Private Sector

A significant aspect of an economic liberalization policy would be a reduction in state bureaucracy and social programs, and withdrawal of the state from the market activities. Yet between 1986 and 1996, the number of state employees increased from 3.5 million to 4.3 million (by 23.3 percent). The rate of growth in the number of state employees was, however, smaller than the rate of growth of the employed workforce in these years, and, consequently, the share of state employees in the workforce decreased from 31.3 percent in 1986 to 29.2 in 1996. As a result, the share of the private sector in the workforce increased only slightly from 68.3 percent to 70.8 percent, as the private-sector employment grew by 36.7 percent. However, the decline in the share of state employment in this period was merely because of a decrease in the number of political functionaries of the state (by 291,000), when the size of the military and paramilitary forces was reduced by 315,000 after the cessation of hostilities with Iraq. In the same period, however, the number of state employees in social services and economic activities increased from 1.6 million to 2.7 million (68.4 percent). By 1996, more than 60 percent of those who worked for the state were in the middle class or working class, providing social services or engaged in economic activities (figure 5.2). Thus, the small decline in the share of state employees in total employment was a result of the postwar demilitarization, and not the consequence of the economic liberalization policy of the government.

The impact of economic liberalization is reflected mainly in the changes in the configuration of social classes, affecting those directly associated with the private sector. Generally, we observe two principal trends. First, there is a distinct decline in importance of the petty-commodity activities and a simultaneous growth in the relative importance of capitalist relations of production, manifested in proletarianization of the workforce and depeasantization of agriculture. Second, we observe a noticeable increase in the managerial and technical complexity of capitalist relations of production, reflected in strengthening of modern capitalist activities and a relative decline in the importance of traditional activities. This condition is accompanied by an increase in the size of the firms and an increase in the size of the administrative, managerial, professional, and technical employees in the rank of private-sector workers.

Proletarianization and Depeasantization

In the decade leading to 1996, the size of the working class increased by 1.8 million to 4.5 million workers,[17] which accounts for one-half of the increase

17. Moghissi and Rahnema (2000, 214–15) estimate the 1996 number of "wage workers" to be 2.6 million in the private sector and 1.3 million in the state sector. They regard "salary" earners in clerical, sales, and service as "the new middle class" just like managers and profes-

Figure 5.2
Composition of State Employees, 1976, 1986, and 1996 (in 1,000s)

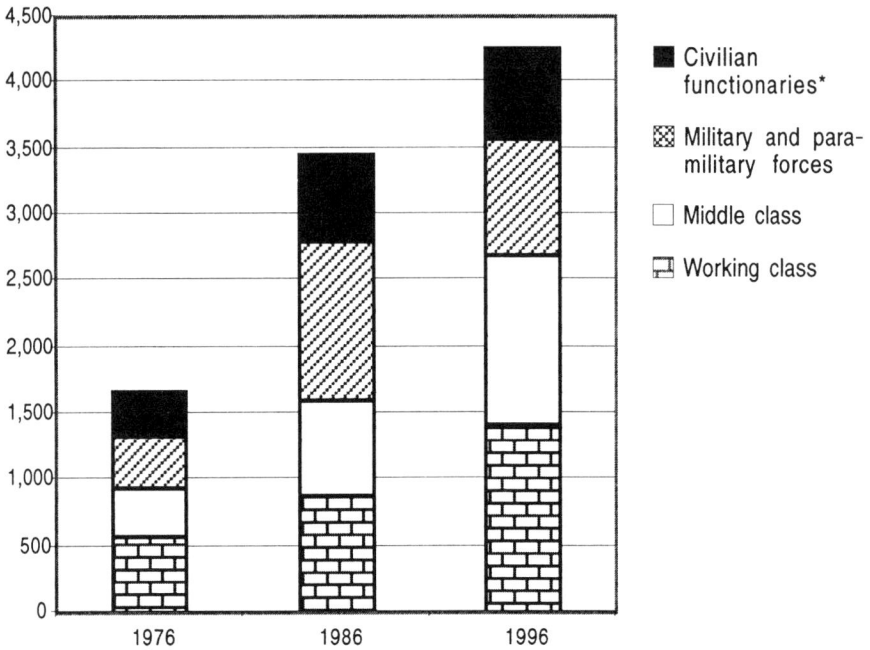

Source: Table A.1 in the Appendix.
*The number for "civilian functionaries" is calculated by subtracting military and paramilitary forces from "political functionaries" in Table A.1.

in employment and represents a rate of growth equal to 67.8 percent. Growing at a rate more than twice the rate of the employed workforce, the relative size of the working class increased from 24.6 percent of the employed workforce in 1986 to 31.1 percent in 1996 (see table 5.1 and figure 5.1). Nevertheless, in 1996 the working class was still a smaller fraction of the workforce than in 1976, when this class location accounted for 40.2 percent of the employed workforce.

As fragmented as in the past, the composition of the working class in dif-

sional employees (202) and effectively include close to a million of the rank and file of the political state, including 881,000 members of the armed forces, in their statistics of the working class. Despite the fact that wage-salary distinction is an important factor in determining the chance for long-run mobility of a small part of the working class, it is not an axis of class determination in either a neo-Weberian or a Marxist approach to class analysis.

ferent occupational positions in 1996 remained more or less similar to the situation in 1986, and in stark contrast to 1976 (figure 5.3). In 1976, only 16 percent of those individuals in the working-class location were in the employment of the state. In 1986 this proportion had more than doubled to 33 percent, when the number of working-class employees of the private sector declined. By 1996, however, the state continued to employ nearly the same proportion of the Iranian working class as in 1986, in spite of a substantial increase in the number in this class location.

In 1996 the working-class population with production or agricultural occupational positions still accounted for the same proportion in the employed working class as they did in 1986. Yet this statement implies that the number of workers in these class locations increased at the same rate as the working class, which grew faster than the employed workforce. At the same time the proportion of sales and service workers and clerical workers in employment in the private sector increased substantially (from 7 percent of the working class in 1986 to 10.3 percent in 1996 for both categories combined). Hence, those

Figure 5.3
Composition of the Working Class, 1976, 1986, and 1996 (in 1,000s)

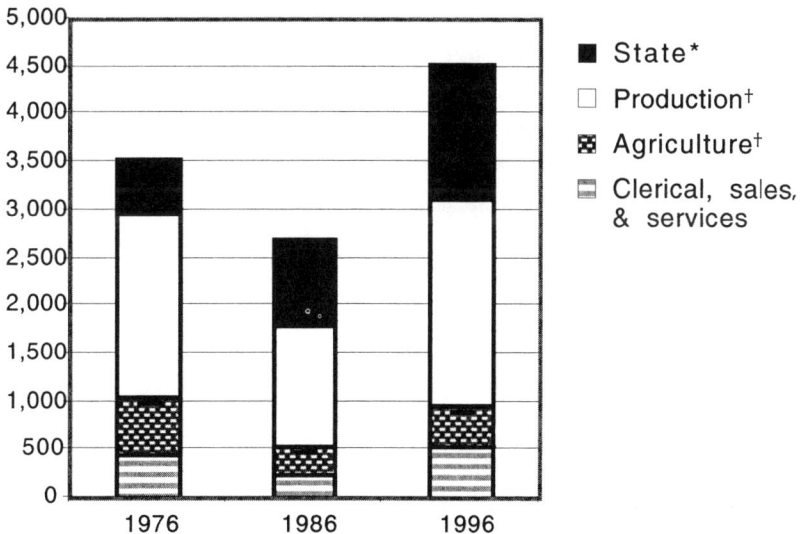

Source: Table A.1 in the Appendix.

*Working-class employees of the state in all major economic activities.

†Working-class employees of the private sector in each major economic activity.

workers in these class locations replaced some of the petty-commodity producers in the similar occupational positions. In fact, in the same period, the petty bourgeoisie grew at the rate of 18.4 percent, significantly less than the rate of growth of the employed workforce (32.4 percent). Thus, the share of the petty bourgeoisie decreased from 39.9 percent to 35.7 percent of the employed workforce. This decrease is the proletarianization trend that we expected to take place in the process of deinvolution in the post-Khomeini period.

A notable change in the petty bourgeoisie subcategories was the absolute decline in the number of those persons engaged in agriculture, from 2.3 million in 1986 to 2.2 million in 1996, in spite of the increase in the size of the employed workforce. In the same period the number in a working-class location in agriculture increased by 41 percent. Recall that in the previous decade, immediately after the revolution, the number of self-employed agricultural workers increased by 36.9 percent, as the absolute number of the agricultural working class suffered an absolute decline of 52.1 percent (see table A.1 in the Appendix).

Between 1986 and 1996, the number of the petty bourgeoisie whose occupational position was identified as production continued to increase somewhat faster (at 37.6 percent) than the size of the employed workforce. At the same time, the number of the working class in the same occupational position increased at a much faster rate (69.2 percent) (see table A.1 in the Appendix). We observe a similar situation for the petty bourgeoisie in sales and services and for their counterparts in the working class.

Therefore, we can make the observation that the increase in the relative size of the working class (proletarianization) in the deinvolutionary process was compensated, most important, by the absolute decline of the agricultural petty bourgeoisie (depeasantization) and the absolute decline in the number of those in military and paramilitary forces (postwar demilitarization). Thus, principally, those workers released from these two declining positions and the new entrants to the employed workforce contributed to the increase in the size of the working-class population in 1996.

Nevertheless, engagement of the unemployed population as self-employed workers in redundant services continued to increase in the 1986–96 decade. In 1996, there were 841,000 self-employed retail shop owners (351,000 more than in 1986). More than 85 percent of these shopkeepers were in the urban areas. The number of self-employed drivers, of various sorts, in 1996 was 486,000 (150,000 more than in 1986). By this account, in 1996, 1.33 million workers, or 9 percent of the Iranian employed workforce, were self-employed shopkeepers or self-employed cabbies. The revolutionary decades added 781,000 to the rank of these two categories of the petty bourgeoisie.

We should note the continuation of the puzzle about the unpaid family workers in the second postrevolutionary period. By 1996, the number of unpaid family workers increased faster than the number of the employed workforce, resulting in an increase (from 1986) in the relative size of this attachment to the petty bourgeoisie. In 1996, the employment of unpaid family workers remained a rural phenomenon, as 83.7 percent of those in this class location were in rural areas. Yet over the years the rural proportion of these workers had slowly declined from 91.7 percent in 1976 to 88.6 percent in 1986. The most significant increase in the number in this class location is for rural women who were under twenty, growing by 81.8 percent, and the smallest rate of increase was for rural men in the same age group, growing by 31.1 percent in the same period. These two trends for young women and men were most probably a response to the recovery of the market for handwoven carpets (placing more women in the unpaid family work) and the creation of employment in the formal labor market (attracting young men to these jobs and away from their existing unpaid family work).

Once we include unpaid family workers in the petty bourgeoisie, their total share in the workforce in 1996 becomes 41.2 percent, which is less than what it was in 1986 (44.3 percent). If we suppose that the most likely employment category of those individuals who are listed as "unspecified" is unpaid family worker or petty bourgeois, then the petty bourgeoisie would have been 48.5 percent of the employed workforce in 1986 and 44.3 percent in 1996, compared to 44 percent in 1976. Considering that even in 1996 more than 96 percent of the petty bourgeoisie were engaged in traditional activities, close to one-half of the Iranian labor force are petty-commodity producers. The 1979 revolution solidified their position and increased the size of their ranks.

Increased Managerial Complexity and Modernization of Class Locations

The deinvolution process in the second postrevolutionary period led to increased modernization of occupational locations and at the same time an increase in the managerial complexity of the firm. These two phenomena are interrelated and are both reflections of advancement of capitalist relations of production. With increased accumulation within the firm and the resulting increase in the size of the firm, division of labor becomes more complex, work relations become more hierarchical, and the need for administrative, managerial, professional, and technical positions increases. We observe that the Concentration Index (the ratio of private-sector working-class and middle-class employees to the capitalists) increased from 5.5 to 6.3 between 1986 and 1996. Granted that in 1996 it was still a much smaller ratio than in 1976 (see table 5.3), but we have to keep in mind that a significant number of the very large corporations were nationalized in the early postrevolutionary years, thus being excluded from the calculation of the Concentration Index.

The increase in the Concentration Index (albeit mild) is observed in all sectors of the economy, except in construction. In the case of manufacturing, for which we have data at the firm level, we can observe an increase in concentration in the structure of firms. Between 1986 and 1996 the number of small firms (with fewer than ten workers) declined from 328,000 to 308,000, the number of medium-size firms (ten to forty-nine workers) remained more or less the same, and the number of large firms (fifty or more workers) increased by 94.3 percent (see table 5.2). In this situation, 53.5 percent of the wage earners in manufacturing activities worked in firms with fifty or more workers. When we add the number of those workers in medium-size firms, this proportion increases to 68.8 percent. Here we should note that between 1986 and 1996 the average size of small firms increased only marginally (from 2.3 to 2.5), medium-size firms remained unchanged at 18, and large firms declined from 407 to 266 workers per establishment, which indicates that the substantial increase in the number of large firms was concentrated at the lower end of the size spectrum for these firms.

In the decade of economic liberalization, the number of modern capitalists (those with administrative, managerial, professional, or technical occupational positions) more than tripled, from 22,000 to 75,000, when the size of the capitalist class increased by 54.8 percent, to 528,000. Hence, by 1996, in comparison to 1986, a much more significant proportion of capitalists were modern. Nevertheless, still 85.9 percent of capitalists were in traditional occupational positions. A similar change in the composition of modern versus traditional petty bourgeoisie is notable in the same period. In spite of more than tripling the number of modern petty bourgeoisie, in 1996 still 96.8 percent of members of this class were traditional.

The postwar demilitarization of the state and rejuvenation of capitalist relations together gave rise to a significant increase (92.9 percent) in the size of the middle class, from 7 percent of the employed workforce in 1986 to 10.2 percent in 1996. From the 719,000 increase in the size of the middle class,

564,000 (or 78.4 percent) was in the growth of professional and technical workers and administrative and managerial employees of the state. Nevertheless, the number in similar class locations in the private sector more than tripled in this decade (to 219,000), constituting 14.7 percent of those in the middle-class location (see table A.1 in the Appendix). Interestingly, the overwhelming majority (87.3 percent) of the middle class were professional and technical employees of the state or the private sector, and only a small group of them (12.7 percent) were in administrative and managerial positions. This situation, especially with respect to the private sector, reflects the relatively low level of managerial complexity of the firm, indicating the existence of only a small proportion of economic enterprises with nonowner managers.

The relatively low level of educational attainment of the capitalist and petty bourgeoisie classes is another indication of the relatively low level of development of capitalism in Iran and the overwhelming traditional positioning of these two classes. In 1996, one-fifth of the capitalist class and more than one-third of the petty bourgeoisie were illiterate (table 5.4). Among the capitalists, 27.9 percent had attended high school, and only 7.2 percent had attended an institution of higher education. For the petty bourgeoisie, these figures were, respectively, 11.2 percent and 1.3 percent.

In comparison, and like before the revolution, employees of the state were the most educated group among all class locations. The census data do not allow us to disaggregate this large group of employees into the middle class, working class, and political functionaries. But the educational attainment data in table 5.4 shows that 58.6 percent of state employees had high school or more education, and 26.6 percent had university education. In fact, 80.7 percent of all university-educated, employed members of the labor force were in employment of the state. This high concentration of educated employees in the various apparatuses of the state constitutes the largest group of the middle-class employees of the state (85.4 percent in 1996).

Among employees of the private sector, the majority of whom (93.9 percent) were in the working class, illiteracy was 23 percent, and "some education," up to the middle school, was 60 percent. The sum of these two groups made up the majority of the working class in the private-sector employment. Only 3.5 percent of the employees of the private sector had some university education. If we assume all of these (116,000) university-educated employees of the private sector were in management or professional-technical capacities, they would make up, approximately, one-half (52.8 percent) of the middle class employed by the private sector. Comparatively, with the same assump-

Table 5.4
Education and Skill Composition, 1996 (in percentages)

	Total	Capitalists	Petty bourgeoisie	Unpaid family workers	Private-sector employees	State employees★	Unspecified
Education							
Illiterate	21.4	20.4	34.0	24.5	23.0	4.7	18.2
Religious school	0.2	0.1	0.2	0.0	0.2	0.3	0.2
Middle school†	50.7	51.5	53.3	70.0	60.0	36.4	52.0
High school and preuniversity	18.0	20.7	11.2	5.3	13.4	32.0	19.4
University	9.6	7.2	1.3	0.2	3.5	26.6	10.2
Total	100.0	100.0	100.0	100.0	100.0	100.0	100.0
Skill							
Unskilled	13.2	2.6	7.7	10.1	31.0	7.9	14.3

Source: MAI 1997.

★Includes rank and file among "state functionaries."

†Includes (1) any level of education (other than religious schooling) less than high school and (2) informal and "adult" education.

tion for the middle-class employees of the state, almost three-quarters (74.5 percent) of managers, professional, and technical employees of the state had university education. That is, the state, with 1.1 million university-educated employees, had a more educated managerial, professional, and technical workforce in both absolute and relative terms than the private sector.

The 1996 census provides the number of unskilled individuals (called "simple laborers" or *"kargaran-e sadeh"*) in different class locations (see table 5.4). Their number is put at 1.9 million (13.2 percent of total employment).[18] Private sector employees made up 1.03 million of these "laborers." If we assume that nearly all of the unskilled employees of the private sector were in the working class, then about one-third (33.2 percent) of the working class are unskilled "simple laborers." Most likely, this population overlaps with the illiterate segment of the class. Here there are three interesting points to note. First, although illiteracy is highest among the petty bourgeoisie and unpaid family workers, the proportion of unskilled among them is relatively low, respectively, 7.7 percent and 10.1 percent, in comparison with the employees of the private sector. Second, illiteracy is amazingly high and educational attainment is quite low among capitalists. This situation is reflective of the empirical fact that a large proportion of Iranian capitalists are traditional and small, in many ways similar to the traditional petty bourgeoisie, with similar life opportunities. Third, a large proportion of the working class is in the market with little skill or education. Many are construction workers, but there are also many in production, services, and agriculture. They can eke out a living in temporary (unstable) work assignments, without protection of the provisions of the labor laws or fringe benefits. Of course, there are also workers who have skills with or without education, working with the benefits that the unskilled-uneducated workers lack.

Conclusions

The postrevolutionary turmoil and transition had notable impacts on the configuration of the class structure in Iran. The disruption of the accumulation process in the first revolutionary decade retarded the capitalist relations of production. This condition was manifested in the deproletarianization of labor and peasantization of the agriculture. This involutionary trend was ac-

---

18. The distribution is 1.09 million in "mining, construction, industry and transportation," 496,000 in services, and 342,000 in "agriculture, forestry and fishery."

companied by an increase in the extent of the activities of the state, most particularly, but not limited to, those individuals in the realm of the "political state." In the post-Khomeini period, the effort toward reconstitution and rejuvenation of the capitalist relations of production via an economic liberalization policy reversed some of the changes observed in the previous decade in the configuration of the class structure. In this period we witnessed, as we expected, an increase in proletarianization of labor and depeasantization of the agriculture. Whereas the first period promoted traditional capitalists and the petty bourgeoisie, in the deinvolution of the latter period we observed a sizable increase in the number of modern capitalists and petty bourgeoisie. Although the reversal trend of deinvolution has not been completed, the new trend in the reconfiguration of the class structure is notable. In a comparison of the class nature of the employed workforce in 1996 with that in 1976 we observe that in spite of some peculiar differences, there are striking similarities between the two periods. If we can regard the changes between 1986 and 1996 as a trend, there is a clear pattern toward reconstruction of the 1976 class configuration.

In the Appendix we have differentiated the absolute and relative magnitudes of each class category (employment effect and class effect, respectively) by applying the decomposition technique (see table A.2). The results confirm the above conclusions.

6

The Nature of Women's
Marginalization in Employment

THE STUDY OF THE CHANGES in the position of women in postrevolutionary Iran has been a vibrant area of social research. The focus of these studies is
mainly legal-jurisprudential, ideological, cultural, and political.[1] In this chapter we will examine gender inequality in postrevolutionary Iran by examining
the extent of exclusion of women from the market, and the class–gender nature of their incorporation into the employed workforce. We will examine
the sources and mechanisms of women's economic marginalization in the
context of involutionary and deinvolutionary processes of the economy in the
postrevolutionary decades.

The current literature on gender and work in Iran has implicitly defined
marginalization as women's exclusion from the market.[2] In this chapter we
will present economic marginalization of women as a multidimensional phenomenon and by a concrete class–gendered analysis of the social hierarchy of
work for the Iranian workforce. Based on this conceptualization of female and
male social hierarchy of work, we will examine the exclusion of women from
the market and the multifaceted segregationist characteristics of the incorporation of the Iranian women in employment. We will use descriptive statistics
and construct indexes to demonstrate the changes in gender inequality in the
workforce by measuring the extent of the exclusion women, and the change
in the segregationist attribute of their incorporation in employment.

1. See among others, Sanasarian 1982, Paidar 1995, Afshar 1998b, Kar 1994, Mir-
Hosseini 1999, Moghissi 1999, Poya 1999, and a vast number of articles in journals and edited
volumes.
2. An important aspect of the debate in the feminist literature has been the change in
women's labor market participation rate, as an indicator of the extent of their exclusion. See,
among others, V. Moghadam 1988, Moghissi 1999, Khatam 2000, and Karimi 2002.

Female Marginalization: Gender, Class, and Social Hierarchy of Work

Our study in this chapter focuses on the nature of the marginalization of women in the workforce in the 1976–96 period. The concept of marginalization was first addressed in the Latin American context. The point of the argument was that in the transition from a "traditional" to a "dependent" capitalist economy, women experience an irreversible process of exclusion from the market economy (for example, Saffioti 1978). Proponents of the thesis argued that the exclusion of women in this process takes place in the form of a long-run, systemic, and irreversible tendency (Benería and Sen, 1982). This proposition has been criticized for its lack of theoretical and methodological clarity and for not being suitable for empirical verification (A. M. Scott 1986). The critics assert that since "any change in the pattern of female employment produces some degree of marginalization, the thesis continues to be supported despite contradictory evidence" (672). Therefore, they argue that the status of this thesis as a theory is suspect (672–73).

Nevertheless, even critics agree that the notion of female marginalization is a useful analytical and political-descriptive concept, if the explanation is based on multicausal structures and concrete analysis. In other words, the female marginalization problem, like the interrelationship between class and gender, cannot be explained at the very abstract system level that leads to generalizations about its variation in different modes of production. A. M. Scott asserts that "gender plays a role in restructuring labour markets not just as cheap labour, but as subordinate labour, docile labour, immobile labour, domesticated labour, sexual labour, and so on" (1986, 673). Thus, under different economic conditions, and under the influence of specific historical, cultural, legal, and religious factors, marginalization as one of the manifestations of gender inequality could have a variety of forms in this or that country. That is, women may be excluded from certain jobs and occupations, incorporated into certain others, and marginalized in others; they might be (or become) segregated in employment and in different occupations and jobs; and they are always marginalized relative to men.

This approach, therefore, emphasizes a concrete analysis of female marginalization in time and space as a multidimensional and multicausal historical phenomenon that would study the problem in comparison with men's positions in employment and occupations (Crompton 1989, 1997). In this approach long-run trends are differentiated from temporary fluctuations. We concur with this view in our study of female marginalization in Iran in 1976–96. Yet because the study of gender inequality and its manifestations in the labor market and work is a complex process, it also requires an integrated examination based on the interlacing of gender and socioeconomic class analysis. This interlacing is inevitable because class and gender are both systems of inequality, or divisions reflecting the interaction of economic and patriarchal relations along gender lines. This system of inequality takes shape in relation to consciousness and struggle of men and women, the study of which requires an analysis in a historical context.

In line with the above theoretical and methodological concerns, we use the term *gender* in the way that it is prevalent, to emphasize the social, rather than biological, foundation of the difference between women and men. As such, gender relations are multidimensional and are shaped in different spheres of social reality and institutions such as the state, labor markets, the law, and the family-household. These relations give rise to gender hierarchies, that is, patriarchal power relations that are dialectically related to class, as well as to other forms of unequal relations such as ethnicity.

Women (or men) do not present a homogeneous category whose members have common interest, abilities, or practices. Therefore, in this study, we rely on our conceptualization of class in economic activities that identifies class locations in terms of three dimensions, which we have identified in Chapter 2. The three dimensions of class are the ownership of productive resources, organizational assets/authority, and skills/credentials in economic processes. However, because class is a multidimensional social phenomenon, it goes beyond an economic relationship, and, therefore, we recognize the importance of the role of human consciousness and all forms of action (struggle) in class and gender relations. Such a view would always require concrete analysis of any phenomenon, and, would look for the interaction of class possibilities, consciousness, struggle, individual choices, and action, in different spheres of life, including the sphere of work hierarchy along gender and, if necessary, racial or ethnic lines. For this reason in our study of women marginalization and its change in the Islamic Republic in Iran we accept the class orientation of the female marginalization analysis, and see class in interaction with gender relations as an important source of power relation, inequality, differentiation, distinction, and stratification.

Islamization, Gender Segregation, and Defeminization of Labor in the Islamic Republic

In the first postrevolutionary decade the feminist literature on Iran was dominated by the study of the implications of Islamic jurisprudence *(fiqh),* and its legal and political consequences on the position of Iranian women. Edited collections such as *In the Shadow of Islam*[3] (Tabari and Yeganeh 1982) and *Women of Iran: The Conflict with Fundamentalist Islam* (Azari 1983) took a militant position toward the Islamic Republic. Their articles dealt with issues like sexuality and women's oppression (Azari 1983), the struggle for emancipation (Tabari 1982), or examination of Khomeini's views on women (Afshar 1982). Some works were specifically focused on the explanations of the Shi'i jurisprudence (Ferdows and Ferdows 1983) or the pronouncements of the leaders of the Islamic Republic (Nashat 1983). These studies underscored the patronizing, male chauvinistic, or even misogynistic ideology of the Islamic Republic and pointed to the severe limitations imposed on women's civil liberties and individual freedom by legislative and policy actions of the state. Haleh Afshar stressed that in the Islamic Republic women are "formally recognized as second-class citizens who have no place in the public arena and no security in the domestic sphere." They are "excluded from most paid employment and chained with ever increasing social and ideological ties to the uncertainties of Islamic marriage." Thus, "Iranian women have little to lose and everything to gain by opposing the regime and its dicta concerning women" (1987, 83).

The early postrevolutionary literature is a critique of suppressive activities of the Islamic Republic, which mobilized its forces to eliminate secular women from the public space and to impose gender segregation upon society. In those days, particularly after the intensification of internal conflict in the Islamic Republic in 1981 (A. Rahnema and Nomani 1990), when Iranian women came under legal and extralegal attacks, few in Iran spoke out in defense of women's rights, and those who had an opportunity to do so preferred not to, for tactical or other reasons (Moghissi 1996). These attacks were particularly harsh on urban women, who had experienced a high degree of secularization in the previous decades. The rapid growth of market relations and urbanization in these decades had brought a considerable segment of Iranian women into the formal urban labor market (Sanasarian 1982; Paidar 1995; Kian-Thiébaut 1998).

These women, and those in educational institutions, were the most obvious target of the state's Islamization project, and the most unfortunate victims

---

3. This book contains a valuable collection of documents, including statements of position of political parties and women's organizations on the question of women in the first two years of the Islamic Republic.

of humiliation and intimidation by the Islamic Republic's formal and vigilante misogynistic battalions. As laws were passed and regulations were implemented to limit the activities of women in the public spheres, dismissal of women from employment became widespread. Women were fired or purged for inadequate compliance with the new rules of the workplace, mainly with regard to female appearance. Many resigned and many others took advantage of the new policy of early retirement for women. Many private employees reduced the number of their women employees because they feared the reprisal of government and paramilitary Islamic organizations for mixing women and men in workshops and offices. Others followed their own gender segregationist preference.

In many workplaces the creation of segregated workspace for men and women was either impractical or too costly. The presence of militant Islamic zealots (male and female) created a hostile environment in the workplace toward female workers. A typical job advertisement in 1980s would announce availability of a position for "brothers committed to Islam and the rule of the jurisconsult (velayat-e faqih)." Obviously, "sisters" need not apply, except for those positions that were specifically viewed as women's jobs, such as teaching female students, nursing women patients, or guarding women prisoners. The trend toward defeminization and gender segregation of labor was compounded by the economic decline, experienced as the result of the impact of social disruption, and external shocks (war, economic sanctions, and the glut in the international oil market) on the production process.

Studies noted these events and conditions as general tendencies and documented them by anecdotal evidence. The first statistical presentation of the changes in women's employment in postrevolutionary Iran appeared almost a decade after the revolution. In this study, Val Moghadam (1988) compared the 1976 census data with the annual population–labor estimate for 1982–83. She concluded rather definitely that "women have not been driven out of the workforce" (228). She also claimed that the share of urban women in state employment ("in twenty-two ministries") remained constant, which in absolute numbers is "four times the number of women employed by these ministries in 1974–1975" (230).[4] This optimistic account was contrary to the prevailing pattern of change in employment of women, particularly when the gender-class implications of the Islamic Republic's segregationist policy is examined in the light of demographic changes in these years. A number of later

4. For a critique of these findings, see Moghissi 1999, 111–17.

studies based on *Census 1986* reveal that in fact women's rate of participation in the labor force and the share of women in employment had declined substantially since the last census in 1976 (F. Moghadam 1994; V. Moghadam 1995; Afshar 1997; and Karimi 2002).[5]

Alizadeh and Harper (1995) took the study of women's position in the Iranian economy a step further by calculating an index of occupational gender segregation for eight occupational groups, based on the one-digit International Classification of Occupations (ILO 1969), using a method suggested by Karmel and Maclachlan (1988). They found that between 1976 and 1986 occupational gender segregation had increased in some occupational groups (mainly in "production") and decreased in others (most important, in the "professional" group), with a net overall increase.[6]

The second postrevolutionary decade was marked with the end of Iran-Iraq War, the death of Ayatollah Khomeini, and a new rise in the international price of oil. These conditions and the Islamic Republic's realization of the failure of its project for the Islamization of the economy provided the background for initiation of a policy of economic liberalization starting in 1990. The general failure of the Islamic project opened avenues for active protest of women, resisting the segregationist policies of the Islamic Republic, demanding reinstitution of their civil liberties and elimination of gender discrimination (Moghissi 1999; Afshar 1998a). The economic liberalization effort, too, in spite of its retardation because of public resistance and factional conflicts within the state has made some employment opportunities more accessible for women than in the previous decade.[7] In a most fundamental way, the Islamic Republic's commitment to gender segregation and patriarchal domination has been at odds with the imperative of capitalist reconstruction of the Iranian economy. Iranian society had experienced a period of rapid secularization in the decades prior to the 1979 revolution. The Islamic Republic's attempt to reverse the previous trend, especially when pushing for economic liberalization, has been a futile effort. This contradiction has brought the women's issue to the forefront of Iranian political arena. Iranian women have

5. A. Khatam, however, challenges these results as "errors and exaggerations" (2000, 134).

6. Among these studies only F. Moghadam (1994) pays attention to the difference in the age for inclusion in the labor force and employed labor force in *Census 1976* (ten years and older) and *Census 1986* (six years and older).

7. For a study of the impact of economic liberalization on women's employment in the Middle East, see Karshenas and Moghadam 1998.

persistently pressed for their civil liberties, and have managed to gain some grounds, albeit in excruciating slow increments.

In a subsequent study, Alizadeh (2000) confirms this expectation and reports an increase in the rate of participation of women in the labor force based on the 1996 census data. She also extends her previous analysis of gender segregation by measuring an "index of dissimilarity" for eight occupational groups. Alizadeh finds that the degree of "dissimilarity" (concentration of one gender group by more than its proportion in the employed labor force in an occupational group) has substantially increased between 1986 and 1996. Her measurement shows that the "professional and technical" occupational group has become more female dominated than the data from previous censuses indicate, and "agriculture" and "production" continue to be male dominated. The secret of the increased domination of women in "professional and technical" occupational groups is ironically in occupational segregation. No less than 82.3 percent of women included in the "professional and technical" group in 1996 were educators and health workers. These jobs were occupational activities that had traditionally employed women more readily, particularly as teachers and nurses. One of the early steps of segregation of the workplace in the Islamic Republic was to make teaching of schoolgirls and nursing of women patients totally off-limits for male workers.

Relying on a combined qualitative, discursive methodology, Poya (1999) examines patriarchal relations in the context of class relations and level of religious beliefs in the Islamic Republic. Her analysis, however, does not present a macroportrayal of the gender-class relations in the postrevolutionary Iran. Moghissi and Rahnema (2000) recognize the importance of class in the study of gender.

In our view, the nature and development of women's exclusion and incorporation in the workforce require a class–gender approach that is explicit about its theoretical class-gender framework, and examines the problem analytically and statistically in the context of the involutionary and deinvolutionary processes in the postrevolutionary period. Our constructed social hierarchy of work in Iran is intimately related to our class typology in line with gender relations. It provides the framework for our study of the nature of women's exclusion and incorporation in a work structure, which manifests the differential access of women and men to means of production, authority and skill in work process.

The involutionary and deinvolutionary changes in the immediate postrevolutionary, and the post-Khomeini periods had pronounced impacts on the class-gender attributes of the workforce, for women and men. In this chapter we will examine how these changes have affected the integration of women in the economy in terms of their participation in the labor market, ownership of productive resources and skills, and their level of authority in work. We will attempt to provide answers for these questions: Do the changing circumstances imply changes in segregation in, or exclusion from, the labor market and segregation in work? Who among women was empowered and who was impaired in the Islamic state? Are there significant differences between the state sector and the private sector in terms of gender employment? Can we measure the segregation level that women have been exposed to in Iran, and can we understand the class nature of employed women's in the Islamic period?

Women's Exclusion from the Market: Trends in Activity Rates

Table 6.1 presents labor force activity rates for women and men and the proportion of the employed women in total employment in Iran in five decennial years of 1956 to 1996. In interpreting the level of female participation rates one should have in mind the problem of underestimation of the rate in all developing countries, especially in Muslim societies, for commonly known reasons. However, in Iran, there is no empirical verification whether the underreporting bias has changed one way or another in the postrevolutionary years. Therefore, we regard the magnitude of changes in the postrevolutionary years just as (un)reliable as those of the prerevolutionary years, after making adjustments for definitional changes (such as age of entering the labor force).

Accelerated development of capitalism in the post-1953 coup d'état period, particularly in the 1960s, expedited the rate of integration of women in the labor market. In 1956, female labor force participation rate was 9.2 percent. A decade later, by 1966, it had increased by 37 percent, to 12.6 percent. In 1976, it was 12.9 percent. The increase in female participation rate took place in spite of more than doubling of the percentage of female students in the ten years and older population, from 3.0 percent to 7.4 percent between 1956 and 1966. By 1976 the percentage of female students doubled again to 14.9 percent. Female labor participation in the 1956–76 period increased as women entered into the growing market. Educated middle-class women entered professional-administrative occupations, especially in the state sector.

Table 6.1
Activity Rates for Male and Female Labor Force, 1956–1996

	1956	1966	1976	1986	1996
Female					
Activity rate	9.2	12.6	12.9	8.2	9.2
Effective activity rate	9.2	11.5	10.8	6.1	8.0
Student-adjusted activity rate	9.5	13.6	15.2	9.8	12.6
Male					
Activity rate	83.9	77.4	70.8	68.4	61.7
Effective activity rate	81.5	70.2	64.3	59.5	56.4
Student-adjusted activity rate	90.9	91.2	92.6	88.8	87.4
Female					
Nonmarket activity rate	90.8	87.4	87.1	91.8	90.8
Students	3.0	7.4	14.9	16.6	26.9
Homemakers and others★	87.8	80.0	72.2	75.3	63.9
Female's relative share					
of employment	9.7	13.3	13.8	8.9	12.1

Sources: MAI 1980, 1988, 1997, *Statistical Yearbook 2000.*
★Includes pensioners and rentiers.

Employment opportunities in clerical, sales, service, and production in urban areas and in agricultural and handicraft industries in rural areas attracted working-class women (Paidar 1995; Kian-Thiébaut 1998).

After the revolution, by 1986, female labor participation rate declined by 36 percent to 8.2 percent (table 6.1). This drop was a reflection of the large absolute decline in female employment from 1.2 million in 1976 to 975,000 in 1986. In contrast, the male labor participation rate, which had been declining along a secular trend, decreased only at a much slower rate (by 3.4 percent) in the postrevolutionary decade. In the same period women's share of employment decreased from 13.8 percent to 8.9 percent, becoming substantially less than what it was in 1956.

Disaggregating the activity rate data into urban and rural area reveals the sources of change more precisely (table 6.2). In the urban areas, between 1976 and 1986, activity rate of male workers increased by 4.5 percent, although the

Table 6.2

Activity Rates, Male and Female, Urban and Rural, 1976, 1986, and 1996 (in percentages)

	Urban			Rural		
	1976	1986	1996	1976	1986	1996
Total male population, 10+						
Activity rate	63.9	66.8	59.4	77.9	70.4	65.5
Effective activity rate	60.7	57.7	54.4	68.1	61.9	59.9
Student-adjusted activity rate	90.8	88.5	86.5	94.1	89.1	88.7
Total inactive	36.1	33.2	40.6	22.1	29.6	34.5
Students	29.6	24.5	31.3	17.2	21.0	26.2
Homemakers	0.0	0.9	0.5	0.0	1.0	0.6
Others★	6.5	7.8	8.7	4.9	7.6	9.0
Total female population, 10+						
Activity rate	9.0	8.4	8.2	16.6	7.9	10.8
Effective activity rate	8.5	5.9	7.2	13.0	6.3	9.3
Student-adjusted activity rate	11.9	10.5	11.9	17.7	9.0	13.5
Total inactive	91.0	91.6	91.8	83.4	92.1	89.2
Students	23.8	20.5	31.2	6.5	11.7	19.7
Homemakers	64.2	66.5	56.8	73.1	71.4	62.5
Others★	3.0	4.7	3.7	3.8	8.9	6.9
Female as a % of total employed	11.2	8.8	11.3	16.0	8.9	13.4

Sources: MAI 1980, 1988, 1997.

★Includes pensioners and rentiers.

increase in the rate of unemployment in 1986 brought down the effective[8] activity rate of male workers to less than what it was in 1976. Activity rate of female urban workers, however, decreased by about 7 percent (from 9 percent to 8.4 percent). Accounting for female unemployment, the effective activity rate of female urban workers dropped by 31 percent between 1976 and 1986. In the rural area, where the activity rate for women has been higher than the urban area, between 1976 and 1986 the activity rate, effective activity rate, and the share of women in total rural employment all declined by about 50 percent.

8. The effective activity rate is the ratio of employed workforce to working-age population.

There is a tendency to attribute the decline of women's participation rate to the decline of unpaid family workers between 1976 and 1986 (see Khatam 2000). We discussed the issue at length in Chapter 5. Here we make the following points. First, unpaid family work is basically a rural phenomenon in Iran. In 1976, more than 91 percent of all unpaid family workers were engaged in the rural economy. We can be certain that there is some underreporting in the collection of census data, but there is no reason to believe that there is more underreporting in urban areas. Therefore, whatever the issue of unpaid family work may be, it would affect urban women's employment only marginally. Second, as the number of female unpaid family workers in the rural areas declined by 248,000 workers (from 445,000 in 1976) in the same period, the number of rural working class women also declined from 190,000 to 70,000. Therefore, there is more to the decline in women participation rate than just the decline in the number of female unpaid family workers. Finally, unpaid family work, for male or female workers, is not useless or superfluous activity. It is a rudimentary form of value creation in a market economy, nevertheless a form of participation in the labor process and enhancement of family's (and ones own) life opportunities. A net decline in labor participation rate, even if it were merely because of the decline in the number of unpaid family workers, would be a decline, and, therefore, significant.

The startling fact is that between 1986 and 1996, in spite of the liberalization effort of the Islamic Republic, the labor participation rate of urban female workers continued to decline, although their effective activity rate increased because of the decline in their rate of unemployment. Thus, whereas the proportion of women in the labor market in fact declined, a larger proportion of women in the market were employed in 1986 than in 1996. Therefore, even in the post-Khomeini decade the impediments on urban women's entry into the labor market were not reduced.

Statistical evidence for the past fifty years shows (tables 6.1 and 6.2) that there has been a definite and continuous upward trend in women's labor market activity rate between 1956 and 1976. This trend turned downward under the Islamic Republic in the Khomeini decade, as revealed by the 1986 census. *Census 1996* indicates that since 1986, in the post-Khomeini decade, there has been only a partial recovery in the activity rate of rural women. The decline in female labor participation rate between 1976 and 1986 (and continued decline for urban female workers) is an aberration in the history of Iran and other Muslim countries in the region (except Afghanistan under the Taliban) in the twentieth century. Meanwhile, in all these periods, similar to the trend in other developing countries, the male participation rate has gradually fallen, except between 1976 and 1986, when the participation rate for urban men actually increased.

The large gap between female and male participation rates, the increase in female share in total employment, despite the steady decline in male participation rates, and the upward trend in the rates for women in the long run are common developments in almost all the developing Muslim countries (Anker 1998, 145–46; Jacobsen 1998, 390–91). The reversal of this trend for women's participation and employment share after the 1979 revolution is, however, peculiar to the case of Iran, where even after the liberalization effort in the post-Khomeini deinvolution period, in 1996, these rates were at best what they were in 1956 (table 6.1).

It may be tempting for apologists to say that the decline in female labor force participation in 1976–86 should be attributed to the notable and noble rise in the proportion of female population of labor force age enrolled in schools. However, the experience of developed and developing countries indicates that the steady rise in female school enrollment is not generally at the expense of the decline in female labor force participation. In fact, as statistics confirm, there was no trade-off between the increased enrollment rate and the rising activity rate in 1956–76 and 1986–96 in Iran. To account for any possible trade-off here we calculate activity rates after adjusting for the changes in the rate of enrollment in population of potential workers. That is, we calculated the "student-adjusted activity rate" by taking out the population of students from the working-age population.[9]

Table 6.1 and figure 6.1 reveal that adjusting the activity rate for the changes in the number of those individuals who have left (or never entered) the labor market to enroll as students only reaffirms our conclusions above. In fact, we can see that the student-adjusted activity rate only magnifies the changes in the activity rate. That is for a simple reason. The very same sociopolitical conditions that may encourage or discourage female adults enter the labor market could also encourage or discourage them from enrolling as students, as well. The macrodata over the past fifty years negate the myth that the sexist and segregationist policies of the Islamic state provided a "safe" avenue for women's education. Not so for adult females (ten years or older). In a country with a rising population, most magnitudes would be increasing. Absolute numbers, and anecdotal information, in abstraction from historical tendencies, could be deceiving.

---

9. We made similar adjustments in Chapter 4.

Figure 6.1
Activity Rates and Student-Adjusted Activity Rates for Female
Workforce, 1955–1996

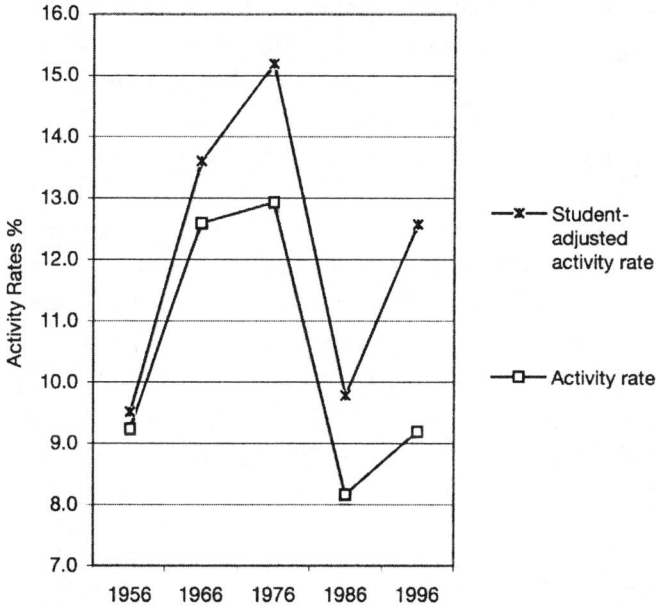

Source: Table 6.1.

Does women's age matter on the rate of their participation in the labor market? Table 6.3 depicts female activity rates for urban and rural women of different ages in 1976, 1986, and 1996. Before examining these changes we need to note that a secular decline in the rate of participation of women (and men) in the young (ten to fourteen years) and old (fifty-five and older) age groups are expected as education of the youth and retirement of the old becomes possible. Our data, however, reveal two different patterns of change in the urban and rural areas. In the urban area, the peak of activity rate, which was 16.1 percent for the twenty-to-twenty-four age group in 1976, shifted to the higher age group (thirty to thirty-four) and became flatter, at 14.2 percent. By 1996, the peak of 14.4–14.7 percent is observed at ages twenty-five to forty-four. That is, in 1996, women in the twenty-to-twenty-nine age group had a lower rate of participation rate than in 1976, while the women in the thirty-to-forty-four age group had a higher rate of participation than in

1976 (figure 6.2). This outcome could reflect two possible situations for urban working women. It could be that the younger (and more likely unmarried) urban women faced a more serious barrier in entering the labor force than the middle-age (and more likely married) women. The higher rate of participation of the middle-age women in 1996 (in comparison to 1976) could also reflect the aging of the cohort of the ideologically accommodating women who entered the career ladder in the 1980s. Shifting the peak of labor participation to the higher age groups between 1986 and 1996 confirms this possibility, though it does not negate the prevalence of discrimination against younger (and single) women.

In the rural economy, the pattern of labor participation for various age groups changed more dramatically between 1976 and 1986. In 1986, the rate of participation of women in all age groups declined in comparison to 1976. The decline in the participation rate for women in the fifteen-to-thirty-nine age group was by as much as 50 percent, and for those in the forty-to-fifty-nine age group by about 30 percent. The single peak activity rate curve in 1976, became double humped, with lower peaks in 1986. By 1996, however, the activity rate curve regained its 1976 shape, albeit at lower activity rates for

Table 6.3

Activity Rates by Age, Urban and Rural Women, 1976, 1986, and 1996 (in percentages)

	Urban			Rural		
	1976	1986	1996	1976	1986	1996
10–14	3.9	2.2	0.9	16.9	6.9	6.0
15–19	7.7	8.0	4.5	23.7	11.3	14.9
20–24	16.1	13.6	11.3	19.8	10.1	16.2
25–29	15.5	13.7	14.7	16.8	7.4	13.1
30–34	12.3	14.2	13.8	15.9	6.8	11.2
35–39	9.5	11.5	14.4	15.6	6.8	10.5
40–44	7.8	8.4	14.4	14.9	9.8	10.2
45–49	6.8	5.2	10.4	14.4	10.5	9.4
50–54	6.5	3.6	5.9	13.4	10.5	9.2
55–59	5.5	3.0	3.5	10.6	7.1	8.6
60–64	5.3	2.7	2.4	7.7	5.9	7.2
65+	3.7	2.1	1.5	5.3	5.5	4.5
Total	9.0	8.4	8.1	16.6	6.7	10.7

Sources: MAI 1980, 1988, 1997.

Figure 6.2
Activity Rates by Age, Urban Women, 1976, 1986, and 1996

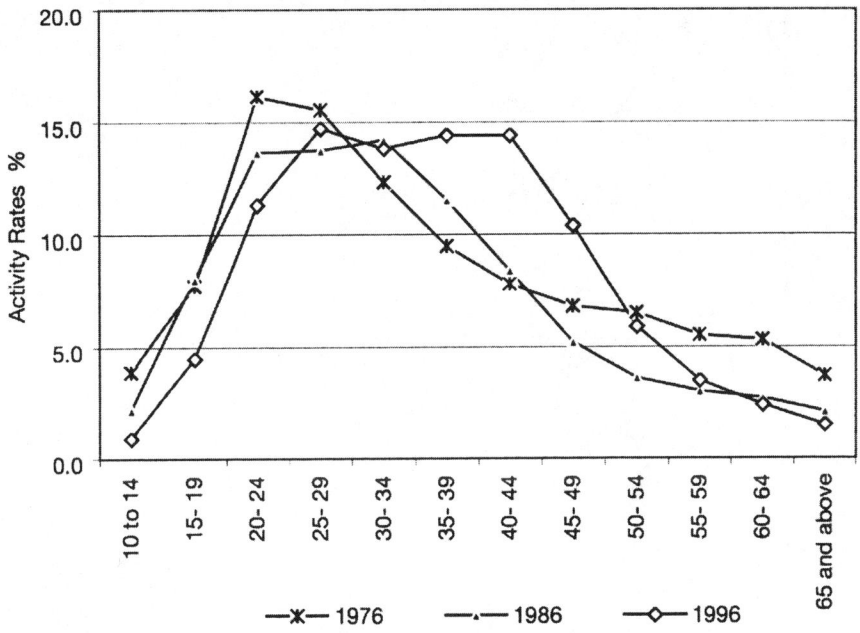

Sources: MAI 1980, 1988, 1997.

all age groups between fifteen and fifty-four. Although there is a general decline in labor participation rate for women of all age groups in the rural area, we do not observe any special barriers for younger (or single) women, as the data for the urban economy suggest (figure 6.3).

In sum, the exclusion of women from the labor force, as measured by female labor force participation rates in 1976 and 1986, clearly indicates the impairment of women in the postrevolutionary decade. However, the modification of the Islamic government policies as a result of the failure of the Islamization of the society, the economic recovery and liberalization in the post-Khomeini period, and the struggle of women have reversed the trend. Nevertheless, in 1996, the female labor force participation rate in Iran was what it was in 1956 (see table 6.1).[10]

10. The ILO data shows that between 1950 and 1990 female activity rate in developed economies shows an upward trend for age groups twenty to fifty-nine (Anker 1998, 141–42).

Figure 6.3
Activity Rates by Age, Rural Women, 1976, 1986, and 1996

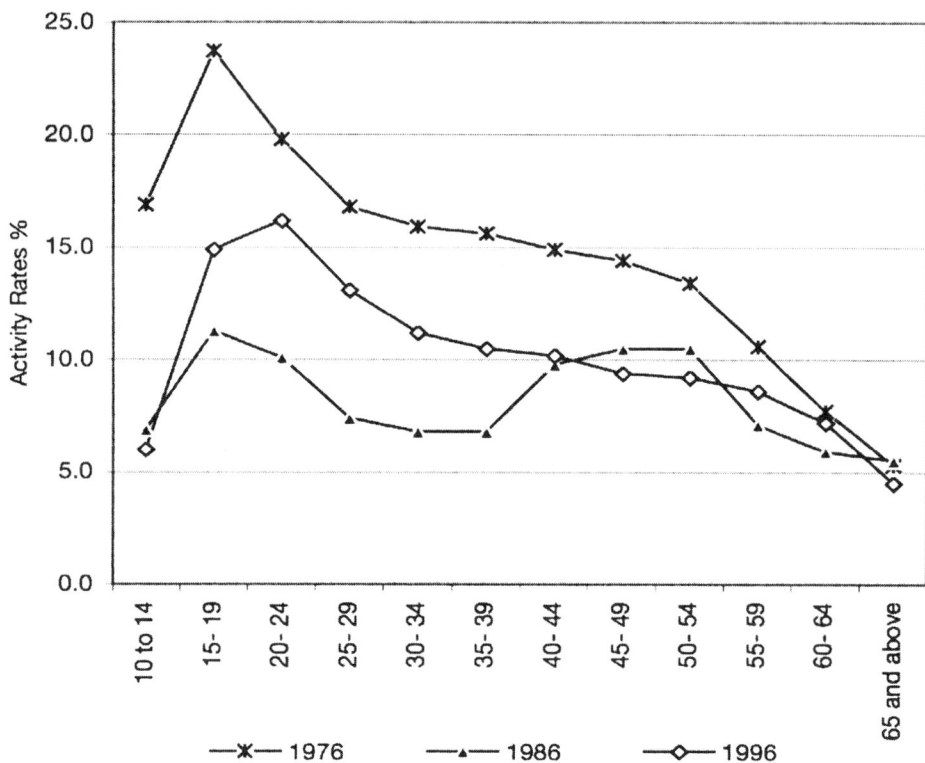

Sources: MAI 1980, 1988, 1997.

The Class-Gender Nature of the Social Hierarchy of Work

The study of changes in the hierarchy of work over time brings together the important sources of women's stratification and employment inequalities relative to men, and enhances our analysis of gender employment empowerment and segregation. The scheme of the social hierarchy of work, presented in table 6.4 and table 6.5 for 1976, 1986, and 1996, has two major advantages. First, it focuses on the differential access of the employed female workforce to ownership of productive resources, organizational assets/authority, and skills/credentials, and, consequently, autonomy and control over their labor, at a point in time and over time. Second, based on the reclassification of occupations according to the three dimensions of class location, this scheme also reveals the class nature of the empowerment process among women, and between men and women in terms of sex segregation, in the private and state sectors.

By examining the differential access of the "haves" and "have–nots" to ownership of productive resources, authority, and skill, we will examine whether women's empowerment in Iran has had a class–gender nature and is affected by state policies associated with the involutionary and deinvolutionary changes of 1976–86 and 1986–96. Such an analysis relies on our categories of the upper- and lower-level work groups that we explained in Chapter 2.

Changes in the Class Nature of Female Work: The Survivors and Losers in Times of Trouble

In 1976, 1.2 million employed women constituted 13.8 percent of the national employment. By 1986, their number had dropped to 975,000, when the employed labor force had increased by 25 percent since the 1976 census. In 1986, women accounted for only 8.9 percent of the employed workforce (table 6.1). Female employment declined by 237,000 in these years, despite the rise in the number of female state employees from 246,000 to 407,000. By 1996, however, the number of employed women increased to 1.8 million, or 12.1 percent of the employed labor force.

In 1976, there were 194,000 (16 percent) employed women in the upper-level hierarchy of work, consisting of capitalists, modern petty bourgeoisie, and the middle class, in contrast to 7.4 percent for male workers. The rest of employed women (1 million, 84 percent) made up the lower-level work group, 41 percent being unpaid family workers. In 1986 the number of female upper-level work group increased to 334,000, making up 34 percent of the female employment. At the same time the number of lower-level female workers declined to 640,000, constituting 66 percent of female employment (table 6.4 and table 6.5). Given the disruptions of the economy and the hostile attitude of the Islamic state toward female employment, the increase in the number and share of those women in the higher-level employment indicates that the women who had the access to financial resources or had high education and skills could stay employed, or enter employment as capitalists, self-employed workers, or skilled employees of the state.

The decline in the number of unpaid family employees occurred most significantly in the rural areas and mainly in carpet weaving because of the ban

Table 6.4
Female Hierarchy of Work: Upper-Level Work Group, 1976, 1986, and 1996

		1976	
	Total	f/F	f/ (f+m)
	(1,000s)	%	%
Upper-level work group	193.5	16.0	25.7
Capitalists	5.4	0.4	2.9
Modern	0.4	0.0	1.9
Administrative and managerial	0.1	0.0	0.8
Professional and technical	0.3	0.0	3.0
Traditional	4.9	0.4	3.1
Clerical and related	0.1	0.0	3.2
Sales and services	0.9	0.1	1.7
Agriculture	0.7	0.1	1.9
Production	3.1	0.3	4.7
Unclassified	0.1	0.0	8.2
Modern petty bourgeoisie	1.7	0.1	5.0
Administrative and managerial	0.0	0.0	0.0
Professional and technical	1.7	0.1	5.0
Middle class	186.5	15.4	34.7
Administrative and managerial	1.2	0.1	4.2
State employees	0.8	0.1	5.9
Private employees	0.4	0.0	2.6
Professional and technical	185.3	15.3	36.4
State employees	173.3	14.3	41.1
Private employees	12.0	1.0	13.7
State employees	174.1	14.4	40.0
Private employees	12.3	1.0	12.1

Sources: MAI 1980, 1988, 1997.

Notes: f = female workers in a category; F = total female employed labor force; m = male workers in a category.

on the export of handwoven carpets, which was (and still is) the main industrial activity of rural women.

Aside from the decline in the number of female unpaid family workers, in the 1976–86 period, the major employment loss for women was among the lower-level employees of the private sector. In this period the number of lower-level female private employees declined from 310,000 to 88,000, when

| | 1986 | | | 1996 | |
Total (1,000s)	f/F %	f/ (f+m) %	Total (1,000s)	f/F %	f/ (f+m) %
334.6	34.3	24.5	591.9	33.5	24.4
13.7	1.4	4.0	16.2	0.9	3.1
1.9	0.2	8.5	2.9	0.2	3.9
0.1	0.0	1.0	1.0	0.1	2.0
1.8	0.2	13.0	1.9	0.1	7.8
11.8	1.2	3.7	13.3	0.8	2.9
0.4	0.0	10.8	0.1	0.0	4.3
0.9	0.1	2.0	2.1	0.1	2.3
7.0	0.7	6.2	5.0	0.3	4.0
2.4	0.2	1.7	4.5	0.3	2.0
1.1	0.1	6.8	1.6	0.1	13.5
3.4	0.3	7.1	9.1	0.5	5.5
0.1	0.0	1.1	0.9	0.1	2.4
3.3	0.3	7.8	8.2	0.5	6.5
317.5	32.6	32.5	566.6	32.1	32.6
1.3	0.1	4.2	37.8	2.1	16.6
1.1	0.1	4.7	34.3	1.9	19.4
0.2	0.0	2.4	3.4	0.2	6.8
316.2	32.4	33.4	528.8	30.0	35.0
307.5	31.5	34.5	495.9	28.1	37.0
8.7	0.9	15.3	32.9	1.9	19.6
308.6	31.6	33.8	530.3	30.0	34.9
8.9	0.9	13.9	36.3	2.1	16.6

the number of low-level state employees increased only from 72,000 to 98,000. Therefore, any gain in employment for the working-class women as the result of nationalization of large private enterprises was merely insignificant. In the same period, the number of upper-level female private employees declined from 12,000 to 9,000, when the number of upper-level female employees of the state increased from 174,000 to 308,000. That is, for every 8.5 women employed who lost their job as a low-level private sector employee,

Table 6.5
Female Hierarchy of Work: Lower-Level Work Group,
1976, 1986, and 1996

	Total (1,000s)	1976 f/F %	f/ (f+m) %
Lower-level work group	1,018.7	84.0	12.7
Traditional petty bourgeoisie	129.0	10.6	4.6
Clerical	0.3	0.0	4.6
Sales and services	10.6	0.9	2.3
Agriculture	17.8	1.5	1.0
Production	100.2	8.3	16.9
Unclassified	0.2	0.0	4.0
Working class	381.8	31.5	9.1
Clerical and related	62.7	5.2	14.7
State employees	47.4	3.9	16.1
Private employees	15.3	1.3	11.6
Sales and services	62.0	5.1	12.6
State employees	10.7	0.9	5.4
Private employees	51.1	4.2	17.4
Agriculture	73.9	6.1	11.3
State employees	0.9	0.1	2.2
Private employees	73.0	6.0	11.9
Production	175.9	14.5	7.9
State employees	6.4	0.5	2.1
Private employees	169.5	14.0	8.8
Unclassified	7.2	0.6	1.8
State employees (military/paramilitary)	6.4	0.5	1.6
Private employees	0.8	0.1	7.3
State employees	71.8	5.9	5.8
Private employees	309.8	25.6	10.4
Unpaid family workers	495.7	40.9	48.5
Sales and services	1.7	0.1	12.6
Agriculture	133.9	11.0	22.8
Production	359.6	29.7	86.0
Others (includes unclassified)	0.5	0.0	18.7
Unspecified	12.2	1.0	30.0
Total female employed workforce	1,212.0	100.0	13.8

Sources: MAI 1980, 1988, 1997.

Notes: f = female workers in a category; F = total female employed labor force;
   m = male workers in a category.

| | 1986 | | | 1996 | |
| Total | f/F | f/ (f+m) | Total | f/F | f/ (f+m) |
(1,000s)	%	%	(1,000s)	%	%
640.6	65.7	6.6	1,173.5	66.5	9.7
175.2	18.0	4.0	338.2	19.2	6.7
0.4	0.0	4.2	0.7	0.0	6.5
13.7	1.4	2.2	35.2	2.0	3.7
65.4	6.7	2.8	81.8	4.6	3.7
93.6	9.6	7.1	210.9	11.9	11.7
2.1	0.2	3.0	9.6	0.5	12.8
187.1	19.2	4.3	390.1	22.1	6.7
42.8	4.4	12.6	97.1	5.5	16.8
38.0	3.9	12.5	77.0	4.4	15.6
4.8	0.5	14.3	20.1	1.1	23.7
25.3	2.6	5.0	56.4	3.2	6.7
17.5	1.8	5.1	37.9	2.1	8.2
7.8	0.8	5.0	18.5	1.0	4.9
29.3	3.0	8.2	45.0	2.6	9.4
1.4	0.1	2.2	1.3	0.1	2.0
27.9	2.9	9.5	43.8	2.5	10.5
62.3	6.4	3.2	151.4	8.6	5.3
16.4	1.7	2.4	23.1	1.3	3.2
45.9	4.7	3.6	128.3	7.3	6.0
27.4	2.8	2.3	40.1	2.3	3.8
25.3	2.6	2.2	28.7	1.6	2.9
2.0	0.2	3.8	11.4	0.6	14.8
98.7	10.1	3.9	168.0	9.5	6.1
88.4	9.1	4.9	222.0	12.6	7.1
209.9	21.5	43.4	366.5	20.8	46.0
0.5	0.1	4.8	1.5	0.1	5.6
153.9	15.8	39.8	161.5	9.1	32.7
54.2	5.6	67.4	196.8	11.1	75.9
1.3	0.1	19.5	6.7	0.4	40.8
68.4	7.0	14.9	78.8	4.5	17.0
975.3	100.0	8.9	1,765.4	100.0	12.1

only 1 gained a job as a state employee in the lower rank. On the other hand, for every woman who lost her job as an upper-level private sector employee, 44.7 gained an upper level job as state employees. We have no way of telling whether those women who lost their job in the private sector were among the ones who gained a job in the public sector. Similarly, we cannot tell from our data if any of those women who lost their jobs in the low-level employment of the private sector found a position as high-level employees of the state. We find the latter unlikely as a general trend because of the skill and educational requirements for professional and technical positions.

The decline in the number of wage and salary earners (working class) in the lower rank of hierarchy of work from 381,000 in 1976 to 187,000 in 1986 reflects a decline in the size of the female working class in every major occupational position, including sales and service, production, and agriculture. Between 1976 and 1986, the number of lower-rank female wage and salary earners in production in employment of the private sector and state declined from 176,000 to 62,000, and those in sales and services from 62,000 to 23,000. In these cases the decline in number of female workers was in spite of some increase in the number of female employees of the state sector. The large majority of women (in 1976, 97 percent in production and 82 percent in sales and services) were employees of the private sector. In clerical occupations the number of females declined from 63,000 to 43,000. In this case the number of employees of both the state and the private sector declined. In none of these occupational positions did the number of women in self-employed categories (traditional petty bourgeoisie) increase appreciably to compensate for the decline in wage and salary employment in those occupational positions. The only exception was agriculture, where a decline in the number of wage and salary earners from 74,000 to 29,000 was compensated by an increase in the number of self-employed workers from 18,000 to 65,000. The exceptional phenomenon in the agricultural occupational positions indicates that the change was a reflection of the de facto redistribution of rural landownership (Schirazi 1993).

Between 1976 and 1986, the proportion of women to the total employment (%f/[f + m] in table 6.4 and table 6.5) in the lower occupational positions declined in every category, except in agriculture and the "unclassified" categories. The most dramatic decline (by more than 50 percent) was the proportion of working class from 9.1 percent to 4.3 percent. In contrast, the proportion of female employed workforce in the upper categories declined only minimally, from 25.7 percent to 24.5 percent, whereas the proportion of female capitalists and modern petty bourgeoisie increased significantly. The most pronounced decline in the proportion of female employment to the total employment in the same category, between 1976 and 1986, was for professional and technical middle class (from 36.4 percent to 33.4 percent). Within this category, the proportion of female professional and technical workers employed by the state declined, from 41.1 percent to 34.5 percent (table 6.4). This information indicates that as the Islamic state was rapidly expanding the size of its bureaucracy, it was increasing the number of its male employees much faster than that of female employees.

Thus, we see that in response to the policies of the Islamic government and the involutionary process the participation of women in many categories of lower-level occupations declined between 1976 and 1986. It is, however, notable that the women in the upper occupational categories, that is, those with capital, skills, and higher education, were able to maintain their position, or enter the job market, whereas those endowed with less education and no capital were ejected from their positions or were unable to find employment.

In response to the deinvolutionary changes and a more liberal cultural and economic policies of the Islamic state in the post-Khomeini years, women's participation in economic activities and employment increased at all levels, as the number of female employed workforce increased by 81 percent to 1.8 million by 1996. How did the opening up of the economic and cultural spheres affect different categories of women?

The proportion of women in each category relative to the total (male plus female) employment in that category reveals the outcome. The overall proportion of women in the upper level of the occupational hierarchy in 1996 remained nearly unchanged. That is, women in the upper occupational category increased in number proportional to the increase in the total number of positions occupied in that category. However, the proportion of capitalist women declined from 4 percent to 3.1 percent, and the proportion of modern petty bourgeois women in the professional and technical positions declined from 7.8 percent to 6.5 percent. In contrast, the proportion of women employed as professional and technical workers by the state and the private sector increased. The substantial increase in the proportion of female middle class workers in the employment of the private sector in the post-Khomeini era (from 13.9 percent in 1986 to 16.6 in 1996, compared to 12.1 in 1976) shows a clear advance for skilled women in that sector. Notably, however, the proportion of middle-class (upper-level) employees of the state in 1996 (34.9 percent) was substantially lower than in 1976 (40.0 percent).

At the same time, the proportion of women in the lower-level occupational category increased significantly, from 6.6 percent of the total (male plus female) employment in that category in 1986, to 9.7 percent in 1996 (table

6.5). The proportion of traditional petty bourgeois women increased from 4 percent to 6.7 percent and the proportion of working-class women from 4.3 percent to 6.7 percent. Although the concentration of women in all these categories is larger than it was in 1986, only for two major categories does the proportion of women exceed those in 1976. The exceptions are the traditional petty bourgeois women in agriculture and those in the employment of the state.

Therefore, as we see, in the deinvolutionary period and in the environment that resistance to the segregationist policies of the Islamic state had forced the state to partially retreat from implementation of some its policies, the women with lower skills and education and with no capital reentered the job market and succeeded in getting jobs. In spite of the increase in the concentration of women in 1996, relative to 1986, in most categories of the lower-level employment, the proportion of women in each category in 1996 was still less than what it was in 1976.

What do women do in these work groups? In 1996, 33.5 percent of female workers were in the upper-level work groups (table 6.4). Among those, 4.9 percent were capitalists, and 93.6 percent were middle-class employees (93.5 percent in employment of the state and 6.4 percent in the private sector). In 1996, 66.5 percent of female labor force was engaged in the lower-level category of employment. These workers were divided among three principal groups (petty bourgeoisie, working class, and unpaid family workers), each engaging about 20 percent of women labor force, in addition to the "unspecified" workers (table 6.5). In terms of economic activities, according to the 1996 census, the first five important female occupations were carpet weaving (27.7 percent of all employed women, compared to 1.3 percent for men), teaching school and educational assistance (23.2 percent), agriculture (14.4 percent), clerical work (4.9 percent), and health care and other technical occupations (4.3 percent). Each of the other categories of major occupational groups employed less than 3 percent of women. In the urban areas 37.8 percent of employed women were in educational occupations. In the rural areas 47.5 percent were in carpet weaving.

In 1996, 50 percent of female capitalists (compared to 1 percent of men), 86 percent of female self-employed workers (compared to 10 percent of men), 80 percent of female private sector employees, 47 percent of female state employees, and 99 percent of unpaid female workers in the industrial activity were in carpet weaving. On the other hand, 54 percent of female employees of the state were teachers.

In other words, the "suitable" employment for women in Iran from a patriarchic and an Islamic point of view are, in order of importance, carpet weaving, teaching female students at the level of elementary and secondary schools, and agricultural, clerical, and health-related occupations.

Upper-Level Women, Lower-Level Women: How Did They Fare?

To capture the importance of the change in the share of each work group and occupational class in 1976–96, and to explore the class-gender nature of employment, we have calculated the Change Ratio standardization index and presented the results in tables 6.6 and 6.7.

A comparison of the size of any category of workers in a given year (say, 1996) to what it was in a previous year (say, 1976) would be meaningful if we account for the change in the size of the employed workforce in that year. That is, if between 1976 and 1996 the number of female capitalists had increased at the same rate as the employed labor force had (65.6 percent), then their number would have increased from 5,360 in 1976 to 8,880 in 1996. But the number of female capitalists had increased to 16,180 in 1996, exceeding the growth of the employed labor force, at the 1978 proportion, by 7,920. One way of presenting the change in the size of any group after adjusting for the increase in the size of the employed workforce is the Change Ratio standardization index. This ratio is defined as the difference between the adjusted value of those in a class category in the current year, relative to the change in the size of the employed workforce, and the actual value of the same category in the initial year, divided by the sum of the same categories (Brown, Mandel, and Lawson 1997, 187–90).[11] It represents the change in the relative size of each male or female class category, or the "class effect."[12]

If any class category increases at a rate faster than the employed work-

11. If

C_{it} = number of employees in class category i in period t,
C_{it-1} = number of employees in the previous period (t-1),
N_t = size of employed labor force in period t,
N_{t-1} = size of employed labor force in period t-1.

Then,

Change Ratio $(t, t-1) = [(C_{it}/(N_t/N_{t-1})) - C_{it-1}]/[(C_{it}/(N_t/N_{t-1})) + C_{it-1}]$

12. "Class effect" in "decomposition approach" measures the size of class effect. See "Decomposition Approach" and table A.2 in the Appendix.

Table 6.6

Change Ratios and Gender Employment Empowerment Index:
Upper-Level Work Group, 1976, 1986, and 1996

| | Change Ratio 1976/1986 | | |
	F	M	Total
Upper-level work group	0.16	0.19	0.18
Capitalists	0.34	0.19	0.20
Modern	0.55	–0.17	–0.13
Administrative and managerial	–0.21	–0.28	–0.28
Professional and technical	0.62	–0.06	–0.01
Traditional	0.32	0.23	0.23
Clerical and related	0.64	0.10	0.14
Sales and services	–0.08	–0.17	–0.16
Agriculture	0.78	0.42	0.44
Production	–0.25	0.26	0.25
Unclassified	0.75	0.79	0.79
Modern petty bourgeoisie	0.23	0.05	0.06
Administrative and managerial	1.00	1.00	1.00
Professional and technical	0.22	–0.01	0.00
Middle class	0.15	0.20	0.19
Administrative and managerial	–0.09	–0.08	–0.08
State employees	0.03	0.14	0.14
Private employees	–0.48	–0.44	–0.44
Professional and technical	0.15	0.22	0.20
State employees	0.17	0.31	0.26
Private employees	–0.26	–0.32	–0.31
State employees	0.17	0.30	0.25
Private employees	–0.27	–0.34	–0.33

Sources: MAI 1980, 1988, 1997.

force, the Change Ratio index will be positive. If a class category shrinks, or grows slower than the rate of growth in the employed workforce, then the Change Ratio index will be negative. The more the rate of growth of a class category deviates from the rate of growth of the employed workforce, the larger would be the absolute value of the Change Ratio index. The change ratio is always less than one, except when the number in a class category in the initial year is zero and in the subsequent year is larger than zero. In that case the index will be equal to one. The Change Ratio index is equal to zero if the

Change Ratio 1976/1996			Gender Employment Empowerment Index		
F	M	Total	1976	1986	1996
0.30	0.33	0.32	0.77	0.75	0.74
0.29	0.27	0.27	0.12	0.16	0.12
0.60	0.31	0.32	0.08	0.32	0.15
0.72	0.43	0.44	0.03	0.04	0.08
0.54	0.10	0.13	0.12	0.46	0.29
0.24	0.27	0.27	0.12	0.15	0.12
0.05	-0.12	-0.11	0.13	0.39	0.17
0.19	0.02	0.02	0.07	0.08	0.09
0.63	0.35	0.36	0.08	0.24	0.16
-0.08	0.35	0.34	0.18	0.07	0.08
0.77	0.63	0.65	0.31	0.26	0.47
0.53	0.49	0.49	0.19	0.27	0.21
1.00	1.00	1.00	0.00	0.04	0.09
0.49	0.37	0.38	0.19	0.29	0.25
0.29	0.34	0.32	0.91	0.88	0.88
0.90	0.62	0.66	0.17	0.16	0.56
0.92	0.73	0.77	0.23	0.18	0.63
0.69	0.34	0.36	0.10	0.10	0.26
0.27	0.29	0.28	0.93	0.90	0.91
0.27	0.35	0.32	0.97	0.91	0.94
0.25	0.04	0.07	0.48	0.53	0.64
0.30	0.39	0.36	0.96	0.90	0.91
0.28	0.10	0.13	0.44	0.49	0.56

adjusted number of workers in a class category in the later year is exactly equal to their number in the initial year.

In the declining economy of 1976–86, the women and the men in the upper-level work groups were relatively better off and the women in lower-level work group were definitely worse off than in 1976. The Change Ratio index for women and men in the upper-level work groups is positive for both and is, respectively, 0.16 and 0.19. In contrast, in the lower-level work groups the Change Ratio index for women and for men is, respectively, -0.33 and 0.01

Table 6.7

Change Ratios and Gender Employment Empowerment Index:
Lower-Level Work Group, 1976, 1986, and 1996

	Change Ratio 1986/1976		
	F	M	Total
Lower-level work group	-0.33	0.01	-0.02
Traditional petty bourgeoisie	0.04	0.11	0.11
Clerical	0.15	0.19	0.19
Sales and services	0.02	0.03	0.03
Agriculture	0.49	0.04	0.05
Production	-0.14	0.33	0.28
Unclassified	0.81	0.86	0.86
Working class	-0.44	-0.07	-0.09
Clerical and related	-0.29	-0.21	-0.22
State employees	-0.22	-0.07	-0.09
Private employees	-0.60	-0.67	-0.66
Sales and services	-0.51	-0.06	-0.10
State employees	0.13	0.17	0.17
Private employees	-0.78	-0.34	-0.40
Agriculture	-0.52	-0.38	-0.39
State employees	0.11	0.11	0.11
Private employees	-0.53	-0.43	-0.45
Production	-0.56	-0.15	-0.17
State employees	0.34	0.28	0.28
Private employees	-0.64	-0.28	-0.31
Unclassified	0.51	0.40	0.40
State employees (military/paramilitary)	0.52	0.39	0.39
Private employees	0.34	0.60	0.59
State employees	0.05	0.25	0.24
Private employees	-0.63	-0.32	-0.34
Unpaid family workers	-0.49	-0.41	-0.45
Sales and services	-0.62	-0.20	-0.24
Agriculture	-0.04	-0.42	-0.31
Production	-0.78	-0.47	-0.73
Others (includes unclassified)	0.39	0.36	0.36
Unspecified	0.64	0.83	0.80
Total employed workforce	-0.22	0.03	0.00

Sources: MAI 1980, 1988, 1997.

| Change Ratio 1996/1976 | | | Gender Employment Empowerment Index | | |
F	M	Total	1976	1986	1996
−0.18	−0.03	−0.05	0.45	0.25	0.35
0.23	0.03	0.05	0.18	0.16	0.25
0.20	0.01	0.02	0.18	0.17	0.25
0.33	0.09	0.10	0.09	0.09	0.14
0.47	−0.14	−0.12	0.04	0.11	0.15
0.12	0.32	0.30	0.57	0.27	0.42
0.94	0.81	0.83	0.16	0.12	0.45
−0.24	−0.07	−0.09	0.34	0.17	0.25
−0.03	−0.11	−0.10	0.51	0.45	0.56
−0.01	0.01	0.00	0.55	0.44	0.53
−0.11	−0.50	−0.44	0.42	0.50	0.73
−0.29	0.05	0.02	0.45	0.20	0.25
0.36	0.16	0.17	0.21	0.20	0.30
−0.64	−0.05	−0.12	0.58	0.19	0.19
−0.46	−0.38	−0.39	0.41	0.31	0.34
−0.07	−0.02	−0.02	0.09	0.09	0.08
−0.47	−0.41	−0.42	0.43	0.35	0.38
−0.32	−0.11	−0.12	0.30	0.13	0.20
0.37	0.17	0.17	0.08	0.09	0.12
−0.37	−0.18	−0.19	0.33	0.14	0.23
0.54	0.22	0.23	0.07	0.09	0.15
0.46	0.20	0.20	0.07	0.09	0.11
0.79	0.59	0.61	0.28	0.15	0.51
0.17	0.14	0.14	0.22	0.15	0.23
−0.40	−0.21	−0.23	0.38	0.19	0.27
−0.38	−0.34	−0.36	1.00	0.99	0.99
−0.31	0.13	0.09	0.45	0.19	0.21
−0.16	−0.39	−0.33	0.71	0.96	0.88
−0.50	−0.22	−0.46	0.47	0.87	0.73
0.80	0.50	0.61	0.62	0.64	0.97
0.59	0.78	0.75	0.85	0.52	0.57
−0.06	0.01	0.00	0.48	0.33	0.43

(table 6.6 and table 6.7). Thus, the number of positions for female employment in the lower-level work groups did not increase in step with the growth in the size of the employed workforce. For men the change in the number of positions was nearly proportional to the change in the size of the workforce in these years.

The changes in subcategories in the upper and lower work groups reveal some interesting patterns. In the upper-level work group, women performed better than men in holding on to their jobs in many occupational positions, particularly as capitalists in professional and technical (0.62 women, -0.06 men) and agricultural occupations (0.78 women, 0.42 men). However, women capitalists in production positions grew in number at a rate much slower than the size of the employed workforce (-0.25), whereas men gained relatively (0.26). While both women and men gained relatively in the upper-level state employee positions (middle class), men's gain (0.30) was larger than women's (0.17). In contrast, neither female nor male upper-level employees of the private sector (the middle class) grew in step with the growth of the workforce, but the loss of women (-0.27) was less than men's (-0.34).

The above results, therefore, indicate that capital, skills, and education enable both men and women to hold on to their positions better than those who do not have them. Moreover, women were more capable than men in keeping their positions. Women, obviously, faced serious difficulties in maintaining their capitalist positions in production, but faced no special barriers in gaining position as agricultural capitalists.[13] Also, in the relative contraction of middle-class employment in the private sector in the 1976–86 period, women were able to hold on to their positions better than men, in spite of the antagonistic environment of the workplace toward them.

The lower-level work groups have a different story to tell. The most serious adverse effects of the social and economic conditions in the first postrevolutionary decade have been on the working class, among whom women lost significantly (-0.44) and men lost slightly (-0.07). Thus, the number of positions for working-class employment in the lower-level work group did not increase in step with the growth in the size of the employed workforce, except

13. We cannot tell from our data if the absence of many rural young and middle-aged men during the war mobilization, at the same time that the land redistribution movement was going on, had anything to do with the increased presence of women as agricultural capitalists. This hypothesis can be tested only with microdata. A decline in the absolute number of women capitalists in agriculture between 1986 and 1996 gives some preliminary support to the hypothesis.

for those in state employment (in production, sales and services, and agriculture). The loss was largest for working–class women in the private sector's employment. In this category the Change Ratio index for female clerical workers is -0.60, for female sales and service employees -0.78, and for female production employees -0.64. Although the Change Ratio index for female agricultural workers in the private sector indicates a significant loss (-0.53), their loss was roughly offset by a large gain (0.49) as self–employed agricultural workers (table 6.7). We can make this claim because the absolute number in the decline of working–class women in agricultural was 44,000, and the gain for self–employed women in agricultural was 48,000 (table 6.7). Of course, we do not claim that there is an individual correspondence between those who lost their working–class positions and those who gained self–employment in agriculture.

In addition to agricultural work, lower–level self–employed women made some relative gains in clerical positions (0.15), and maintained their positions in sales and services (0.02). But the absolute number of these gains was much smaller than the loss of positions by the working–class women in these positions.

The large absolute decline in the number of unpaid family workers gives rise to a negative Change Ratio index for all of its subcategories, except for "others," which includes "unclassified." Relative decline is largest in production (-0.78), which is mostly related to decline in the market for handwoven carpets in these years. The number of unpaid family workers in agriculture declined only slightly relative to the growth of the employed labor force (Change Ratio -0.04).

Overall, in the 1976–96 period, we note that the pattern revealed in 1976–86 prevails, although we observe some attenuation in the magnitude of changes. In the upper–level work groups all Change Ratios indexes are positive, except for capitalists in production positions (-0.08). Most notable changes are the improvement in the position of self–employed professional and technical female workers (from 0.22 in the 1976–86 period to 0.49 in 1976–96), and the middle–class female employees of the private sector (from -0.27 to 0.28).

The bleak story remains for the disadvantaged lower–level group of female workers. The Change Ratio index for lower–level workers for 1976–96, as a group, remains negative (-0.18), albeit smaller than what it was in the 1976–86 period (-0.33). The Change Ratio index for the working–class women (-0.24, versus -0.07 for men) indicates that in spite of the liberalization effort, working-class women suffered not only because of their class but also because of their gender, as gender discrimination continued in the workplace for women who did not have access to capital and had low levels of skills and education. Yet by 1996 they were better off in holding their positions than in 1976–86 when the Change Ratio index relative to 1976 was -0.44 (table 6.7). All Change Ratio indexes for 1976–96 for subcategories under low-level working groups are negative for female workers, except for those employed by the state (0.17) and "unclassified" working-class women (0.54). The large negative Change Ratio index for female production workers (-0.37) and sales and service workers (-0.64) in the private sector is most distressful. It reflects the continuation, and perhaps institutionalization of, gender discrimination in the workshops and factories in the Islamic Republic.

In contrast to the position of the working-class women, the self-employed women show a noticeable advance in their position. The Change Ratio index for all categories of lower-level self-employment in 1996 is positive, and larger than what it is for 1986.

The analysis of the Change Ratio index clearly indicates the advantaged position of women in upper work groups relative to women in lower work groups in terms of employment possibilities. Given the decline in women's labor force participation rates, these trends also confirm our thesis that exclusion and the gendered-oriented incorporation process within female employment are mostly experienced by less skilled and less privileged women relative to more privileged women, and relative to men, employers, or employees.

Discriminatory policies of the Islamic state against the labor force in general, and the female labor force in particular, is reflected in the movement between labor groups and individual categories, such as the relatively stronger decline in the private sector's employment of female sales and services and production workers. Many small capitalist and self-employed activities that were created in 1979–86 were initiated by women and men who had lost their jobs during the period of Islamic cleansing, particularly between 1980 and 1989. Some left their job "voluntarily" or accepted early retirement in order to relieve themselves from the Islamists' harassment. However, protracted stagnation also had an important role in the rise of small-scale business in this period (Behdad and Nomani 2002).

At the same time, the Change Ratio indexes at both upper and lower levels of aggregation indicate a clear difference in terms of female employment policy between the state and the private sector. The state sector prefers male employees at the upper-level work groups, reflected by the 1976–96 Change

Ratio index of 0.30 for female and 0.33 for male state employees at the upper level. They prefer men because the state has a firm ideological requirement for its employees, and many professional and highly skilled women refuse conformity to the code of Islamic conduct. On the contrary, the private sector's female employment in the professional and technical work group enjoyed a strong growth (0.28 for women and only 0.10 for men) in the same period. Yet while female state employment growth is positive in all categories at the lower level of work group (except in agricultural employment), the private sector has shunned working-class women, as indicated by the negative Change Ratio indexes in table 6.7. The segregationist policy of the state has made it costly for private enterprises to employ women, because providing separate workspace is costly and impractical. This factor above all has institutionalized a sexist employment practice for women, particularly in production activities.

Moreover, the comparison of Change Ratio indexes for the lower-level work groups for women for 1976–86 and 1976–96 indicates some improvement in the position of women between 1986 and 1996. Timid economic and social liberalization and economic recovery in the post-Khomeini period and women's resistance to regain its prerevolutionary position in the workforce after the death of the leader of the Islamic Republic explain this positive change. The trend in defeminization of the labor force, particularly in employment of working-class women in the private sector in the Khomeini decade, was mitigated in the post-Khomeini decade of economic liberalization and increased women's resistance.

The marginalization of women through defeminization of the workforce was partly moderated in the post-Khomeini decade through increased activity rates and employment of women in lower-rank occupational categories. However, the process of marginalization of women continued through gender segregation in occupations. We will examine the process of marginalization of women by segregation by relying on the Gender Employment Empowerment Index (GEEI) in the following section.

Class-Gender Nature of Empowerment-Impairment

Gender Employment Empowerment Index was introduced by the United Nations Development Program (UNDP 1996, 107–8). It reveals the degree of empowerment of women in the labor market by measuring for each occupational category the adjusted share of female and male workers by their share in the working-age population (in the case of Iran, the female and male population ten years or older).[14] We apply this descriptive index for detecting the changes in differentiated segregation within different work groups, reflecting different class locations, in the period under study. A value of 1.0 for this index implies that the share of employed women and men in a given work group is equal to the percentage of their share in the working-age population.

Tables 6.6 and 6.7 depict the GEEI for various occupational categories in the upper and lower hierarchy of work for 1976, 1986, and 1996. The GEEI for all women falls from 0.48 in 1976 to 0.33 in 1986, and then moves up to 0.43 in 1996. This movement indicates overall impairment of women in the involutionary years, and some improvement in the subsequent deinvolutionary, post-Khomeini years. Nevertheless, the value of the overall GEEI in 1996 is less than what it was in 1976.

A comparison of the GEEI for upper and lower work groups reflects the class dimension of the gender empowerment and impairment in Iran in the twenty years considered in this study. In 1976 women in the upper-level work group were significantly more empowered in employment (GEEI 0.77) compared to women in the lower-level work categories (0.45). In the involutionary years, when the economy faced serious disruptions and women became the targets of the segregationist policies of the Islamic state, women in the upper-level work groups, as a group, nearly maintained their position. However, the women in the lower work levels lost significantly as their GEEI fell to 0.25. This decline is what we observed in the previous analyses. The GEEI, however, reveals that in the upper-level work group women capitalists in 1976 had a very low GEEI as a group (0.12) and particularly in administration (0.03), sales and services (0.07), and agriculture (0.08). The highest GEEI for capitalist women in 1975 was 0.31 for the "unclassified" category; next was 0.18 in production.

---

14. If

    FP = Female population ten years or older,
    MP = Male Population ten years or older,
    TP = Total population ten years or older,
    f_i = Number of women in category i,
    m_i = Number of men in category i.

Then

$$GEEI_i = [1/((FP/TP) \star (1/(f_i/(f_i+m_i)))) + ((MP/TP) \star (1/(m_i/(f_i+m_i))))]/0.5$$

See UNDP 1996, 107–8.

By 1986, in spite of adverse economic and social conditions, the GEEI for capitalist women increased, in all occupational groups, except for those in production and "unclassified" groups. On the other hand, upper-level working women in middle-class positions who enjoyed an almost equal position in comparison with men (GEEI 0.91) in 1976, suffered a loss (0.88) in 1986, and as a group did not experience any improvement by 1996. It was state employment where upper-level salary women experienced the loss (from 0.96 in 1976 to 0.91 in 1996). This evidence is contrary to the apologists' perception considering the Islamic Republic as the vehicle for empowerment of professional women. It is in the private sector where professional women have gained empowerment, even in the hard years of the 1978–86 (GEEI 0.44, 0.49, and 0.56, respectively, in 1976, 1986, and 1996).

In the 1976–86 period, in the lower-level work group, most categories suffered a decline, a few that already had a low GEEI remained the same, and only two categories enjoyed an improvement. Among those whose GEEI declined were self-employed women in production (from 0.57 to 0.27) and working-class women in production in the private sector (from 0.33 to 0.14). The working-class women in the private sector lost as a whole (from 0.38 to 0.19), as did the state employees (from 0.22 to 0.15). Self-employed women in agriculture benefited from employment empowerment (from 0.04 to 0.11), but their GEEI indicates that they suffer from a very low level of empowerment to begin with. The only major winner among the lower-level female workers were clerical workers employed by the private sector (from 0.42 to 0.50). It is noteworthy that in the lower categories, in all cases in 1976 and 1986, the GEEI was below 0.6 (except for unpaid family workers). In 1996, wage-earning female clerical workers passed the 0.60 mark and attained 0.73 for their GEEI.

The post-Khomeini decade brought some improvement in the GEEI for some in the lower-level work group. Some even exceeded their 1976 level, including self-employed women (except in production) and private-sector clerical workers. Others were major losers compared to 1976, especially working-class women in sales and service, agriculture, and production, employed by the private sector.

The change in the GEEI position of upper-level working women by 1996 is mixed. By 1996, it is clear that the upper-class women, as a whole, had been slowly sliding down, from 0.77 in 1976 to 0.74 in 1996, but still doing significantly better than the lower-level working women, who began at a lower GEEI (0.45) and fell much lower (to 0.35), in spite of their improvement between 1986 and 1996. Female capitalists lost some of their 1986 gains by 1996, and so did the middle-class women in state employment, while they continued to gain, mainly as professional and technical workers in the employment of the private sector.

Once we place the GEEI index next to our previous finding in this chapter we see that although among the employed workforce women in the upper-work level managed to pass through the adverse condition of 1976–86 relatively less harmed, in comparison to the lower-level working group, they too experienced some losses once we account for the increase in the number of women in the potential workforce (ten years and older). Moreover, we observe that the upper-level working women were clear victims of the state's gender segregationist policy, even though initially they scored some gains in finding new opportunities as the result of the very same gender segregation policies (female teachers for female students). Of course, the heavy brunt of the pain of economic disruption and gender discrimination was borne by the lower-level working women, who had little skill and no capital to pass through the storm. They lost all over. Their only win was for the very small number who became self-employed, or even capitalist in the agricultural activities, and the clerical workers employed by the private sector.

Conclusions

Our study demonstrates that because of a protracted economic crisis, and with the aggressive and oppressive gender-segregationist policy of the Islamic state, women's economic marginalization and impairment have been manifested partly as exclusion from the labor market and employment, and partly in the form of segregation within the labor market and employment in different forms. Our study indicates that the way women were excluded from, or integrated into, the market and employment in the involutionary and deinvolutionary processes period was affected by their access or lack of access to the ownership of productive resources, organizational assets/authority, and skills/credentials. However, women's choice of occupations and their ranks in these occupations and in jobs within these occupations were limited by the religiously and culturally motivated forces and institutions.

A Note on Our Statistical Method:
Why We Did Not Use Some Popular Indexes

There is much debate about the adequacy of various indexes measuring segregation and concentration of various categories of workers in the workforce and in different categories of employment. There is even more controversy in interpretation of theses indexes. We have no intention of contributing to that controversy. We used indexes that we think are most appropriate for our analysis. We refer the readers interested in this controversy to Anker (1998, 68–94) and Jacobsen (1998, 213–14). However, we feel obliged to explain why we did not use two prevalent indexes in our study. These two indexes are the Dissimilarity Index and the Representation Ratio.

The Dissimilarity Index is highly aggregated, and, therefore, is class blind. It masks the complexities associated with segregation. Moreover, the Dissimilarity Index does not reflect the changes in the participation rates that could be a strong bias against women employment in some Muslim societies (Anker 1998, 69–78). Besides, over time, this index must be adjusted for the change in integration of women across work groups or occupations, and changes in the occupational structure of the workforce (Blau and Hendricks 1979, 198–200; Jacobs 1989, 160–64; Anker 1998, 76–78). The widespread confusion about the intuitive interpretation of the Dissimilarity Index has been already examined (see especially Anker 1998, 89–92).

We do not use the Representation Ratio because it measures the percentage of women in an occupational category, relative to the percentage of women in the (employed) labor force. This measure would be reliable in indicating changes in gender representation in various work categories over time only if women's activity rate, relative to men's, remains stable over the period of study. In the case of Iran, where the activity rate of women, relative to men, fluctuates significantly, this index could not be reliable. Between 1976 and 1986, the activity rate of women declined significantly. Therefore, any change in the Representation Ratios calculated for 1986 would have an upward bias. In contrast, in 1996 women's activity rate, relative to men's, increased in comparison to 1986. Therefore, the Representation Ratios for women for 1996 would have a downward bias, compared to 1986.

7

Modes of Production and Classes

Urban and Rural Division

ON THE EVE OF THE IRANIAN REVOLUTION, more than half of the workforce was engaged in rural regions. This spatial division of the workforce has been reversed in the postrevolutionary years in the midst of the involuntary and deinvolutionary transformation of the economic structures. These changes have affected the configuration of production relations, or the modes of production, in rural and urban areas, and their corresponding class relations.[1] The overall outcome of these developments as reflected in the class nature of the employed workforce and the peculiarity of its gender division were examined in Chapters 5 and 6. Yet this aggregate transformation was the end result of specific patterns of change in the configuration of modes of productions and the associated class nature of the employed workforce in urban-rural division in the context of involuntary and deinvolutionary processes. These peculiarities identify the changing socioeconomic balance of power in the class nature of the workforce in its spatial division and indicate the tendency for their future development. Although the involutionary and deinvolutionary processes have been more or less similar in urban and rural regions, the weight and the pace of change in the urban and rural configuration of relations in economic activities and their associated socioeconomic balance of power were distinct. The delineation of the

1. Cohen asserts that production relations are "relations of effective power over persons and productive forces" (2001, 63). We noted in Chapters 1 and 2 that, as a matter of convenience, we may present production relations as relations of ownership. As such, the mode of production or "economic structure of a society is the whole set of its production relation," and not a way or manner of production, or even a process, even though it is subject to process (ibid.; see also 78–87). For example, in 1976–96 the economic structures or the sets of production relations under the domination of capitalist relations in Iran were subject to the processes of involution and deinvolution.

changing peculiarity of the urban-rural class nature of the employed work-force in correspondence with changing combination of modes of produc-tion in 1976–96 is the objective of this chapter. Such a focus, at the same time, lays the ground for the study of certain important factors that impact the differentiation of lifelong opportunities of the Iranian workforce in Chapter 8.

The Prerevolutionary Conditions

In 1976, 4.1 million people were employed in urban areas and 4.7 million were working in rural regions. They constituted 46.6 percent and 53.4 per-cent of the total employed workforce, respectively. In the urban economy capitalism was the dominant mode of production in an uneven and combined coexistence with petty-commodity economic activities and with a strong state sector. Table 7.1 depicts that 41 percent of the workforce was engaged in capitalist economic relations and 24.8 percent in petty economic activities, despite a notable relative decline in these activities in the 1970s. Moreover, similar to many developing economies that rely on the export of important state-owned natural resources, the share of the government in the ownership of resources and employment was significant. More than one-third (34.2 per-cent) of the urban workforce was employed by the state, including the mid-dle-class professional and technical employees, the working-class wage earners, and the political functionaries (bureaucrats and the military and para-military personnel). About 84 percent of state employees were in the urban economy, where more than three-fourths (78.5 percent) of the middle class and less than a quarter (22.8 percent) of the working class were state employ-ees. Nearly 16 percent of the urban workforce were political functionaries, about half of them in the armed forces.

The traditional petty bourgeoisie, along with family workers and those in the "unspecified" category, made up nearly a quarter of the urban workers. Modern petty bourgeoisie (professional and technical workers) constituted only a tiny portion of the urban workforce (0.7 percent). The urban workers were concentrated in Tehran, other large cities, and their surrounding areas.

In our examination of the class divisions in the rural economy we do not present a detailed class differentiation schema applicable to the agrarian mode of production. We limit our analysis to the generalized classifications of capi-talist economic relations, petty economic activities, and the commodified and

Table 7.1
Modes of Production, Urban Economy, 1976, 1986, and 1996

	1976 Total (1,000s*)	%	1986 Total (1,000s*)	%	1996 Total (1,000s*)	%
Private capitalist relations	1,687	41.0	1,278	21.5	2,500	28.4
Capitalists	142	3.5	206	3.5	385	4.4
Private employees: middle class	88	2.1	57	1.0	200	2.3
Private employees: working class	1,457	35.4	1,014	17.0	1,916	21.8
(Employees per capitalist)	(10.9)		(5.2)		(5.5)	
Petty economic activities	1,020	24.8	2,082	35.0	2,947	33.5
Petty bourgeoisie: modern	29	0.7	41	0.7	141	1.6
Petty bourgeoisie: traditional	887	21.6	1,700	28.5	2,394	27.2
Unpaid family workers	86	2.1	46	0.8	113	1.3
Unspecified	20	0.5	294	4.9	299	3.4
State employment	1,405	34.2	2,594	43.6	3,352	38.1
State employees: middle class	323	7.8	603	10.1	1,101	12.5
State employees: working class	430	10.5	886	14.9	1,081	12.3
Political functionaries	652	15.9	1,106	18.6	1,170	13.3
Military and paramilitary	346	8.4	749	12.6	588	6.7
Total employed urban workforce	4,113	100.0	5,953	100.0	8,799	100.0

Source: Table A.1 in the Appendix.
*Except those in parentheses.

decommodified economic activities of the state.[2] We contend that this generalized classification conceptualizes the agrarian mode of production in Iran adequately. The classes related to these modes of economic activities, that is, capitalists, middle and working classes in the private sector, petty bourgeoisie (and the unpaid family workers) in the petty economic activities, and the middle and working classes employed by the state capture the most important features of the rural economy. Nevertheless, we recognize that this study may be extended to the examination of the strata within each of these primary and contradictory class locations, in agrarian or nonagrarian economic relations. Data limitation imposes constraint on further disaggregation in our analysis.

In 1976, in sharp contrast to the urban economy, the rural economic

2. For a study of the agrarian social structure in the prerevolutionary Iran, see Khosravi 1972 and 1979.

structure was under the quantitative predominance of petty agricultural commodity production (table 7.2). Sixty-one percent of the rural employed workforce was engaged in petty commodity production. The majority (84 percent, 1.6 million) of the rural petty bourgeoisie were self-employed peasant farmers who worked primarily on their own land, and alongside small capitalist farmers relied on the help of 573,000 unpaid family workers (77 percent male). The relative share of unpaid family workers in total rural employment was 20 percent, compared to 2.1 percent in urban employment. We noted before that unpaid family work is predominantly a rural phenomenon in Iran.

Table 7.2
Modes of Production, Rural Economy, 1976, 1986, and 1996

	1976 Total (1,000s*)	%	1986 Total (1,000s*)	%	1996 Total (1,000s*)	%
Private capitalist relations	1,567	33.4	938	18.6	1,354	23.5
Capitalists	40	0.9	135	2.7	143	2.5
Agriculture	27	0.6	96	1.9	96	1.7
Private employees: middle class	13	0.3	7	0.1	19	0.3
Private employees: working class	1,514	32.3	796	15.8	1,193	20.7
Agriculture	541	11.5	251	5.0	335	5.8
(Employees per capitalist)	(38.2)		(5.9)		(8.5)	
Petty economic activities	2,852	60.8	3,251	64.4	3,512	60.8
Petty bourgeoisie: modern	5	0.1	6	0.1	23	0.4
Petty bourgeoisie: traditional	1,890	40.3	2,643	52.4	2,641	45.8
Agriculture	1,582	33.8	2,016	41.7	1,904	33.0
Unpaid family workers	936	20.0	438	8.7	684	11.9
Agriculture	574	12.2	374	7.4	472	8.2
Unspecified	21	0.5	163	3.2	163	2.8
State employment	268	5.7	859	17.0	906	15.7
State employees: middle class	63	1.3	100	2.0	173	3.0
State employees: working class	126	2.7	289	5.7	344	6.0
Political functionaries	79	1.7	470	9.3	389	6.7
Military and paramilitary	43	0.9	421	8.3	300	5.2
Total employed rural workforce	4,686	100.0	5,048	100.0	5,772	100.0

Source: Table A.1 in the Appendix.
*Except those in parentheses.

In 1974, in spite of the dominance of capitalist relations of production in the nonagrarian economy, according to the *Survey of Agriculture* of the Statistical Center of Iran, 61 percent of all rural landholdings relied solely on family labor (petty bourgeoisie), 33 percent relied primarily on family labor (small capitalists), and only 5 percent used primarily wage-earning workers. Similarly, 51 percent of all farms did not sell any of their output in the market, 27 percent sold less than half, and only 22 percent sold more than half of their output. In contrast, among the largest rural agricultural units (those 50 hectares or larger), constituting 1.0 percent of all units (26,000 in total), 97 percent reported selling more than half of their output to the market (MAI 1977, 7, 9).

Thus, the agrarian sector in 1974, five years before the revolution, was dominated by petty-commodity activities, by peasant farmers, relying primarily on family labor and producing mainly for consumption, rather than exchange. This petty-commodity mode of production coexisted with a growing commercialized agriculture in the rural economy (in large rural corporations and agribusinesses) and a predominantly capitalist relations of production in the urban areas.

In table 7.3 we present the distribution of landholdings in the rural economy of Iran as an index for agrarian strata. We recognize, however, that class is a relational concept and that the size of landholding is not the sole criterion for agrarian class analysis or the major attribute of peasant and capitalist farms. Size of landholding influences the scale of farm production, and only in relation to other factors[3] are we able to quantify strata within agrarian classes. We, therefore, present the size distribution of landholdings with much caution and only to reflect the general structural framework of the class formation in Iran.

The land reform of the 1960s had already distributed a large portion of agricultural land among 1.8 to 1.9 million tenant cultivators (Majd and Nowshirvani 1993, 443–45). In 1974, 64.4 percent of all (2.48 million) rural agricultural units (farms) held less than 5 hectares of land, adding up to no more than 14.8 percent of Iran's agricultural land (table 7.3). The area of land needed for maintaining the subsistence of a family of five in Iran, on the average, in the 1970s was estimated about 7 hectares (Hooglund 1982, 77), whereas this group of farms had, on the average, only 1.5 hectares of land.

---

3. Such as the number of labor hired and unpaid family labor within the household, area under cultivation, degree of mechanization, quality of soil and seed, the number of animals and machines, the degree of irrigation, amount of rented-in land, and so on.

Table 7.3

Distribution of Agricultural Landholdings by Size, 1974, 1988, and 1993

Unit area (H)*	1974 % of units†	1974 % of total area†	1974 Avg. area (H)	1988 % of units†	1988 % of total area†	1988 Avg. area (H)	1993 % of units†	1993 % of total area†	1993 Avg. area (H)
Less than 1	29.6	1.6	0.4	26.8	1.7	0.4	30.9	2.0	0.4
1–less than 2	42.6	4.3	1.4	41.7	4.8	1.3	46.0	5.5	1.3
2–less than 5	64.4	14.8	3.2	66.1	17.1	3.1	69.4	18.5	3.0
5–less than 10	81.7	32.8	6.9	83.2	36.0	6.7	84.8	37.2	6.7
10–less than 50	99.0	78.5	17.5	98.9	81.2	17.5	99.0	82.5	17.6
50–less than 100	99.6	85.1	66.0	99.7	89.6	63.5	99.8	90.9	63.0
100+	100.0	100.0	256.8	100.0	100.0	202.6	100.0	100.0	204.9

Sources: MAI 1977, 1992, 1999d.

*H = hectares.

†Cumulative percentages.

Thus, those who depended for their livelihood principally on these farms had to supplement their income by having some members of their household working as laborers in other farms, in other economic activities of the village (working as a driver on a small pickup truck—*vanetbar*—was an attractive possibility), or working on the household's account (as unpaid family workers) weaving rugs (mostly women). Moreover, migration of one or several members of the household (mainly men) to the cities seasonally, or more permanently, was the alternative chosen by many.

Another 17.3 percent of Iranian rural farms in 1974 had between 5 to 10 hectares of land. Nearly all of the first group and many of those in the second group of landholdings (together 81.7 percent, or 2 million in number of all rural farms) constituted the majority of "poor peasants" *(dehqanan-e faqir)* of Iran, the large majority of them among the rural petty bourgeoisie. According to the official statistics (MAI 1977, 7), 65 percent of these farms were run solely by family labor, 31 percent primarily by family labor, and only 4 percent primarily by hired workers.[4]

The holdings with 10 to 50 hectares of land had, on average, 17.5

4. There were those who possibly owned more than one landholding. The number of these cases was small, although not insignificant.

hectares, or more than twice the minimum necessary for sustenance of a family. Among these 44 percent ran their farms solely by family labor and 48 percent primarily by family labor. Only 7 percent managed their activities mainly with hired labor. They represent the relatively "well off" *(dehqanan-e miyaneh-hal)* peasant as well as capitalist farmers.

Farms with more than 50 hectares of land made up 1 percent of Iranian agricultural units and owned more than one-fifth (22 percent) of agricultural land of the country (table 7.3). They included the "wealthy farmers" *(dehqanan-e muraffah)* and various forms of corporate farms, each landholding working, on average, with 135 hectares of land. Among these units, representing the backbone of capitalist agriculture of Iran, only 47 percent relied primarily on hired labor, and 16 percent relied solely on family labor (MAI 1977, 7, 9).[5]

The land–distribution statistics reveal a number of significant points. First, a large majority of Iranian landholdings in 1974 were very small. Their small size is an indication of the predominance of petty-commodity peasant production, which is also revealed by the statistics of category of labor employed and the proportion of their output taken to the market. Second, the small size of landholdings indicates that most farming households could not rely solely on their land and had to engage in other activities to supplement their farm income. This need has led, most important, to the migration of some members of households to urban centers. Third, although most peasant farmers operated on small landholdings, there are others who had large holdings of land. Therefore, not all petty bourgeois landholdings were necessarily poor; a small percentage of them were quite wealthy. The opposite is also true for the "capitalist" farmers. Some, albeit a small percentage, of landholdings were capitalist farms. As we will show in the study of income distribution, there are in fact some capitalists who are among the rural poor (as it is also the case in the urban economy).

Capitalist relations made up 33.4 percent of employment in rural Iran in 1976, and the state employed only 5.7 percent of the rural workforce (table 7.2). In the rural economy, 40,100 capitalists employed 1.5 million working-class workers and 13,400 middle-class (managers and professional and technical) workers. That is, 38.2 workers per capitalist. This number is a startling high "concentration index" for the rural economy in comparison to 10.9 employees per capitalist in the urban economy. The absence of disaggregated

5. For a discussion of grouping of agrarian petty bourgeoisies, see Ashraf 1982.

data prevents us from scrutinizing the size (employment) distribution of firms in the rural and urban economy. Calculation of the sectoral "concentration index" reveals that this seemingly paradoxical disparity is particularly large in construction activities, where there are 358 employees per capitalist in the rural economy and only 27 in the urban economy.[6] The reason for this large disparity in the number of employees per capitalist in the two regions of the economy is the dominant position of the large firms operating outside the urban areas, as defined by city zonings. These firms are counted along side the large number of small shops, artisans' workshops, retailers, and farmers who employ one or two workers (thus being counted as capitalists) in the rural areas. The disparity was as large as we showed above in construction in 1976 because rural construction activities was dominated by road building and other state infrastructural projects, which were always contracted to large construction companies.

Tables 7.1 and 7.2 show this disparity decreased significantly in 1986 and 1996 for a number of reasons. First, in construction many infrastructural projects were curtailed in the postrevolutionary period. Second, many large firms in all major economic activities were transferred to the state or parastatal foundations by nationalization or confiscation. And third, urban development (or just extending the city limits) brought some of the activities of the enterprises within the boundaries of cities. Nevertheless, the concentration index (employees per capitalist), both in the urban and rural economies changed (tables 7.1 and 7.2) according to the pattern that we noted in Chapter 5. Indexes decreased in the involutionary process (shown by the index for 1986) and increased only slightly in the subsequent decade as the economy experienced the process of deinvolution (revealed by the index for 1996).

Agriculture accounted for 67 percent of rural capitalists and only 36 percent of the rural working class. The large proportion of nonagricultural working class in the rural areas reflects the phenomenon that we addressed above. More than one-third of the rural working class were counted as construction workers (Behdad and Nomani 2002, 677). Obviously, they were not all constructing buildings for the rural population of Iran.

The state had a limited direct role in rural employment in comparison to the cities. It employed 63,000 middle-class employees. The majority were

6. For calculation of concentration index of the private sector in various major economic activities (agriculture, industry, construction and services), see Chapter 5 and Behdad and Nomani 2002, 680.

teachers and health-care professionals. The working-class employees of the state were about 126,000, only 2.7 percent of the rural labor force. The state employed 79,000 political functionaries (including 43,000 in the armed forces) in the rural economy, compared to 652,000 (346,000 in the armed forces) in the urban economy. Only 16 percent of the state's activities and 11 percent of its political functionaries were placed in the rural area. The remaining majority were in the urban areas.

The Involutionary Changes

In the involutionary period, the urban and rural configuration of relations in economic activities, and the corresponding class structures, changed notably. By 1986 private capitalist relations, measured by the number of those engaged in these relations, contracted in both urban and rural areas. The number of wage and salary earners (working class and the middle class) of the private sector in urban and rural areas decreased as the domain of activities of the state in the economy and the number of those in petty economic activities increased. Thus, the overall share (and absolute number) of the workforce directly employed in private capitalist relations dropped from 41 percent to 21.5 percent (1.7 million to 1.3 million) in urban areas, and from 33.4 percent to 18.6 percent (1.6 million to 900,000) in rural areas (tables 7.1 and 7.2).

These dramatic declines were accompanied by large increases in the number of urban and rural capitalists. Urban capitalists increased in number by 45 percent, and the number of those in the rural economy more than tripled. Thus, an average urban capitalist employed only 5.2 workers, and an average rural capitalist had only 5.9 workers on the payroll. Nearly three-fourths (72 percent) of the new rural capitalists were in agricultural positions, and the rest were mainly in production, whereas in the cities the increase in the number of capitalists was concentrated in production. We can make a similar note about the increase in the number of rural and urban petty bourgeoisie and the decline in the number of the working class. We called this deproletarianization of the labor force in Chapter 5, which in the rural sector implied peasantization of agriculture, as a significant portion of the rural working class became the new self-employed peasant farmers.

The private capitalist relations shrank mainly by a decline in the size of enterprises, when in fact the number of enterprises (nearly corresponding to the number of capitalists) increased. We alluded to this situation by noting the changes in the number of urban manufacturing enterprises in this period in

Chapter 5. The same pattern took shape in the rural areas, particularly in rural agriculture, where land redistribution had a dramatic effect in increasing the number of land owning farmers. In the early postrevolutionary years about 800,000 hectares of prime agricultural land (6 percent of the total) was confiscated by rural population, and about 100,000 hectares of state land was distributed among peasants (Schirazi 1993, 195). Moreover, the Construction Mobilization Corps (Jahad-e Sazandegi) and various state agencies engaged in rural development concentrated their effort on promoting small agrarian entrepreneurship and petty-commodity production.

The census of agriculture shows that by 1988 the percentage of agricultural units in the less-than-5-hectare category increased to 66.1 percent of the total (from 64.4 percent in 1974) holding 17.1 percent of land area (instead of 14.8 percent in 1974). Although there were more small peasant farms occupying a larger area of land, the average size of a small farm remained unchanged at 1.5 hectares. The increase in the area of land allotted to those smaller than 5 hectares came as a result of the appropriation of the larger landholdings (50 hectares and larger) in the initial postrevolutionary years. The area of land held by these units declined from 21.5 percent to 18.8 percent as their average landholding declined from 137 hectares to 103 hectares (from 66 to 63.5 hectares for 50–100 hectare holdings and from 256.8 to 202.6 hectares for 100+ hectare holdings; see table 7.3).

Thus, with the decline of private capitalist relations in economic activities (coinciding with the deproletarianization of the workforce), the share of petty-commodity production increased sharply. In the urban economy, the proportion of those engaged in petty-commodity activities increased from 24.8 to 35 percent between 1976 and 1986. In the rural areas petty-commodity activities, which was already more than 60 percent, increased to 64.4 percent, in spite of a sharp decline (about 500,000) in the number of unpaid family workers.

The decline in the share of middle-class employees in the urban and rural private sector was more than compensated by the rise of middle-class employment in the state sector. Yet this situation was not the case for urban and rural working-class employees who suffered most in terms of employment during the Khomeini period.

By 1986 the relative share of the state in urban and rural employment had risen to 43.6 percent and 17 percent of employment, respectively (from 34.2 percent and 5.7 percent, respectively, in 1976). Although the increase in the number of the middle-class and working-class employees of the state in both

urban and rural areas was large, the increase in the number of political functionaries (especially the armed forces) was most dramatic (tables 7.1 and 7.2).

The Deinvolutionary Trend

In the 1986–96 decade the involutionary process of the previous decade was
noticeably reversed. By 1996, in the urban economy, the overall share of the
private capitalist employment increased to 28.4 percent. It was notably higher
than in 1986, but still much less than what it was (41 percent) in 1976 (see
table 7.1). Similarly, the share of petty economic activities and the share of the
state declined significantly, but they were still higher than what they were in
1976. Between 1986 and 1996, although the absolute number of the traditional petty bourgeoisie in urban economy increased by almost 700,000, the
share of this class category declined from 28.5 percent to 27.2 percent. Meanwhile, the number of the urban working class in the employment of the private sector increased by almost 900,000 in contrast with a 450,000 decline in
the previous decade. Thus, their share in the urban workforce increased from
17 percent to 21.8 percent between 1986 and 1996. Adding those workers in
the employment of the state, the urban working class accounted for 34.1 percent of the urban workforce, more than in 1986 (31.9 percent), but still less
than in 1976 (45.9 percent). This slow rate of proletarianization in the deinvolutionary process reflects the low rate of capital accumulation resulting
from the failure of the liberalization policy of the Islamic state in this period.

The urban middle class grew considerably in the deinvolutionary decade.
The number of workers in the private sector increased by 248 percent, but
with their absolute number at only 200,000 in 1996 it was no more than 2.3
percent of the urban workforce. In contrast, more than 1 million urban middle-class workers (12.5 percent of the workforce) were in the employment of
the state. Thus, by 1996, the size of the urban middle class, employed by the
private sector and the state together, had increased to 14.8 percent of the
urban workforce, in comparison to only 9.9 percent in 1976. These changes
were accompanied by the decline in the size of the armed forces following the
cease-fire agreement with Iraq.

Thus, in 1996 and in comparison with 1976, the urban economy had experienced a rapid growth in the absolute and relative size of the middle class
(mainly in employment of the state), a much larger class of smaller capitalists,
and similarly a large class of traditional petty bourgeoisie. The working class
had declined, while the state functionaries had become more numerous.

Between 1986 and 1996, in spite of the sizable decline in the relative share of rural employment in total workforce of the country (from 45.9 percent to 39.6 percent), we observe an expansion in the capitalist relations and a relative decline in the share of state and petty economic activity in the rural sector. The relative share of capitalist relations in the rural economy increased to 23.5 percent (from 18.6 percent in 1986) at the expense of state and petty economic activity, which declined to 15.7 percent and 60.8 percent, respectively (from 17 percent and 64.4 percent).

The observed trends in rural areas were the result of several important changes that at a more disaggregated level of class-employment classification shed light on important long-run processes in the Iranian economy. The main reason for the expansion of employment within rural capitalist relations was the increase in the relative share of the private-sector working-class employees from 15.8 percent to 20.7 percent of the rural workforce. This trend was, however, accompanied with a relative decline in the number of rural capitalists, indicating an increase in the concentration of ownership and capital in the rural economy. The ratio of employees per employer in the rural economy increased from 5.9 to 8.5, when this ratio increased only minimally in the urban economy (from 5.2 to 5.5).

The change in the class configuration of the rural agriculture is particularly revealing. Between 1986 and 1996, the number of capitalists in rural agriculture remained constant, while the number of working class in their employment increased by more than 84,000 (33.4 percent). More important, in this period the number of petty bourgeoisie in rural agriculture declined by 202,000 (9.6 percent). This depeasantization of rural agriculture is a clear reversal of the peasantization process that we observed in the previous period.[7]

Nevertheless, in 1996 capitalist agriculture was considerably smaller in scale in comparison to 1976. From data in table 7.2 we can calculate the number of hired laborers per employers in the rural agriculture in census years. This ratio in 1976 was 20.2. By 1986, after some large agribusinesses were parceled out by peasant farmers, and others were taken over by the *bonyads* (thus moved into the state sector), this ratio declined to 2.5. In the deinvolution process the average number of hired workers per capitalist in rural agriculture increased to 3.5 in 1996. The slowness of the rate of expansion of capitalist agriculture in rural Iran is also reflected in the size distribution of

7. See also Ajami's findings in a study (2005) of a village near Marvdasht on peasantization and the subsequent depeasantization of rural agriculture in postrevolutionary Iran.

landholdings. Between 1988 and 1994 the process of land fragmentation continued as the percentage of farms smaller than 5 hectares increased (table 7.3). In the absence of disaggregated data, and based on observations in a limited number of case studies (for example, Hooglund 2001 and Ajami 2005) we can suggest that the capitalist development has been concentrated mainly in small- and medium-size farms.

Conclusions

In 1976–86 the private capitalist economy in both urban and rural areas contracted, was deproletarianized, peasantized, and, as we have shown also traditionalized and defeminized. At the same time, the state and petty economic activity expanded. All these trends were in harmony with the dominance of the petty bourgeois, populist ideology in the Iranian revolution.

Our analysis indicates a slow process of revitalization of capitalist relations in the post-Khomeini decade, following the retardation of these relations in the first revolutionary decade. The revitalization of the capitalist relations is manifested, more than anything else, in the growth of the urban and rural working class (proletarianization) and the relative decline of the urban and rural traditional petty bourgeoisie. In the rural economy, this trend is most significantly noted in the depeasantization of agriculture. The speed of the revitalization of capitalist relations is, however, limited by the rate of capital accumulation. The low rate of proletarianization in the urban and rural economy is an indication of the slowness of the rate of accumulation of capital.

8

Classes and Unequal Life Opportunities

ACUTE SOCIAL INEQUALITY is a distinct characteristic of Iranian society. The manifestations of inequality are varied and complex, and may be delineated and measured only in fragments, where data exist. Yet the persistent use of common expressions such as *bala shahri-ha* and *pa'in shahri-ha* (uptowners and downtowners), *dara-ha va nadar-ha* (the haves and the have-nots), *tabagh-e bala* (upper class), and *zahmatkeshan* (toilers) in Iranian discourse reflects the awareness of the people about existence of some kind of class cleavage and the inequality resulting from it.

The conceptualization of social inequality based on class and its related differential life opportunities unveils an important structural source of inequality and its reproduction. The class nature of economic relations between employees and employers, in mediation with family-kinship, gender, educational system, and state, manifests itself in differential life opportunities for those individuals involved in these relationships. In the study of the access to scarce resources, as well as the study of different dimensions of social inequalities, class matters. John Western, in a study of inequality in Australia, notes that "the 'higher up' the hierarchy one is, or the greater 'control' over the productive processes of the society one can exercise, the greater one's access to scarce and valued resources" (1989, 129). Over time, this, in turn, generates differential life opportunities for different classes.

Those persons who are more or less in the same position in terms of ownership of the means of production, organizational assets, and credentials will have access to a similar set of opportunities in their life. The primary mechanism for the unequal distribution of life opportunities is economic relations. Over time, surplus appropriation in relations of production provides a rising capacity for the owners of economic assets to consume more (and more discriminately), to invest in the education of their children, to acquire for them cultural capital, and to transfer property to them by bequest. The acquired capital (physical, financial, or cultural) enhances the lifelong opportunities of the propertied class and facilitates reproduction of social division. Moreover, part of the resources that are either acquired through the distributive and regulatory power of the state or in private productive and distributive activities are invested in political ventures, to gain influence and benefit from the power of the state for ensuring the flow of economic rents.

Class relations are reproduced in interaction with the mediating factors, that is, family, gender, educational system, and state. They limit the have-nots in acquiring the essential qualifications, support, and information necessary for upward mobility.

Family has a fundamental role in reproduction of class and inequality. It is the basic mechanism for the transfer of ownership and control of property, material, and cultural capital. It determines individuals' initial conditions and their expected projectile of lifelong opportunities.

Economic, social, and cultural capital empowers the advantaged classes in periods of economic recovery and prevents their fall in times of general economic hardship. These factors, in addition to the ability for surplus appropriation in economic relations, enhance the lifelong opportunity of the propertied class and reproduce its advantaged position vis-à-vis the have-nots. Class analysis identifies quantitative and qualitative variables that detect the nature of the production and reproduction of inequality in the form of differential life opportunities in the long run.

Differential life opportunities that facilitate reproduction of class inequalities through time are realized by means of many variables (Korpi 1978, 19–20). Some of these variables, like employment possibility and income, are related to occupations and labor market. Others are wealth, cultural capital, education, leisure, and social and economic security.

In postrevolutionary Iran, the pattern of the class nature of employment has been transformed along with the changing composition of interrelated modes of production. The transformation of class relations and differentiated life opportunities associated with these classes have reproduced many of the old structural inequalities of the Iranian socioeconomic system, intensified some, and modified others. Here we will examine a broad picture of the differential life opportunities of the workforce with the help of only a few direct and indirect measurable indicators of life opportunities, namely, employment opportunity (unemployment) and distribution of income-expenditures. We have discussed gender inequality, as an important attribute of the workforce, in Chapter 6. The study of the role of family, cultural capital, distribution of

wealth, social-economic and political actions, and the specific role of the Islamic state in the reproduction of the structure of inequality, although important in this context, are beyond the scope of this book.

Unlevel Grounds in Employment

Between 1976 and 1996, every year, on average, 1.1 million were added to
the working-age population (ten years or older) of Iran. From this, each year,
410,000 were added to the rank of students. Therefore, each year 712,000
were added to the nonstudent working-age population. At the same time, in
these years, total civilian and noncivilian, paid and unpaid employment increased by 5.8 million. That increase amounts to 290,000 new jobs per year.
The discrepancy between the increase in the nonstudent working-age population and increase in paid and unpaid job creation points to the increase in
the number of those persons who remain nonactive, or unemployed.

We can gain a deeper understanding of the problem of employment in
Iran by disaggregating these numbers in terms of the access of the workforce
to scarce recourses and types of employment. We can examine the increase
in employment in the past two decades in the context of our class typology
and the social hierarchy of work (tables A.1, A.3, and A.4 in the Appendix).
From the total increase of 5.8 million in employment in 1976–96, 4.7 million
was in the urban economy and 1.1 million in the rural areas.

State employment constituted 44 percent (2.6 million) of the total increase in employment. More than one-third of this increase (898,000) was in
the number of middle-class employees of the state. Petty-commodity economic activity made up another 41 percent of the increase in employment
between 1976 and 1996. These figures demonstrate the bureaucratic and
petty bourgeois nature of the growth in employment, and the dependence of
the middle class on state employment in the postrevolutionary period.

Table 8.1 indicates the proportion of the employed workforce in the
upper and lower occupation categories in 1976 and 1996, and the average annual rate of growth in the number in each category. We can draw a few points
from this table. First, employment growth in the rural areas has been dramatically less than in urban areas (average annual rate of 1.0 percent versus 3.9
percent). This trend has been a general characteristic of the Iranian economy
in the past decades (as in most other developing countries) and has been a
major source, and a reflection of, the continued rural-urban migration. Second, the rural workforce has been engaged overwhelmingly in the lower-level

occupational category. With the low level of capital accumulation in the rural economy, and the concentration of the bureaucratic functions and economic activities of the state in the urban economy, this outcome is inescapable. Third, over the past twenty years, in both urban and rural areas, the employment growth has been predominantly concentrated in the upper-level occupational category, especially in the state sector. This finding is the generalized situation of what we observed in the case of female employment in Chapter 6.

In 1976, 15.2 percent of the urban employed workforce was in the upper level of the social hierarchy of work, having access to means of production, or in possession of managerial and skills and credentials (table 8.1). They include the urban capitalists, modern petty bourgeoisie, and middle classes in the employment of the private sector or the state. The remaining 84.8 percent of the urban workforce and 97.3 percent of the rural workforce were in the lower-level occupational category. In the urban economy 71 percent of the lower-level workforce belonged to the working class, employed by the private sector or the state. Another 25 percent were the traditional petty bourgeoisie (see table A.4 in the Appendix). In the rural economy, in 1976, only 2.7 percent of the workforce was engaged in higher-level occupational category. In the lower-level occupational group, 62 percent were traditional petty bourgeois and unpaid family workers, and 37 percent were in the working class (see table A.6 in the Appendix).

By 1996, however, the number of individuals in the upper-level occupational category, both in urban and rural areas, especially in the state sector, had

Table 8.1

Summary of Social Hierarchy of Work Categories, Urban and Rural, 1976 and 1996 (in percentages)

	1976	1996	Average annual rate of growth
Total		2.6	
Urban	100.0	100.0	3.9
Upper level	15.2	23.3	6.1
Lower level	84.8	76.7	3.4
Rural	100.0	100.0	1.0
Upper level	2.7	6.6	5.6
Lower level	97.3	93.4	0.8

Sources: Tables A.3, A.4, A.5, and A.6 in the Appendix.

increased by a rate higher than that of those in the lower work category (table 8.1). In 1996 almost a quarter of the urban workforce (23.3 percent) was in the upper category. In the rural economy, while the proportion of those in the upper level was still very small, it had nevertheless grown at a rate several times higher than the rate of growth of rural employment.

Revolutionary changes in this period had a moderating effect on the distribution of wealth and income (Behdad 1989), and replaced the elite of the ancien régime in the state and economic sector mostly with Islamist activists, many of whom were not previously located at the upper level of the social hierarchy of work. Soon after the 1979 revolution, many valuable economic assets were redistributed, as we noted in Chapter 3. In the rural area, peasants took over and parceled out some larger landholdings. In the urban economy, the disruptions in the working of existing enterprises, particularly the large oligopolies owned by the close associates of the Shah's regime, opened new avenues for some small capitalists.

Two particular groups took advantage of this opportunity. First, the ideological cleansing of the state apparatus in the Khomeini era resulted in a large replacement of the many upper- and mid-level bureaucrats and professionals with the newly appointed or promoted Islamist activists to these positions. Cleansing Committees (Komiteh Paksazi) were established in all governmental organizations from the army and the police to ministries, bureaus, universities and schools, and large state-owned or private enterprises. These committees were packed with the most aggressive Islamist zealots, and each had a special representative of the Imam (Ayatollah Khomeini). Those who were considered antirevolutionary, associates of the ancien régime, non-Islamic, or just not respecting the new Islamic ordinance or protocol, such as taking part in public prayer in the office or following the rules of *hejab* (for women), were expelled, given leave without pay, or were retired. Early retirement arrangements were made especially attractive to encourage those who did not actively support the Islamic state to leave state employment.

Many of those who were purged or retired sought employment in the private sector. With little possibility for wage employment in the disrupted private sector, these former employees of the state sought refuge in entrepreneurship. Some became successful purveyors of specialized services or innovative producers in a market plagued with widespread shortages of industrial inputs and outputs. Many others joined the mushrooming retail trade. A sardonic expression of this phenomenon with a reference to the social origin of many elites of the Islamic state was this joke in the early revolutionary years that "the *baqqals* (grocers) have become the state, and the state bureaucrats have become *baqqals*." Failing *baqqal* or successful entrepreneurs, this story is the one that we alluded to in Chapters 5 and 6. Those who had financial capital or skills and credentials sought their livelihood in petty-commodity or small capitalist activities. For many, entrepreneurship was a career parachute after their ejection from state employment and a way of making a living in desperation. Some, however, became quite successful in their new ventures, but many dropped out. We do not know of a systematic study of this phenomenon. Our assertion is speculative and based on our own observations.

There was also another group of new entrepreneurs. They were state cronies, who benefited from the postrevolutionary redistribution of assets and from rent-seeking activities in the new power structure. Soon after the revolution, the state nationalized some major manufacturing and agricultural enterprises, banks and insurance companies and brought them under its own ownership (Nomani and Rahnema 1994, 160–69). The wealth of those who were declared "corrupt on earth" was confiscated by the Islamic Revolutionary Courts and came under the ownership of the parastatal foundations *(bonyads),* under the direct control of the political elite of the Islamic state, without being subject to the general auditing requirement of the state. Thus, the access to the state and its *bonyads* became an important source of rent-seeking activities for Islamist political elites and their offspring, in-laws, and cronies, who have been dubbed *aqazadegan* (a title for sons of high-ranking clergies).[1]

The large number of economic entities under the ownership of the state or the *bonyads* gave rise to a vast network of enterprises that fed these entities and were fed by them. This nontransparent network of enterprises is the black hole of the Iranian economy, the nexus of power breaking, and node of capital accumulation. Many young and not-so-young *aqazadegan* (and even *aqayan*—the clergies—themselves) and cronies of the state came to hold and control these enterprises and established new ones in response to the growing needs. There was no Chinese wall separating these enterprises from the successful among the first group. The privatization process that began in the early 1990s gave rise to more extensive private ownership of public enterprises. Meanwhile, the need for managers and technical workers in the newly established or refurbished enterprises gave rise to employment of many skilled professionals and technical workers in both the state-owned and the private enterprises.

1. See Maloney 2000, Rashidi 2002, and Assadi 2003 for rent-seeking activities.

To them we must add the large cadre of professionals needed for increasing the educational and health network in response to the high rate of population growth. More teachers, nurses, and doctors, as well as more information technology experts, accountants, and managers, were needed to run the growing network of the state apparatuses. The relatively small middle class began growing very rapidly in the post-Khomeini decade, more rapidly than any other major group in Iranian society.

Moreover, the rejuvenation of the private sector in the post-Khomeini decade has given rise to an increase in the employment of the urban working class. At the same time, the rapid growth of the traditional petty bourgeoisie has also dampened in the latter decade. It is apparent that a large segment of the petty-commodity activities is a substitute for wage employment of the working class. When wage employment is not a possibility, petty-commodity activities become an alternative strategy for survival for those who have some skills or some financial means (albeit small) to work in "their own business." Thus, a portion of those who are counted as petty bourgeoisie are in fact disguised members of the working class, waiting hopefully for a job opportunity, to become employed and receive wages. Therefore, in any way that we measure the unemployment rate, we need to keep in mind that we are missing not only those who have given up searching for work or see no hope in looking for it ("discouraged workers") but also a large proportion of the traditional petty bourgeoisie who are where they are because they cannot be somewhere earning a wage.

Who Is Unemployed?

According to the census, there were 1.46 million unemployed workers in 1996. Given the 16 million economically active population of Iran in that year, we will have a rate of unemployment equal to 9.1 percent. All the general reservations with respect to the counting of the unemployed workers apply here, as well. That is, this figure does not include all those who work part-time and seek full-time employment. Anyone who has worked for two days in the week before the census is counted as employed. Nor does the unemployment rate include those who have been discouraged in the labor market and have given up looking for work. These issues are the general problems of measuring unemployment. What is specific to the case of each country is the extent of these biases. That is, how large is the proportion of those who are working only part-time but seek full-time employment, and what is their average hours of work per week, how large is the number of discouraged workers, and how many are seasonally unemployed?

In this study, in contrast to macroeconomic analyses, we are concerned not merely with the absolute level of unemployment but rather with its variation among different social groups. As long as the margin of bias does not vary significantly, or the direction of bias is known for different social groups and occupational categories, our analysis would be reliable.

In the case of Iran we should, however, point to two additional structural considerations. First, in the absence of a social security system and unemployment insurance, "unemployment" is simply not an option for the poor. They must eke out a living one way or another. Some, and perhaps many, among those who are counted as self-employed are in fact unemployed, in search of a "real" job.[2] The proportion of the unemployed considered as "self-employed" workers tends to be higher in the urban areas, where a large number of recent immigrants seek employment and the absence of extended family relations makes "unemployment" a nontenable situation.

Second, *Census 1996* does not count the seasonally unemployed among the unemployed. The number of those seasonally unemployed is characteristically large relative to the size of official unemployment and is strongly biased toward the rural workforce. According to the *Census 1976,* there were 644,000 seasonally unemployed workers. Ninety-five percent of these workers were in the rural economy. If we assume that between 1976 and 1996 the number of seasonally unemployed remained a constant proportion of the rural labor force, then in 1996 we must have had about 785,000 seasonally unemployed workers. Hence, the national unemployment rate in 1996 would be 14.0 percent. The difference between the official and the adjusted rates of unemployment is pronounced in rural areas, 9.4 percent versus 21.2 percent, respectively. In the urban area the two figures are 8.9 percent versus 9.3 percent, respectively (table 8.2).

One may argue that in the past two decades seasonality of rural employment has declined. That argument is tenable. In that case, our adjusted rate presents an upper bound for the unemployment rate, and the official figures would determine a lower bound.

In both urban and rural areas the rate of unemployment for women is distinctly higher than for men whether we rely on the official or adjusted rates of

---

2. See Ra'is-Dana, Shadi-Talab, and Piran 2000 for a collection of studies on poverty in Iran.

Table 8.2
Unemployment and Unemployment Rates, 1996

	Unemployment (1,000s)	Adjusted unemployment* (1,000s)	Unemployment rate (%)	Adjusted unemployment rate† (%)
Total country	1,456	2,240	9.1	14.0
Urban	855	895	8.9	9.3
Male	713	746	8.4	8.7
Female	142	149	12.5	13.2
Rural	596	1,340	9.4	21.2
Male	467	973	8.6	18.0
Female	128	367	14.4	41.1

Source: MAI 1997.
*Adjusted by adding the estimates of seasonal unemployment.
†Calculated based on the adjusted unemployment for each category.

unemployment. In the urban economy, the unemployment rate of women is 49 percent higher than for men if we rely on the official rates, and 52 percent if we adjust the rates for seasonal unemployment. In the rural areas the unemployment rate of women is 67 percent more than that of men by the official figures, and 128 percent more by the adjusted figures (table 8.2). The difference in rates of unemployment between men and women in the rural and urban areas is a manifestation of gender inequality in the labor market, which is even more magnified when we take into account the lower activity rate of women in comparison to men (see Chapters 4 and 6).

Unemployment in the urban and rural areas is concentrated among the youth. Thirty-two percent of the unemployed are younger than twenty years, and another 39 percent are between twenty and twenty-nine years old. To these percentages one must add the youth who are prolonging their education or are simply idle, living in their parents' dwellings and relying on their financial support, in the absence of employment opportunities. Among those who are counted as unemployed in the official figures, 73.9 percent are the new entrants to the labor market (were "not previously employed"), the majority of whom are the young workers. These are the baby boomers searching with disappointment for the fruits of their parents' revolution.

The incidence of unemployment among various social classes is of interest to us. Unfortunately, we do not have the necessary data to present the rate of unemployment based on social hierarchy of work. The available data, however, allow us to examine the incidence of unemployment on the basis of occupational status and occupational position for those unemployed workers who were previously employed. However, because the majority of unemployed workers were never employed, the census cannot specify their occupational status. These workers were obviously seeking wage employment. If they become successful in their job search, they would become, most likely, an employee of the state or the private sector (mainly as working class, and a minority with skills and credentials as middle class). Some of those who fail to find a wage-paying job may start their own "business," and as such join the rank of the petty bourgeoisie.

Among the unemployed workers who previously had a job (veteran unemployed), the largest group was the wage earners of the private sector (32.8 percent). The next-largest group was the "self-employed" (30 percent). An "unemployed" self-employed worker is most likely one who has lost his or her "business" and is seeking another comeback to the market. Commonly, a large majority of them are in search of a "steady" wage employment in the state or the private sector. To those, the unpaid family workers must be added. They constituted 2.2 percent of the unemployed.

Former state employees made up 19.9 percent of the veteran unemployed group, and those with the "unclassified" occupational status accounted for 12.5 percent of the unemployed. The latter group is generally made up of the unskilled workers who drift at the margins of the labor market, never having any defined occupational status. If the term *unemployment* may be applicable for capitalists, they made up 2.6 percent of the veteran unemployed (table 8.3).

By examining the classification of the veteran unemployed population on the basis of their occupational position we can make some inferences with respect to their technical or managerial skills. Production workers and agricultural workers constituted the largest group of veteran unemployed workers (56.5 percent and 14.5 percent, respectively). These two groups plus "sales and services" (10.2 percent) and the "unspecified" group (8.2 percent) made up 89.4 percent of the veteran unemployed workers. Administrators and managers, professional and technical workers, and sales and service workers, altogether, made up 10.6 percent of the unemployed.

On the other hand, the educational credentials of the unemployed reveals that in 1996, 41.9 percent of all unemployed workers (veterans or new entrants) were either illiterate or had only elementary education, 49.8 percent

Table 8.3
Unemployment by Occupational Status, 1996

Previous occupational status	All unemployed (1,000s)	(%)	Unemployed with previous occupation (%)
Capitalists	9.8	0.7	2.6
Self-employed	114.1	7.8	30.0
Unpaid family workers	8.4	0.6	2.2
Private employees	124.9	8.6	32.8
State employees	75.8	5.2	19.9
Unspecified	47.5	3.3	12.5
New job seekers	1,075.2	73.9	–
Total	1,455.7	100.0	100.0

Source: MAI 1997.

had middle school or high school education (equal percentages in each group), and 8.4 percent had some post–high school credentials.

Thus, the census data reveal that in 1996 the youth and the new entrants to the labor market constituted the overwhelming majority of the unemployed population who were actively seeking employment. The data also reveal that among those who were actively seeking employment and did not even have a seasonal or part-time job, the rate of unemployment in the urban and rural areas was higher for women than for men. Moreover, the majority of veteran unemployed workers were production and agricultural workers. If the level of education may be regarded as a relevant determinant of the potential occupational position of the unemployed population, the census data reveal that about one-half of the population with less than middle-school education would most likely expect working-class positions, with the other half vying for administrative, managerial, or technical employment.

The increase in the rate of schooling and military mobilization of the Islamic state has partially delayed the crisis of unemployment. However, the rising level of education of the new entrants to the labor market and the sense of entitlement among the military veterans tend to increase their expectation for "suitable" employment. Therefore, the state has found itself faced not only with an unemployment problem but also with a problem of increasing expectations. This trend is a characteristic of the labor markets in the intermediate phases of development in many developing counties. In the prerevolutionary

Iran, the rapid oil-induced economic growth of 1960s and 1970s created a growing demand for labor, especially for skilled and managerial positions. The high unemployment and rising expectation of the new entrants to the labor market are the special challenges of the state in the present decade.

Class and Income Distribution

Household income enables members of the household to function within the existing class structure by maintaining "appropriate" patterns of consumption and lifestyle. As such, income level is a relevant factor in mapping individual's (or their family's) class-determined differential life opportunities.

Income is determined by access to scarce resources. Financial assets and income-earning property of capitalists and petty bourgeoisie, as well as skills, credentials, and the quality of intellectual or physical labor of wage and salary earners, are the important determinants of income. In addition, cultural assets, social network, and political connections of those in the upper-level work categories contribute to their ability to place themselves in the important economic nodes to gain special privileges and benefits from rent-seeking activities. The Islamic state in Iran is notoriously known for regarding allegiance to state ideology as a criterion for employment or distribution of rent. Even requirements for entrance to the university (thus access to skills and credentials) is skewed in favor of those committed to the state ideology, and disqualifies those suspected of nonadherence to the state ideology (Habibi 1989).[3]

At the aggregate level we have access to data on expenditures-income of households, the occupational status, and the educational attainment of the "heads of households." Indexes of physical, financial, and cultural capital; social position; and access to political power do not exist. Our study is limited to the data available from annual surveys of income-expenditures of urban and rural household by the Statistical Center of Iran (MAI, *Expenditures-Income Survey,* annual). Given our interest in the class nature of income and expenditure, our study focuses on the functional (source) distribution of income and

---

3. This, too, was especially severe in the Khomeini era. In addition to a test of ideology, which was, and still is, a part of the national entrance examination, each applicant's background was checked in the neighborhood. The imam of the neighborhood mosque and the local *komiteh* (security committee) were the most important sources of information for these investigations.

the expenditures of different occupational categories in the social hierarchy of work.[4]

Table 8.4 reveals the source of income of an "average" household in urban and rural areas of Iran for selected years between 1977 and 2001. Although MAI's *Expenditures-Income Survey* is published annually, in some years survey samples have been especially small to be comparable with other years. Here we have selected the years for our study of income distribution as close as possible to our years of attention in the previous chapters. We have also included the data for 2001 to provide the continuity of the trend into the most recent year for which the data are available.

We have calculated the index of average real household income (in 1995 prices, 1995 income is equal to 100) in the urban and the rural areas (table 8.4). Urban households, on average, suffered a decline in their real income following the revolution, from 169 in 1977 to 100 in 1995. In the subsequent years, however, particularly after 1997, because of the increase in oil prices, average urban household income continued to increase, and in 2001 the index reached 143. In contrast to the urban households, rural households did not suffer from a declining income in the postrevolutionary years. In fact, because of some increase in output and productivity in agricultural activities, in most of these years, the rural households have been doing as well as the prerevolutionary years, and even better in some years.[5] As a result of these opposite tendencies in changing income of average households in urban and rural areas, the ratio of urban to rural household income (in current prices) fell continually from 2.7 in 1977 (before the revolution) to 1.6 in 1997. The latter ratio has remained relatively stable, although the tendency toward reversal of this trend is beginning to emerge, as expected.

The changes in the sources of income for the average urban and rural households demonstrate some aspects of the changes in the interclass relations in these years (table 8.4). In 1977, nearly one-half (46 percent) of the income of an "average" urban household was from wages and salaries of the middle and working classes. For the "average" rural household the share of wages and

4. For a more general study of the extent of inequality in postrevolutionary Iran, based on the size distribution of household income (expenditures) and the measurement of Gini Ratios, see Behdad 1989, Toudeh-Roosta and Ramezani 2002, Esfandiari 2002, Alavi 2002, and Mehryar, Tabibian, and Gholipour n.d.a, n.d.b.

5. See Behdad and Nomani 2002, 676, 681, for value added and employment changes in major economic activities in 1976–96.

Table 8.4

Sources of Income for the Average Urban and Rural Household,
1977–2001 (in percentages)

	1977	1985	1991	1997	2001
Urban					
Wages and salaries	46	42	29	33	34
State employment	NA	29	19	20	20
Private employment	NA	13	11	13	14
Profit and proprietors' income	23	24	36	30	28
Miscellaneous income	31	33	35	37	38
Nonmonetary income	22	26	28	27	15
Rural					
Wages and salaries	33	30	26	28	29
State employment	NA	12	11	11	11
Private employment	NA	17	16	17	19
Profit and proprietors' income	50	51	54	55	48
Agricultural activities	38	37	37	37	31
Nonagricultural activities	12	14	18	18	17
Miscellaneous income	18	19	19	18	22
Nonmonetary income	14	17	15	13	13
Average household income (1995 = 100)					
Urban	169	128	116	109	143
Rural	101	106	103	108	136
Ratio of urban to rural average household income*	2.7	2.0	1.8	1.6	1.7

Sources: MAI, *Expenditures-Income Survey: Urban,* annual; *Expenditures-Income Survey: Rural,*
    annual; IMF 2001.

*In current prices.

salaries was 33 percent. Existing data do not differentiate the income of the
middle class from the working class.

    From 1977 to 1991 the share of wages and salaries in both urban and rural
households declined. For the average urban household this decline was most
serious between 1985 and 1991, and was mainly in the share of wages and
salaries from state employment. In the rural area, however, wages and salaries

from private sector and state employment declined, more or less, together. In 1997 and 2001, the share of wages and salaries in income of average urban and rural households increased. The deinvolutionary process, as expected, made some recovery possible for the wage and salary earners.

The MAI's statistics on the source of income do not disaggregate the income of capitalists from the income of the petty bourgeoisie. In 1977, these two sources, together, made up 50 percent of income of the average rural household and 23 percent of the income of the average urban household. The reason for the much higher share of this source of income in the rural area was the extensive petty bourgeois landownership in the agricultural activities. Nevertheless, in the postrevolutionary years, both in rural and in urban economies, the share of income of the average household from capitalists and petty bourgeois activities increased. This trend was much pronounced in the urban areas, where it began to reverse after 1991. A similar but milder trend continued in the rural area for a longer period, but it, too, was reversed by 2001.

It is unfortunate that we cannot disaggregate the income of capitalists from the income of the petty bourgeoisie. We can suspect that the changes in the importance of the proportion of the two sources of income changed in opposite directions throughout the entire period. That is, it is expected that in the early postrevolutionary years, as the economy experienced the involutionary process, the share of income from capitalist activities declined, whereas the share of income from petty bourgeois activities increased. However, when the economy began undergoing the deinvolutionary process, the share of income from petty bourgeois activities began declining. We can expect that in this process, some petty bourgeoisie joined the rank of the wage-earning working class (proletarianizaton in general and depeasantization in agriculture), and the profit-earning ability of capitalists increased. The precise examination of this pattern of change would be possible only with more disaggregated data, which are not available in the MAI publications.

About one-third of household income in the urban areas and one-fifth in the rural areas is categorized as miscellaneous income (table 8.4). It is composed of income from rent, absentee ownership, interest, and retirement pensions, in addition to various kinds of transfer payments. The importance of this source of income increased throughout the postrevolutionary years. As income from wages declined in urban and rural areas, the share of income from miscellaneous sources increased for urban and rural households. This trend may be also attributed to the increase in the number of retirees (mainly in the urban areas) and the importance of rent-seeking and illegal activities. Moreover, the rising share of miscellaneous income in the postrevolutionary periods was from nonmonetary sources. This trend demonstrates the increase in in-kind transfer payments made through family networks.

We measure the distribution of household expenditures by class categories and education of "the head of the household" to show the importance of ownership of physical and financial resources and skills and credentials in providing for the life opportunities of different classes. We use expenditure data, rather than income data, because MAI's expenditure data are more comprehensive and consistent. Moreover, in low-income countries, households' shares in expenditures is more meaningful than household income (Swamy 1967, 161) in reflecting households' welfare. However, in relying on expenditure data we underestimate the share of higher-income households by not including the importance of the flow of savings. Thus, our measure of inequality would be smaller than it actually is.

Table 8.5 depicts the distribution of household expenditures by occupational status as a proxy for social classes, in urban and rural economies, in four selected years, 1977, 1985, 1997, and 2001. The expenditures-income survey data use the categories "capitalist" and "petty bourgeoisie" as we have used in our previous analysis. However, the data do not allow us to disaggregate the working class and the middle class in the private sector, these classes employed by the state, and the political functionaries of the state. All private-sector employees and all employees of the state are lumped together in two categories of private-sector and state employees. In addition, the expenditures-income surveys have an "others" category, which includes heterogeneous groups of unemployed, retired (pensioners), rentiers, and various kinds of absentee owners.

We have calculated the percentage distribution of each employment group within the various categories of household distribution. For example, our calculation in table 8.5 indicates that in 1977, 40 percent of urban capitalist households were in the top 20 percent urban expenditure group.

An overview of the distribution of households of different employment groups indicates that capitalists and state employees, as it is expected, have been (and are) in a privileged position in the economy (table 8.5). In the urban area, capitalists, as a class, are most privileged. They have the smallest percentage of households among the lowest expenditure groups, and highest percentage of any other employment category in the high-income bracket. Nevertheless, 17 percent of the urban capitalists were in the bottom 40 per-

Table 8.5

Expenditures Distribution of Households by Occupational Status of Heads of Households, 1977–2001 (in percentages)

	Capitalists				Petty bourgeoisie				Private-sector employees				State employees				Others			
	1977	1985	1997	2001	1977	1985	1997	2001	1977	1985	1997	2001	1977	1985	1997	2001	1977	1985	1997	2001
Urban																				
1st 40%	17	17	21	21	40	40	37	41	49	52	53	54	25	26	29	15	48	57	50	54
2nd 40%	42	38	37	40	43	42	43	40	38	37	35	35	45	47	47	54	33	30	34	32
Top 20%	40	45	42	40	18	18	20	19	13	10	13	11	29	27	24	31	19	14	15	14
	100	100	100	100	100	100	100	100	100	100	100	100	100	100	100	100	100	100	100	100
Bottom 10%	3	2	4	4	8	9	8	7	12	11	13	13	3	3	5	1	19	24	17	20
Top 10%	22	29	27	25	8	9	9	10	6	4	6	5	15	14	12	15	9	7	7	7
Rural																				
1st 40%	23	17	24	21	36	38	35	34	46	46	48	47	18	18	20	8	70	70	71	70
2nd 40%	43	37	44	45	42	42	42	45	40	41	40	41	47	49	52	46	21	22	21	23
Top 20%	34	46	32	34	22	20	23	22	14	13	12	12	35	34	29	46	9	8	9	7
	100	100	100	100	100	100	100	100	100	100	100	100	100	100	100	100	100	100	100	100
Bottom 10%	4	2	3	3	7	3	7	6	10	4	9	8	3	1	2	1	39	23	34	31
Top 10%	20	29	19	21	10	10	12	8	18	5	5	24	19	16	13	17	4	4	4	3

Sources: MAI, *Expenditures-Income Survey: Urban,* annual; *Expenditures-Income Survey: Rural,* annual.

cent of households in 1977, and some 3 percent were among the "very poor" (bottom 10 percent) households. Obviously, not all capitalists are wealthy.

Over the past two decades, as reflected in our data for selective years, there have been some changes in the relative position of urban capitalists.[6] The percentage of capitalists in the lower 40 percent of households increased from 17 percent in 1977 and 1985 to 21 percent in 1997 and 2001. We should note that these capitalists were poor not only relative to other capitalists but also in comparison to the aggregation of urban households. That is to say, in 2001, more than one-fifth of urban capitalists were as poor as many petty bourgeois or even wage earners. In 2001, 4 percent of capitalist households were in the bottom 10 percent of all urban households.

The data also show that in 1985, when the dire economic conditions pushed down many urban households in other classes, particularly the wage earners of the private sector, a larger percentage of capitalists were in the top 20 percent of urban households in comparison to 1977, and the years subsequent to 1985.

The next well-off group of urban households was state employees. Only a quarter of households of urban civil servants were in the lowest 40 percent of urban households in 1977, when 29 percent of them were among the top 20 percent urban households. In the subsequent years there were minor changes in the relative position of state employees in the urban sector, except in 2001, when we observe a notable improvement in their position. The proportion of state employees' households in the lowest 40 percent urban income group declined, and their percentage in higher expenditure groups increased (table 8.5).

The households of the urban petty bourgeoisie, mostly considered "traditional," have been distributed nearly the same as those of total urban population over the past decades. That is, just about 40 percent of their households have been in the 40 percent low-income households, 40 percent in the middle-income households, and so forth. It is therefore inaccurate to consider the petty bourgeoisie either rich or poor. They have managed to keep their proportions in every income group in the urban economy.

Private-sector employees, as a category, includes the lowly paid working-

6. For a more detailed study of the changes between 1977 and 1984, in the immediate aftermath of the revolution, see Behdad 1989. In these turbulent years some significant U-shaped changes took place in the distribution of expenditures, some contrary to the general trend observed over the longer postrevolutionary years.

class employees, as well as the middle-class professional and technical workers, administrators, and managers who receive mid- to high-level salaries. Private-sector employees, too, similar to the petty bourgeoisie, include a wide spectrum of households, except that their percentage in the bottom 40 percent group is larger than proportional, and in the top 20 percent group is smaller than proportional.

Our calculations show that since 1977, the proportion of the private-sector employees' households in the bottom 40 percent of urban households has increased and their proportion of those in the middle 40 percent has declined (table 8.5).

The pattern of distribution of household expenditures for major rural social groups has been similar to the trend of the urban economy, only with some minor variations. In the rural economy state employees, including both middle and working classes, were as privileged as the rural capitalists. Between 1977 and 1997 only one-fifth of state employees were in the bottom 40 percent of rural households, whereas about a quarter of rural capitalists were in this category. More than one-third of capitalists, and about the same proportion of state employees, were in the top 20 percent of rural households, composing the majority of the upper-class household groups. Between 1997 and 2001, however, the situation of the state employees improved significantly. By 2001, nearly one-half of the state employees in the rural economy were in the middle-income group, another half were in the top 20 percent of the rural households, and only 8 percent were in the bottom 40 percent of rural households.

Rural capitalists and rural petty bourgeoisie were distributed in a pattern similar to their urban counterparts. The notable difference was that the percentage of rural petty bourgeois households in the lower 40 percent expenditure group was less than those in the urban areas, and the percentage of households in the top expenditure groups was slightly more than that for their urban counterparts.

Employees of the private sector in the rural economy, in comparison to their urban counterparts, were positioned slightly better, although they were both the least-privileged group among the four employment categories.

Among those in the "other" category, about one-half in the urban area and about three-quarters in the rural economy were in the bottom 40 percent expenditure groups. This group is the poorest category of households in booth urban and rural areas. It includes the majority of the cyclical and structural unemployed population. In the selected years, 17–24 percent of urban "others" were in the bottom 10 percent of urban households. In the rural areas, about one-third of the households of this occupational category were in the bottom 10 percent of the households.

Table 8.6 depicts the pattern of expenditure distribution of urban households on the basis of the level of education of the head of the households. Our estimates, based on MAI's data, reveal that, in general, the level of education of the head of the household is an important determinant of the welfare position of the household. The majority of the illiterates were among the lowest 40 percent of the urban households, whereas the majority of those with a university education were in the top 20 percent expenditure groups. Those with an intermediate level of education fell between these two extremes.

Between 1977 and 2001, there was a notable increase in the educational attainment of heads of households as the overall rate of literacy continued to increase in Iran (table 8.7). The proportion of illiterate heads of households declined from 45.9 percent to 22.8 percent, and the proportion of households of high school diploma holders and university educated individuals increased from 11.6 percent to 28.5 percent in the same period. The result of this increase in the overall level of educational attainment of heads of households in this period has been increasing the concentration of the poor and very poor among the illiterate group. The percentage of the poor (lowest 40 percent) and very poor (bottom 10 percent) households increased from 55 and 16 percent to 62 percent and 22 percent, respectively, between 1977 and 2001. At the same time, as the poor attained literacy, and the illiterate category became smaller in number, the proportion of the poor among the other groups increased.

In particular, the period between 1997 and 2001 is characterized by a relative worsening of the households of the illiterates and those who had less than a high school diploma, and a notable improvement in the position of the household of those with a university education (see table 8.6).

Conclusions

Our examination of social inequality in Iran demonstrates that, first and most important, class makes a difference in differential control over society's output. Second, observed trends in employment-income-consumption variables within classes and in the interclass relations changed in harmony with the at-

Table 8.6

Expenditures Distribution of Urban Households by Educational Attainment of Heads of Households, 1977–2001 (in percentages)

	Illiterate				Less than high school diploma				High school diploma				University education			
	1977	1985	1997	2001	1977	1985	1997	2001	1977	1985	1997	2001	1977	1985	1997	2001
1st 40%	55	54	58	62	31	33	41	43	17	22	23	21	2	11	16	8
2nd 40%	35	35	32	30	47	45	42	41	42	43	46	48	19	31	35	41
Top 20%	10	11	10	9	22	22	17	16	41	34	31	31	79	58	49	50
	100	100	100	100	100	100	100	100	100	100	100	100	100	100	100	100
Bottom 10%	16	17	19	22	5	5	9	8	3	4	4	4	0	3	3	2
Top 10%	4	5	4	4	10	11	8	7	21	19	16	16	50	36	33	32

Sources: MAI, Expenditures-Income Survey: Urban, annual; Expenditures-Income Survey: Rural, annual.

Table 8.7

Educational-Attainment Level of Urban Heads of Households,
1977–2001

	1977	1985	1997	2001
Illiterate	45.9	42.5	24.1	22.8
Less than high school diploma	41.1	40.8	49.7	48.2
High school diploma	7.9	13.5	18.7	20.6
University education	3.7	3.2	7.0	7.9
Unspecified★	1.4	0.0	0.5	0.5

Source: MAI, Expenditures-Income Survey: Urban, annual.
★In 1997 and 2001 includes religious education.

tributes of involutionary and deinvolutionary processes. Third, each class constitutes a wide spectrum of households in terms of levels of income and expenditures that are a reflection of segmentation within classes and are partly responsible for the lack of class cohesiveness in each class.

9

Revolution and Labor

Concluding Remarks

THE 1979 REVOLUTION toppled the existing political order to establish a new one. It ruptured the existing social relations and institutions to reconstruct them in a new mold. It was an idealized expression for social change and progress. Its slogans, deliberate or spontaneous, were epitomes of the expected orientation of the revolutionary movement by the mass of its participants and its leaders. Yet a revolution, like a forest fire, a hurricane, or a tornado, once it takes shape, its form, direction, and extent have more to do with the internal dynamics of the interaction of its forceful momentum with the social landscape in which it traverses than with its origin or initial orientation. Such is the story of the Iranian revolution, seeking to establish the rule of the oppressed; to eradicate poverty, exploitation, and excessive wealth; to do away with "imperialism of East and West"; and to replace Iran's "dependent capitalism" with a hitherto undefined utopian Islamic economic order under a petty bourgeois Shi'i theocracy, in the deeply polarized Iranian society.

Upon its initial victory in toppling the existing political order, the Iranian revolution, like other modern revolutions, confronted an economic crisis of the postrevolutionary type. In our analysis we defined a postrevolutionary economic crisis as the outcome of open social confrontations. It is the outward manifestation of the disruption in the production and accumulation processes, when the sanctity of property rights and security of capital are jeopardized by the contending social forces, and the legitimacy of the existing outcome of the accumulation process and fairness of distribution of wealth and means of production come under question. With the antagonism expressed toward capital and property, and the state's inability to facilitate the production process, capital withdraws, seeks refuge, and attempts to minimize the exposure to political risk. In these circumstances capitalist relations of pro-

191

duction shrivels and petty-commodity activities thrive. This is a degenerative process, creating tangles within the existing economic structure, obstructing the accumulation process, and aggravating the economic crisis. It gives rise to what we have called "structural involution."

The postrevolutionary economic crisis continues until a new economic order is established and the production and accumulation processes can be resumed undisturbed. The Islamic state has attempted to overcome the postrevolutionary economic crisis by rejuvenating the capitalist relations of production through its economic liberalization policy. This move is a reversal of the involutionary process; hence, we have called it "deinvolution" of the economic structure.

However, defining and establishing the postrevolutionary economic order are matters of struggle among contending social forces. This process is nonlinear and uneven, involving shifts and shuffling in the relative positions of various social groups, vying to promote their interests and to defend or improve their absolute or relative life opportunities, individually or as a class.

For many, it is a struggle for survival in the midst of social turmoil; for others, as the Persian saying goes, it is "catching fish in the muddied water," or taking advantage of the opportune moments. For the capitalists and the well-off petty bourgeois entrepreneurs, it is a struggle to hold on to their physical and financial capital, to minimize the heightened risk while maintaining a sustainable rate of accumulation, and to avoid bankruptcy and financial dissolution. For the working class and the middle class, it is the struggle to improve their lot, to hold on to a wage- or salary-earning position, and, above all, to avoid poverty and destitution. For the youth and women who are about to enter the labor market, and for those who have become unemployed, it is the struggle for finding a job, a source of livelihood and an occupational status. Yet the turmoil and disturbance, the shifts in the power structure and nodes of decision making, make many new opportunities for rent-seeking activities and new monopoly advantages, black marketeering, outright confiscation, and theft, as well as upward mobility for some, when others are purged or demoted. In short, some will gain, some will lose, and a few will find ample occasions for "primitive accumulation," all in the midst of a crisis of accumulation.

Our Conceptualization of Class Analysis

In this study we sought to quantify the impact of the involutionary and deinvolutionary processes on the class nature of the workforce and to reveal the manifestations of the class attributes of the workforce in the pattern of inequalities in postrevolutionary Iran. However, any empirical analysis of the class nature of the workforce must be explicit about its theoretical framework for class analysis, and its method of operationalizing the existing data.

We believe that work and the occupational structure are defined in reference to class and gender. In our study we have asserted that those who seek work enter the labor market with a baggage, a bundle of resources, containing their ownership (differentiated access and control) of scarce economic resources. The ownership of resources is not only a legal disposition for its owner but, more important, also a means for controlling economic activities. Hence, ownership of resources gives rise to three axes of class locations in a market economy, depending on the peculiarity of each category of resources: (1) the means of production, (2) organizational assets/authority, and (3) skills/credentials. In this sense the workforce, employed and unemployed, is an asymmetrically divided entity, shaped in the process of production in constant interaction with the market. The reproduction of this asymmetric relationship in time and space is largely affected in mediation with family, gender, and state. The cumulative aspect of these complex processes gives rise to unequal lifelong opportunities for individuals. This class outlook and its three axes of class locations enable us to detect the following class locations in the census data of the Iranian workforce: capitalist and working-class locations, petty bourgeoisie (self-employed proprietors), and the middle class (owners of organizational assets/authority or skills/credentials) locations.

Monopolistic access to oil revenues has enabled the Iranian state to become a major owner of means of economic activities and to run a giant bureaucracy. We view the state's activities in terms of its apparatuses, defined as the political state (for political administration, national defense, and domestic surveillance), nonmarket (decommodified) services (providing social services such as public education and health), and economic activities (producing goods and services for the market). Based on ownership of organizational assets/authority and skills/credentials, we distinguished the state middle-class from the state working-class locations in different state occupational positions. However, because of the absence of disaggregated data on "administrative and defense" employment of the state, and the ambiguity of the situation of members of the armed forces (professionals, draftees, and volunteers), in our empirical construction of class composition in Iran we included all those engaged in the political state in the ambiguous category of political functionaries of the state.

An important objective of our class approach to the study of the workforce in Iran is the identification of structured inequalities in economic activities. These structured inequalities, especially in the form of classes, are the sources of conflict of economic interests of the workforce. We have argued that work, or broadly speaking the occupational structure, cannot be defined without reference to class and gender. Class and gender are both about power relations, and in that sense, the asymmetric-hierarchical occupational structure is also gendered. This asymmetric-hierarchical relationship is approximated with reasonable certainty in our constructed social hierarchy of work based on the three axes of class locations by interlacing of employment-occupational census data. This complex structure is a modified version of our class structure of the employed workforce. However, its significance as an empirical tool of analysis is not only that it sheds light on the class-gender nature of the workforce but that it can also focus on class-gender-spatial, class-gender-ethnic, and class-gender-religious divisions in the workforce. However, in this study we examined only class-gender-spatial divisions. Data on ethnicity and religious affiliation in Iran are limited and do not provide a basis for a class analysis.

Moreover, we have argued that differential access to scarce assets is the foundation of class inequality not only in what people do in production relations and what they receive in a given period of time but also how their access to resources is reproduced over time. In other words, class analysis is about the analysis of not only economic roles and of differential returns, but also differential economic opportunities over time. Because of limitation of data, we relied only on the analysis of unemployment and income-expenditures distribution among classes for approximating unequal lifelong opportunities of the workforce.

We recognize that the explanation of the changes in the complex socioeconomic structure of the postrevolutionary decades in Iran has to take into account the effect of many important variables other than the revolution and its redistributive impact on wealth and property. Populist economic policies of the Islamic state, a protracted war, economic sanctions, fluctuations in the international oil market, women's resistance to their marginalization, and the economic liberalization policies of the state have had distinct impacts on the workforce and its class nature. On the other hand, demographic variables influence the present and future supply of labor and its composition, and in turn are influenced by the conditions of the labor market in the long haul.

What Happened to the Class Nature of the Workforce in Postrevolutionary Iran?

Our quantitative class analysis of the workforce reveals that in the first postrevolutionary decade the involutionary process was in full effect. We noted that both in urban and in rural economies of Iran, capitalist relations of production receded and became deproletarianized, defeminized, and traditionalized. These changes were accompanied by the peasantization of the rural economy. The involutionary process led to a fall in the number of those directly engaged in capitalist activities, and the decline of the concentration of capital. The number of working-class and middle-class employees of the private sector decreased, when the number of capitalist employers increased. However, the majority of the new capitalists were small in terms of the size of their capital, number of employees, and the extent of their activity, and were nearly all in the traditional occupations, a characteristic of the early development of capitalism. Thus, in many ways, the majority of the new capitalists were quite similar in their character to the petty bourgeoisie.

Meanwhile, the petty bourgeoisie, who already constituted a little less than one-third of the employed labor force at the time of the revolution, increased in number both absolutely and relatively. The increase in the number of the petty bourgeoisie was also concentrated in traditional occupational positions.

Our study shows that the decline in the size of the working class in the private sector was significantly larger than the increase in the number of working-class employees that the state employed in providing decommodified social services and production of economic goods and services. It is true that in the first postrevolutionary decade the number of state employees increased immensely. Their increase, however, was above all in the number of political functionaries in administration of the political affairs of the state, and in its military and paramilitary forces. Thus, the total number of those in the working class (employed by the state and the private sector) shrank not only relatively but also absolutely. On the other hand, the increase in the number of the middle-class workers in government employment, mainly in social services (health and education), more than compensated for the decline of the middle class in the private sector. The decline of the middle-class employees of the private sector was closely consistent with the weakening of capitalist activities, decline of concentration of capital, and traditionalization of capitalist activities. The middle-class employees of the private sector are commonly in management and technical positions. Small capitalist firms are generally run by owners-managers and have little use for professional managers-administrators or professional-technical workers.

By 1988 the populist utopian project of Islamization of the economy had reached its dead end. The oil-market glut of the mid-1980s and the high cost of the war with Iraq had put the Islamic state under a heavy financial burden. Scarce foreign exchange was principally allocated for defense and other purposes of the state, and the rest was the valuable prize of the cronies of the political state, who also benefited from the many schemes of the government for controlling the market. Corruption, clientalism, and the war economy had accelerated the accumulation process in certain activities, in spite of the persisting crisis in the economy. The bourgeoisie, who as a whole felt deprived of its fair share, resented the new trend in formation of oligopolies by the close affiliates of the Islamic state. They began a murmur of resistance, demanding privatization and liberalization of the economy.

The urban population, too, tired of standing in lines for their rations, and longing for a kinder and gentler social and political environment, began expressing dissatisfaction. The decline in foreign-exchange earning had reduced the state's ability to provide subsidies. Lines were becoming longer and rations smaller. The death of Ayatollah Khomeini helped to break many social policy taboos, and the discourse of economic liberalization began. In 1993 the liberalization policy was accelerated, and its impacts soon became apparent in every corner of the economy. Public opposition mounted and the state retreated. In the subsequent years the state has followed a timid, zigzag liberalization strategy.

Although the liberalization effort has had only limited impact in accelerating the accumulation process, it has been an effective move toward reconstruction and rejuvenation of the capitalist relations of production. The sanctity of property and security of capital have been recognized and protected by the state, and the populist discourse of "the rule of the oppressed" and "Islamic economic system" have been nearly totally abandoned. The institutions of market have been reconstructed and rejuvenated. Banks, chambers of commerce, and the stock market have become functional; the markets operate with much less intervention by the state and its vigilantes; and the international financial links have been reinstituted. A reversal of the involutionary process, that is, a deinvolutionary trend, has been in motion since the early 1990s. The Islamic state that once wanted to establish Islamic economic justice viewed profit making as an antisocial preoccupation, and regarded foreign investment and borrowing as satanic acts, is now promoting trickle-down economic policy, encourages profit-making investments, and tries its best dancing to the tune of foreign investors to attract them to take part in lucrative projects, in spite of the United States' persistence in upholding its prohibitive economic sanctions. How successful the state has been in pursuing these policy objectives is a different issue. What matters is that the Islamic-revolutionary discourse has changed and if the high-rise luxury apartments in the skyline of Tehran reflect anything, the "oppressed" *(mostazafan)* are "out" and the "arrogants" *(mostakbaran)* are back "in," all thanks to the Bonyad Mostazafan, the largest real estate developer in the country.

The analysis of 1986–96 data reveals that the timid liberalization effort has not yet offset the principal effects of the involutionary entanglement fully, but the reversal of the trend is, nevertheless, manifested in many areas in the economy. The capitalist relation of production in the private sector has grown, and the overall share of those on its payroll in the middle-class and working-class locations has increased since 1986. The increase in the relative size of the traditional petty bourgeois workforce in employment has been curbed, even though its share in the workforce is still above what it was in 1976. Thus, the most significant indications of expansion of capitalist activities in urban and rural areas have been the increase in proletarianization, and the trend toward depeasantization of the rural workforce. These trends are also associated with the comeback of the middle class in the private sector along the continued growth in the number of the middle class in socioeconomic activities of the state, and the rise of modern capitalists and modern petty bourgeoisie.

The slow rate of proletarianization in the urban and rural economy of Iran is an indication of the low rate of capital accumulation in the deinvolutionary period. Consequently, in 1996, both in the urban and in the rural economy, the proportion of the workforce engaged in capitalist activities of the private sector was still significantly smaller than in 1976.

In 1996 in the urban economy, the share of the workforce engaged in petty economic activities and in the employment of the state were both smaller than in 1986. In the rural economy, the proportion of those engaged in petty economic activities in 1996 had dropped back to the already high level of 61 percent of the workforce in 1976.

What Happened to Women's Marginalization?

Iranian working-age women suffered from double jeopardy in the postrevolutionary period. Similar to their male counterparts they were affected by the impacts of the structural involution. However, and more important, Iranian women became the unfortunate targets of the state's Islamization project. Laws and official declarations regulating women's presence in the public space, and especially at work, resulted in an acute defeminization of the workforce, except in areas where gender segregation barred the presence of male workers. By 1986 the rate of participation of women in the labor force, even after adjusting for the increase in the number of female students in the working-age population, had dropped to about what it was in 1956.

We argue in our analysis that marginalization of female labor is a multidimensional, multicausal historical phenomenon, requiring a concrete class analysis. We also point out that marginalization cannot be examined only by a summary measure, such as the rate of participation in the labor force (activity rate), as important as such a measure is. Hence, we rely on the scheme of social hierarchy of work, reflecting the three dimensions of class, namely, property ownership, authority, and skills in economic activities, and constructed statistical indexes that detect different facets of women's marginalization. With the help of these indexes we delineated the class-gender nature of women's economic marginalization. Our examination of the changes in the social hierarchy of work reveals that women's marginalization and impairment have been manifested partly in exclusion from the labor market and employment, and partly in the form of segregation within the market. We show that working-class women were subject to exclusion from employment not only more than men but also more than the women who either possessed financial means or had valuable skills. The women with financial means or high skills could better resist the gender segregationist policies of the state or employers by becoming engaged in economic activities as capitalists or self-employed petty bourgeois, or could distinguish themselves with their skills and remain in their middle class employment positions. Nevertheless, women's choice of occupations has been limited by religious and cultural definition of acceptable female employment. Our study also indicates that women at the higher-level work groups in the social hierarchy of work could increase their share of employment relative to men, whereas the working-class women experienced relative employment impairment.

The quick and quiet demise of the Islamization project in the post-Khomeini era, punctuated by the state's turn-around from its populist-utopian objectives, opened the political arena for women to express their indignations toward the repressive, segregationist policies of the Islamic state. Concurrently, the economic liberalization policies made the enforcement of the segregationist objectives of the Islamic state increasingly more costly for the private sector and less defensible for the state. Consequently, the avenues for entry of women into the workforce became gradually less daunting, albeit still not encouraging.

In 1986–96, women in disadvantaged classes came back to the labor market more than before, and more advantaged women who had access to means of production and skill and credentials took a more active part in economic activities, in urban and rural areas. However, the relative share of upper-level female work groups in urban and rural areas, unlike the share for men, declined in favor of the share of lower work groups. This change was due to a slowdown in the growth of the number of female capitalists and those in middle-class occupations, relative to the faster growth in employment of working-class women.

Who Are the Unemployed?

The unemployed are by definition those who seek employment from those who own the means of production. Hence, it is class determined by the nature of labor market in a capitalist economy. The unemployed are, therefore, generally those seeking working-class or middle-class occupational positions (wage- or salary-paying jobs) in the private sector or the government. Although a capitalist or a self-employed petty bourgeois may be out of work for some period of time, they should not be considered unemployed unless they seek a wage- or salary-paying occupational position.

In the postrevolutionary decade the involutionary process led to a general decline in employment opportunities, reflected in the higher rate of unemployment and lower activity rate of the working-age population. The decline in employment opportunity was, therefore, concentrated among the working-class and middle-class employees of the private sector, where the production process was severely disrupted. Few government workers became unemployed because of economic or political disruptions. However, many government employees lost their jobs because of ideological cleansing *(paksazi)* throughout the state-run institutions, from the military and the police to schools, hospitals, and the state-owned enterprises. They were replaced, however, by ideologically "committed" individuals. As we have shown, the number of state employees increased in all three apparatuses of the state.

Among those who lose their wage or salary employment some may seek means of survival by engaging in some form of entrepreneurial activities in the market. Those who have some savings or marketable technical skills may become engaged as small capitalists or petty commodity producers. The disruptions in market activities may provide golden opportunities for some, filling in for the existing acute shortages in the market, or becoming engaged in the thriving black markets. On the other hand, the absence of a comprehensive system of unemployment insurance would make unemployment an impossible option for the poor. Thus, the rise in petty-commodity activities in the face of the crisis of accumulation in the involutionary process is, in part, nothing but disguised unemployment. The large number of street vendors and many of the others engaged in redundant service activities, recorded in the census as "self-employed," are in fact unemployed workers. When economic disruptions are overcome, and accumulation process accelerates in the deinvolutionary period, employment opportunities would increase, and the sudden growth in the number of small capitalists and petty bourgeoisie will subside. This is the pattern that we observed in the involutionary decade and the subsequent deinvolutionary years.

We realize the limitation of official unemployment statistics. They generally underestimate the actual unemployment rate. Yet, even according to the official reports, the unemployment rate in 1996, although less than in 1986, was still significantly higher than in 1976, before the revolution. Moreover, our study shows that the overwhelming majority of the officially unemployed are the young new entrants to the labor market. The persistence of the high rate of unemployment, particularly among the youth, reflects not only the low rate of job creation because of the slow rate of capital accumulation (demand for labor) but also the impact of the baby boom of the immediate postrevolutionary years on the labor market (supply of labor). The postrevolutionary babies are reaching the working age, and have begun flocking to the labor market. Some youths of the financially better-off families (mainly the urban middle class) are delaying their entry to the labor market by seeking more education, or just "hanging around" their parents' households. But that cannot last for long and is not possible for children of the poor. Every generation must eke out its own living.

Income-Expenditures Inequality

Our analysis of the sources of income of urban and rural households shows that in the involutionary years (until 1991) the share of wages-salary in income of the average household declined notably, and despite its reversal since 1991, it is still below what it was in 1977. Throughout the 1977–2001 period, however, the combined share of proprietors' income (of the petty bourgeoisie) and profits (of capitalists) increased. Unfortunately, we do not have access to disaggregated data, separating the share of proprietors' income from that of profits. The huge increase in the number of the petty bourgeoisie in the urban and rural economies in the involutionary decade is expected to be the major source of the increase in the combined share of proprietors' income and capitalists' profit in the average household's income. In contrast, in the deinvolutionary period, we expect an increase in profits to give rise to the increase in the combined share of proprietors' income and profits. In the absence of disaggregated data, this assertion remains a hypothesis to be tested empirically.

Despite their similarities, these trends were more pronounced in urban areas than in rural areas. However, in the rural economy, proprietors' income and profits already made up about half of the average household's income before the revolution. This proportion increased in the involutionary years. We note a fundamental difference in the pattern of structural involution between the urban and rural economies. Although the social contestation over property rights and antagonism toward wealth and capital in the urban economy resulted in disruptions in the production process, the same conditions gave rise to increased production and economic growth in the rural economy. This seemingly paradoxical situation reflects the differences in property relations and technical conditions of production in the petty commodity agricultural production in the rural economy and the predominantly capitalist urban industries. Most important, the divisibility of agricultural land, and the prevailing Islamic jurisprudential view on land and crop ownership, made redistribution of land possible and encouraged peasants to cultivate the appropriated land immediately to establish their ownership. Thus, in the rural economy, the increased peasantization of agriculture and small-scale farming led to economic growth, whereas deproletarianization of the urban economy reflected the disruption in the accumulation process and led to economic stagnation. As a result, in the postrevolutionary decade the income gap between average urban and rural households became narrower, as the real income of an average urban household declined sharply and that of a rural household increased mildly. This trend seems to have begun reversing in more recent years.

In our study we also examined the income-expenditures distribution of households within each class and in comparison with the size distribution of household income-expenditures in the urban and rural economies. Our data do not allow us to separate the households of the working class from those of the middle-class employees, either in the private sector or the state. The results show that a large proportion of the employees of the private sector are among the poor and very poor, reflecting the low lifelong opportunities of the private sector's working class. On the other hand, a large proportion of state employees (including working class, middle class, and political functionaries of the state) are among the better-off and the wealthy households in the urban and rural areas, only next to the households of capitalists. Thus, many among the small middle class of the private sector and the comparatively large middle class of the state remain among the privileged social classes. The middle class, particularly those employed by the state, also benefit from some valuable nonmonetary privileges, such as subsidized housing, or low interest home mortgages.

We found the petty bourgeoisie divided proportionally along the spectrum of income-expenditure groups, pointing to the acute fragmentation of this class. Capitalists, as expected, constitute the wealthiest households in the urban and rural economies. However, not all capitalists are wealthy. The fragmentation of the bourgeoisie is reflected in the wide distribution of their household expenditures. There are in fact some poor, or even some very poor, capitalists.

Our examination also reveals that skills and credentials pay. The study of urban household expenditures indicates that those with a higher level of educational attainment are generally better off. However, as the literacy rate and the level of educational attainment increases in the population, skills/credentials become a less reliable indicator of income, as the proportion of the poor households among those of the literate and the more educated workers increases.

The Existing Class Structure

The bird's-eye view of the class nature of Iranian workforce in 1996 indicates a society of petty bourgeoisie, workers and bureaucrats. The composition of the class locations of the employed workforce indicates that 41 percent are in the petty bourgeoisie class locations (including the unpaid family workers), 31 percent are working-class employees of the private sector and the state, 4 percent are capitalists, 10 percent are in the middle class (85 percent are employed by the state), and 11 percent are political functionaries of the state. Compared to 1976, the proportion of the working class and that of unpaid family workers in the workforce have declined, and for all other major class locations have increased.

The Petty Bourgeoisie

In spite of the deinvolutionary trend in the post-Khomeini era, the fragmented petty bourgeoisie is Iran's largest social class. Only 3 percent of this petty bourgeoisie is modern. The rest are in the traditional petty economic activities. They are concentrated in rural agricultural and urban production, and sales and services. In the past twenty years the proportion of the petty bourgeoisie in agriculture has consistently declined, and in production and services has increased.

Traditionally, a large segment of the urban petty bourgeoisie in production and services (mainly retail trade) were congregated in the bazaar, alongside small and large merchant capitalists. The rapid capitalist development of Iran in the post-1953 period and the spatial extension of commercial activities beyond the limited arena of the bazaar in the old section of the cities and into the newly developed streets and shopping *"pasazhs"* (small malls) led to acute marginalization of the bazaar. Nevertheless, bazaars have remained as a cohesive congregation of culturally and religiously traditionalist petty bourgeoisie and merchant capitalists *(bazaaris)*,[1] with extensive financial ties with the *hawzehs* (religious centers) and the clerical establishment.[2] In the prerevolutionary years Ayatollah Khomeini gained the support of the politically active bazaaris, in competition with the religiously more prominent and politically more conservative clergies such as Ayatollah Kho'i and Ayatollah Shari'atmadari.

The bazaaris were influential in the revolutionary movement and the postrevolutionary period. In alliance with the clerical establishment, they mobilized and organized the Islamic movement to gain the leadership of the revolutionary struggle. Upon the 1979 victory of the revolution, they formed the organizational skeleton of the Islamic Republic. They and their male offspring were the first to be placed at different levels of the apparatuses of the Islamic state, as simple clerks and jail keepers, up to managers of state-owned enterprises and Islamic foundations, Revolutionary Guard's top brass, ministers and members of the Islamic parliament. An important consequence of the

1. Bazaars and the bazaaris were, however, active participants in the Constitutional Revolution of 1906, and in the oil nationalization movement of 1950–51, which were both liberal secular movements.

2. There are several scholarly studies on the subject of the financial relations between the bazaar and the clerical establishment. See, among others, Arjomand, 1988, Akhavi 1980, and Fischer 1980. However, one of the most revealing documents on this subject is Ayatollah Hosein Ali Montazeri's memoir (Montazeri 2000).

revolution has been the access of those with a petty bourgeois or small capitalist merchant background to Islamic state power and its economic resources. It has inevitably increased the bargaining position of this class in the state's policies, as reflected in the cultural and economic policy orientation of the Islamic Republic, particularly in the Khomeini decade.

However, many of those who gained access to the power of the state found lucrative opportunities for personal gain, which they did not hesitate to take advantage of in spite of their puritanical revolutionary and Islamic claims. With their political power and their leverage at the nodes of rent-seeking activities, and little fear of any political risk, they successfully managed a high rate of capital accumulation and constituted the nucleus of the new elite capitalist class in the newly formed oligopolistic structure surrounding the *bonyads,* state-owned enterprises, and government bureaucracy. The expropriations, nationalizations, war mobilization, and the extensive control of the state over the market in the Khomeini decade accelerated *embourgeoisement* of the selected few among the petty bourgeoisie. Some became monopoly capitalists all at once.

But that is the story of the few who found the golden goose in the turmoil of the revolution. The mass of traditional petty bourgeoisie has become more fragmented in the post-Khomeini decade. Economic liberalization and its deinvolutionary outcome have helped to open avenues of capitalist accumulation through more vibrant price competition. With the disappearance of the black markets, emergence of newly formed or refurbished capitalist enterprises, and the general normalization of market activities, the more dynamic petty bourgeois producers may find increase in profitability and room to grow. But those whose market niche depended on shortages, black markets and other manifestations of the postrevolutionary crisis would be confronting their decline, or even doomsday. The reversal of the process that brought around the new wave of the petty bourgeoisie in the first decade after the revolution is now at work in depressing their activity. The losing petty bourgeoisie, more than any other group, is fired up in opposition to the economic liberalization policy and the Islamic Republic's abandonment of its populist slogans in defense of the *mostazafan*. Increased job opportunities in the rank of the working class would have made happy many who have been engaged in petty commodity activities in absence of a wage-paying job. But the prospect of increased employment opportunity, especially with the wave of new entrants to the labor market, is anything but grim.

As the Islamic state has begun taking a capitalist posture less abashedly in the post-Khomeini decade, its ideological power base among the traditional petty bourgeoisie and even small traditional bourgeoisie has been diminishing. After all, it was they who were the most ardent proponents, believers, and perhaps even beneficiary of the rule of the *mostazafan*.

The modern petty bourgeoisie, however, characteristically had little attraction toward the Islamic state, perhaps most important because of the projected cultural and religious traditionalism of the Islamic Republic, and also because of its extensive interference in the domain of their professional activities. The Islamic associations of professionals, such as engineers, physicians, or accountants, never became totally encompassing, nor could the operators of the Islamic state democratically gain control of associations such as the Lawyer's Bar Association, Medical Association, Publishers' Guilds, Association of Engineers and Contractors, or the Writers' Society. Some associations were taken over through heavy-handed tactics of the state; some others were banned for noncompliance with intrusive state's regulations, or just for political reasons. The weakening of the state's cultural and religious traditionalism and economic interventionism would be a source of relief for the modern petty bourgeoisie, whose rank has been expanding both absolutely and relatively in the post-Khomeini decade.

The Working Class

We have argued that working class includes all those employed as semiskilled to unskilled workers in production or service activities. They do not own the means of production and have little or no authority, or skills and credentials. Based on property-authority-skill axes of class location typology (in contrast to wage-salary distinction that is purely a market distinction for the classification of the working class) we counted those with clerical, low-level administrative, sales, and service occupations in the working class. Yet the potential career trajectory of a very small portion of salaried employees, their subjective view of themselves, and the subjective views of the society about their status do not fully correspond to their objective class location within the working class. However, objectively, they do not own the means of economic activity, and they all contribute to the realization of capital accumulation of the propertied class, just like others in the working class.

In two decades of the Islamic Republic's rule the share of the working class declined from 40 percent of the workforce in 1976 to 31 percent of that in 1996. That is, given the growth of the workforce, the size of the working class in 1996 was 1.3 million smaller than what it would have been if their share in the workforce had remained what it was in 1976 (table A.2 in the Appendix). We called this "class effect" in our decomposition analysis. The class effect loss of the working-class employment in the private sector in this period was 1.8 million. Thus, in 1996 a smaller proportion of the workforce was in the working class than in 1976, and even a smaller proportion of that was employed by the private sector. In 1996, more than half of the private sector's working class (57 percent) was in production, and about half of them were in construction. A high share of unskilled employed working class in different economic sectors demonstrates the relative undeveloped aspect of the Iranian capitalist economy.

The Iranian working class is among the least privileged, alongside the low strata of the petty bourgeoisie, and the unemployed. There is only a tiny aristocracy among the skilled workers, in the oil industry, large manufacturing establishments and financial sectors, mostly employed by the state. Our study shows that the workers in large enterprises have managed to have their wages keep pace with the official rate of inflation in the years of economic liberalization. Most of the others had no such success. The official statistics, however, have their known limitations, particularly in underestimating the true rate of inflation, and thus the changes in the real wages. Over the past years, workers, even in large state-owned enterprises, have suffered from differed wage payments. This issue, at times, has led to strikes and work stoppage to gain the attention of the authorities.

The Islamic state has been vigilant in preventing formation of a labor movement and its independent organizations and unions. One of the early acts of the Islamic Republic was dissolving the Workers' Councils, established by the workers in the early days of the postrevolutionary year. They were replaced by Islamic Workers' Councils and the House of Workers (Khaneh Kargar), under direct supervision of the government. The formulation of the labor law was one of the controversial issues in the early revolutionary years. The law that was passed by the Majles was never approved by the Guardian Council, even after several revisions by the Majles. The Guardian Council upheld the laissez-faire view that the state should not impose any restrictions or regulations on the contractual relation between the employer and the employee. Finally, in 1990 the Labor Law was enacted by the authority of the newly formed Expediency Council (Posusney and Pfeifer 1997). In the past years, the proponents of economic liberalization have insisted that the existing Labor Law, with limitations that it places on the employers and rights that provides for the workers, is a barrier to business investment in general, and to direct foreign investment, in particular. They propose its revision with the objective of limiting its coverage and eliminating some of the clauses favoring workers. However, it would be construed as a formal repudiation of the Islamic state's populist position and may entail a direct confrontation with Iranian labor.

Capitalists

In 1976–96 the number of capitalists almost tripled to 528,000. About 35 percent of capitalists were engaged in business services, mostly in wholesale and retail trade, 24 percent were involved in industrial activities (60 percent of whom were in carpet, clothing and textile business), 24 percent in agriculture, and 16 percent in construction activities.

An overwhelming number of the new capitalists are quite small, with one or two wage employees. The Concentration Index of 6.3 paid workers per employer in 1996 underscores the fragmentation of the capitalist class, some of whom, at the lower end of the spectrum, are not characteristically all that different from the petty bourgeoisie. This point reveals the existence of a petty bourgeoisie orientation among some in the capitalist class. These individuals are the small, traditional capitalists with a low productivity and accumulation capability, struggling alongside a network of highly concentrated state-owned enterprises (including those owned by the *bonyads*), and their private-sector affiliates.

The majority of Iranian capitalist establishments are managed by their working owners and rely principally on their own capital for financing their investment. This situation obliges those firms that do not have rent-seeking links to Islamic state and cannot benefit from the low interest loans of the nationalized banks to rely on their own retained earnings and short-term usurious loans of the bazaar. In 2003, the stocks of only about 350 firms were offered in the Tehran stock market, where more that 50 percent of daily transactions were related to the stocks of 7 firms. About 80 percent of the existing stocks in the market are owned by state enterprises, state banks, and the *bonyads*.[3] Thus, ownership of big private capital is mainly direct (many family owned) and not dispersed. Some of the more successful and larger firms belong to the nouveaux riches, the elite of the Islamic Republic *(aqazadegan or aqayan* themselves), or the traditional bourgeoisie of the past and the heirs of former wealthy families of the ancien régime.

3. *Eqtesad-e Iran,* June–July 2003, no. 54, 25.

The capitalist class is in the process of taking form. It is slowly recuperating from the blows of the revolution, but it is still under the heavy hand of the monopolistic practices of the state and the *bonyads*. Nevertheless, capitalists own and control a substantial part of the economy, which still lies in the private sector, especially in small- and medium-size manufacturing, construction, trade, and agriculture concerns. In the post-Khomeini years the bourgeoisie has become more assertive and vocal in influencing the economic orientation of the state. They constitute an influential economic elite that is critical of the vestiges of populist tendencies of the Islamic state, its downright inefficiency, corruption, nepotism, rent-seeking clergy-administrators, and their monopolistic paramilitary-economic complexes and niches. Their ideological gurus have become the spokespersons of Iran's Chamber of Commerce and other influential institutions, and have had strongholds in the cabinets of Hashemi-Rafsanjani and Khatami, the Majles, and the media. If capitalists and capitalism were pejorative nouns among the revolutionary shibboleths, they are now viewed by some ideologues of market reform as the warriors of the new age of economic and political liberalism. A few in the rank of the populist ideologues of the early days of the Islamic Republic have now become proponents of a Hayekian laissez-faire market economy.[4]

Those in the upper-level strata of this class, especially its modernist faction, continue to enjoy their lifestyle of opulence and affluence, in many ways similar to what they enjoyed before the revolution. They have become more assertive in demonstration of their immense wealth. They have their luxury automobiles and incredible mansions, and their club memberships and means of networking. Conspicuous consumption, which had become a sign of decadence and arrogance *(estekbar)* in the revolutionary days, has now gained legitimacy, at least politically. Many elite of the new regime *(aqayan* and *aqazadegan)* and the their close associates have joined the rank of capitalist. They, too, openly enjoy the lifestyle of affluence. One should feel politically safe in such a company.

The Middle Class

The career opportunities for the middle class have increased after the revolution, especially in the state's employment. For those with Islamic credentials ("commitment"), or with connection to the state's elite, the ladder of upward mobility to managerial and administrative positions in the Islamic officialdom has been an easy climb.

4. See as a prominent example Akbar Ganji 2002.

In 1996, 10 percent of the workforce was in the middle class. Among them, 85 percent were employees of the state. In addition, 11 percent (1.6 million) of the workforce was state's political functionaries. Thirty-nine thousand of them (95 percent male) occupied the high and middle rank of political-administrative positions of the Islamic Republic. A small circle among these constitute the political ruling elite, the Islamic political official-dom of the country in the executive, judiciary, and legislative branches, and the top brass of the armed forces.

At a lower stratum, an army of professionals and technicians (88.4 percent of the state middle class) were engaged in different activities, especially in education (74 percent of all state middle class were K–12 educators), health care, engineering and technical functions, and management of enterprises, in social services and economic activities of the government. To these occupations, we may add those among state political functionaries who served as bureau chiefs, midlevel administrators, and technical workers.

Together, the middle-class employees of the state, and administrator-managers and professional-technical employees of the state political apparatus, made up 1.5 million, or 10.4 percent, of the employed workforce, whereas the middle class of the private sector was no more than 219,000 in number, or 1.5 percent of the employed workforce. Among the latter group, three-fourths are professionals and technical workers. Only one-forth (51,000) were in administration and management of private enterprises, indicating the low level of complexity of management and administration of Iranian private enterprises, which are generally managed by capitalist owners.

The Iranian growing middle class, like the middle class in any other society, is vastly fragmented. It includes the highly skilled, well-paid professionals, managers, and administrators, in the urban centers (mainly in Tehran), and the low-skilled, low-paid personnel, such as educators and paramedical workers (many in rural areas). There are, however, two special characteristics for the Iranian middle class. First, they are mainly employees of the state. Thus, they enjoy job security, a pension, some health care, and, thanks to the oil income, an assurance for receiving their paycheck on time and in full. These benefits have made state employment attractive to the new entrants into the job market in the past several decades since the formation of the modern state in Iran in the 1920s–1930s.

Second, the Iranian middle class, in the private or state sector, is not professionally organized. With some minor exceptions (mainly physicians, lawyers, accountants, and journalists), the members of the middle class are not engaged in professional associations in an effort to promote their professional interests. In the past several decades, the middle class has shown that it can become politically charged quite quickly, as it did in the oil nationalization movement of the early 1950s and the 1979 revolution. But it is also known that it is quite susceptible to quietism and passivity, as it was in the post-1953 coup d'état years, and in the Khomeini decade.

Thus, the Iranian middle class can remain a content and obedient group as long as there is no spark in the political theater. But when open political confrontations take shape, they could easily become a rebellious group of free agents, floating toward the emerging political poles. Their high level of education tends to make a large group of them sympathetic toward the university student movement with its generally radical political disposition (Parsa 2000, chap. 4).

Our Final Words

Our study presents the fragmented nature of the workforce in a state-dominated capitalist society with a vast, but subordinated, petty-commodity relation of production. Iran has 40 percent of its employed workforce engaged in traditional petty-commodity activities. The rest are almost equally divided between a frail and highly fragmented capitalist private sector and a state with overextended apparatuses of administration and coercion, social services, and economic activities. The capitalist private sector, severely battered and pushed over in the revolution and the structural involution of the postrevolutionary decade, has been struggling to make advances on the political and economic terrains. It has been trying to promote the cause of economic liberalism, and to accelerate its rate of accumulation in the deinvolutionary process that commenced over a decade ago. But so far its success has been limited. Most important, for its own frailty. The low concentration index indicates that capitalist enterprises are mostly very small. They are mainly engaged in traditional activities, and their characteristics are similar in many ways to the establishments of petty-commodity producers. As such they have little potential for growth in a dynamic economy. Many of these small firms are themselves threatened by the economic liberalization policy and wish to seek protection from the market competition, to continue benefiting from subsidies and price control for their inputs. They have been a vocal opponent of the Labor Law, which in March 2000 the Majles modified by excluding enterprises with five or fewer workers from its coverage.

At the other end of the spectrum, the market is dominated by the ghastly presence of the *bonyads* and the overt and covert economic activities of various military, paramilitary, and "intelligence" organizations of the state (particularly the Islamic Revolutionary Guards), who seek off-budget sources of income. Hand in hand with a network of their affiliates, they constitute a Mafiaesque underworld of aggressive oligopolistic market. They have been the main buyers of the state-owned enterprises in the privatization undertaking of the government. They themselves are, however, exempt from being privatized. No adventurous capitalist would dare entering this treacherous domain, without protection of one of the several godfathers. Many aspiring capitalists have stated it openly that their growth and development are conditional on dismantling this oligopolistic segment of the market. But doing so is tantamount to dismantling the structure of the "Governance of the Jurisconsult" (Velayat-e Faqih), as these two interrelated structures are the pillars of the existing political regime. Muhammad Khatami, with all his claims for reform in the eight years of his presidency of the Islamic Republic, never acted or even spoke openly in opposition to these two "satanic" constructs, using the favorite term of Ayatollah Khomeini, who was the architect of both. It is apparent that the capitalist class, with its serious infirmity, is in no position to advance even its own cause. The *bonyads* and their affiliated capitalists have formed a formidable barrier to the capitalist development of Iran.

The appearance of Khatami on the political scene, with his unexpected landslide victory in the May 1997 presidential election, was a manifestation of the intensified cultural confrontation in the Iranian society. In two decades of its rule, the Islamic Republic had not succeeded in compelling the Iranian population to submit to its restrictive traditionalist Islamic norms of conduct. Khatami, by the softness of his speech, his kind smile, and his expressed reception to diversity of world views *(degarandishi)* and norms of conduct, appeared to represent a kinder and gentler face of the Islamic state. It was appealing to the majority of the population, particularly the youth, women, and the seculars, who rushed to the polls to elect him twice.

Khatami and his "reformist movement" had no economic agenda (Behdad 2001b). He benefited from a rather long period of high oil prices in the international market, which brought Iran high oil revenues. In his eight years of presidency, Khatami brought forth no economic policy debates and proposed no economic policy reforms. He followed the zigzag of economic liberalization that Hashemi-Rafsanjani retreated to in the last years of his presidency. Some policy organs of the government promoted and implemented economic liberalization measures (for example, the Central Bank), while others opposed them (including the Ministry of Finance). Khatami was elected only for his presumed cultural agenda, which he tried to implement in the face of ferocious opposition of the traditionalist faction of the Islamic Republic. He failed in reforming the Islamic state, as his proponents and his optimistic followers expected (Behdad 2001a). He, however, succeeded in mitigating an intensifying political crisis in the Islamic state by establishing the discourse of limited political criticism, and providing a wider space for cultural expressions.

The election of Mahmud Ahmadinejad to the presidency of the Islamic Republic in June 2005, with the orchestrated effort of the military machinery (the Revolutionary Guards and Basij), on a populist platform, has introduced further complexity to the political economy of Iran. Ahmadinejad represents the culturally and politically conservative faction of the Islamic Republic. He is strongly supported by the Islamic foundations *(bonyads)* who have special interests in maintaining the strong hold of the state on the economy, and to preserve their monopolistic domination of the market. At the same time, in running against Hashemi-Rafsanjani (the champion of economic liberalization in the mid-1990s and an alleged symbol of corruption and nepotism), Ahmadinejad attracted many among traditional petty bourgeoisie and the less privileged and poor urban and rural populations to vote for his populist social justice, anticorruption platform. The vote for Ahmadinejad was, at least partly, a vote against the economic liberalization of Hashemi-Rafsanjani.

In our evaluation of economic liberalization policy, we noted the inflationary impact of the economic liberalization. In these circumstances, the functional distribution of income changes in favor of capital (profit) and against labor (wages). Certainly, not all capitalists were winners. Some, particularly the small and inefficient establishments (capitalist or petty-commodity producers), either have perished or have been seriously threatened. Others have had a higher profit. Similarly, not all wage earners lost real income. Those with scarce skills or with market power have been able to keep up with the inflation, and the successful enterprises have gained a stronger position in the market place. This process has been at work in the zigzag policy of economic liberalization not only during the Hashemi-Rafsanjani presidency but also during the eight years of Khatami's administration. The rising price of oil in the international market, consequently the increasing oil income of Iran in the past several years, has lubricated the wheels of the Iranian economy, by providing the input to the Iranian industries and augmenting the supply of consumer goods and food supply. Exhilarated by the rising oil prices in the world markets, approaching seventy dollars a barrel, Ahmadinejad's minister of economy and finance has pledged "bringing the oil income to the table of Iranian households" *(Entekhab,* October 5, 2005). Those who know the ups and downs of the oil market would be hesitant betting their fortune on the future of oil prices.

Unemployment, especially the unemployment of the new entrants into the labor market, will remain the Achilles heel of the regime. The baby boomers are entering the labor market. They have a higher literacy rate and higher education than their parents and expect at least as much in terms of employment opportunities. In past generations, a high school education was leverage for entering into a middle-class occupational position. For the new generation of youth, such possibilities appear quite limited. The bureaucracy, in the various apparatuses of the state, is already highly bloated with redundant employees. There is special pressure on the state to downsize its bureaucracy. The low rate of accumulation by the private sector, dominated by the vast number of small capitalist firms, creates limited absorptive capacity for employment of managers, administrators, and technical workers. Our study of household distribution of income-expenditures reveals that, in general, skills/credentials place the workers at a higher level of earning. In the past two decades, however, an increasing proportion of those with high school or higher level of educational attainment has fallen into the group of poor households. With the limitation on the continued expansion of state employment, a smaller proportion of "the educated" young workers will be able to secure a middle-class occupational position to enjoy its job security, relatively higher pay, and social prestige.

So far, in the history of the Islamic Republic of Iran, women's contestation has been principally in cultural and legal arenas. While the gender-segregationist policies of the Islamic state remain a critical target of popular opposition to the state, the problem of female unemployment, and gender discrimination in employment, will tend to gain more prominence. Women suffer from a larger increase in their rate of unemployment, and the pressure of women for entering the labor market is mounting. The economic hardship of households, and the increase in the literacy and educational attainment of women over the years, will accentuate their employment demand.

As the peak of the baby boomers is entering the labor market in these years, the best that the overwhelming majority of the youth ("educated" or otherwise) can expect would be a working-class position. Many will not be able to secure even that, and will have to join the rank of the unemployed or seek refuge in petty economic activities. The failed expectation of the youth, who see unemployment, or at best a factory job or driving a cab in one of the large cities, and cultural and political restrictions as the bitter fruit of their parents' revolution, will be the major political and social dilemma of the current decade in Iran.

Appendix

Bibliography

Index

Appendix

Table A.1
Class Composition of the Employed Workforce, 1976, 1986, and 1996

	1976		1986		1996	
	1,000s	%‡	1,000s	%‡	1,000s	%‡
Capitalists	182	2.1	341	3.1	528	3.6
Modern	23	12.8	22	6.5	75	14.1
Administrative and managerial	12	6.5	8	2.4	50	9.5
Professional and technical	11	6.3	14	4.1	24	4.6
Traditional	159	87.2	319	93.5	453	85.9
Clerical and related	3	1.4	4	1.2	3	0.6
Sales and services	53	29.0	47	13.9	91	17.3
Agriculture	36	19.5	113	33.1	124	23.5
Production	66	36.5	138	40.5	223	42.2
Unclassified	2	0.8	16	4.8	12	2.2
Middle class	477	5.4	774	7.0	1,493	10.2
Private-sector employees	102	21.3	64	8.3	219	14.6
Administrative and managerial	14	3.0	7	0.9	51	3.4
Professional and technical	87	18.3	57	7.4	168	11.2
State employees: economic and social	376	78.7	710	91.7	1,274	85.4
Administrative and managerial	5	1.1	12	1.5	138	9.2
Professional and technical	371	77.6	698	90.2	1,136	76.1

(continued on next page)

Sources: MAI 1980, 1988, 1997.

*Includes rank-and-file workers in administration and defense who are not counted in the total for "working class."

†Included in the other subcategories of political functionaries.

‡Percentages for major class categories add up to 100. Percentages for subcategories within each category add up to 100 for the corresponding category.

Table A.1 *(continued)*
Class Composition of the Employed Workforce, 1976, 1986, and 1996

	1976		1986		1996	
	1,000s	%‡	1,000s	%‡	1,000s	%‡
Petty bourgeoisie	2,810	31.9	4,390	39.9	5,199	35.7
Modern	34	1.2	48	1.1	164	3.2
Administrative and managerial	0	0.0	5	0.1	38	0.7
Professional and technical	34	1.2	43	1.0	126	2.4
Traditional	2,776	98.8	4,343	98.9	5,035	96.8
Clerical	6	0.2	11	0.2	10	0.2
Sales and services	470	16.7	621	14.1	948	18.2
Agriculture	1,704	60.7	2,333	53.1	2,199	42.3
Production	592	21.1	1,310	29.8	1,803	34.7
Unclassified	4	0.2	69	1.6	75	1.4
Unpaid family workers	1,021	11.6	484	4.4	797	5.5
Sales and services	14	1.4	11	2.2	28	3.5
Agriculture	587	57.5	386	79.8	494	62.0
Production	418	40.9	80	16.6	259	32.5
Others (includes unclassified)	2	0.2	6	1.3	16	2.1
Working class	3,536	40.2	2,702	24.6	4,533	31.1
Private-sector employees	2,970	84.0	1,810	67.0	3,109	68.6
Clerical and related	132	3.7	33	1.2	85	1.9
Sales and services	294	8.3	157	5.8	380	8.4
Agriculture	614	17.4	294	10.9	416	9.2
Production	1,919	54.3	1,271	47.0	2,151	47.4
Unclassified	11	0.3	54	2.0	76	1.7
State employees (all rank and file)★	1,238	35.0	2,539	94.0	2,739	60.4
State employees: economic and social	566	16.0	892	33.0	1,424	31.4
Political functionaries	731	8.3	1,851	16.8	1,560	10.7
Administrative and managerial	9	1.2	11	0.6	39	2.5
Professional and technical	51	6.9	192	10.4	205	13.2
Rank and file	672	91.9	1,647	89.0	1,315	84.3
Military and paramilitary forces†	386	52.7	1,197	64.7	881	56.5
Unspecified	41	0.5	458	4.2	463	3.2
Total‡	8,799	100.0	11,002	100.0	14,572	100.0

Decomposition Approach: Accounting of Changes in Class Sizes

In Chapter 5 we presented the changes in the absolute and relative sizes of different class locations in the employed workforce of Iran between 1976–86 and 1986–96.

The decomposition technique[1] measures the rate of change in a class category against the rate of change in the size of the employed workforce. That is, any observed change in the number of those in a class category between two points of measurement could be construed as the combined result of two simultaneous changes in that period: First, *employment effect* (pure effect) or the change in the number of those in a specific category as a result of change in the overall level of employment (size of the workforce), given the relative share of that class is held constant. That is, by how much would the size of the specific class category have changed if the relative size of that category within the workforce had remained constant? Second, *class effect* (structural effect) or the extent by which the rate of change of a class category deviated from the rate of change in the size of the workforce. A positive (negative) sign indicates an increase (decrease) in the absolute or relative size of a class category.

The sum of the employment effect and class effect constitutes the observed change in the size of the specific category. Furthermore, the sum of all employment effects in all categories would be equal to the change in the number of the employed labor force, and the sum of all class effects should be equal to zero.

If C_1 an C_2 are the number of those in C category in years 1 and 2, and N_1 and N_2 are the employed labor force in these two years, respectively, then $C_2 - C_1 = Y + X$ decomposes the change in C into the employment effect (Y) and class effect (X). Y is the change in the size of C if rate of change of C were the same as the rate of change in the employed labor force (N). X is the deviation of the actual size of C from the expected trend (Y). Therefore, $X = C_2 - C_1 - Y$. We know $Y = C_1 (N_2 - N_1 / N_1)$. Hence, after some manipulation we get $X = N_2 (C_2/N_2 - C_1/N_1)$. That is, $C_2 - C_1 = C_1(N_2 - N_1/N_1) + N_2(C_2/N_2 - C_1/N_1)$.

Based on this relationship, we calculate the employment effect and the class effect of the changes in various job categories in the involutionary and deinvolutionary period in Iran.[2] The results are shown in Table A.2.

The application of this technique to the case of Iran in the involutionary period confirms our observations in Chapter 5 about the massiveness of the deproletarianization of the working class, the immense increase in the size of the traditional petty bourgeoisie, and the huge rise in political functionaries of the state. The timid economic liberalization effort in the post-Khomeini decade was associated with the rise of all classes, except the petty bourgeoisie. Nevertheless, the initial impact of the revolutionary change on reconfiguration of classes is still apparent.

1. Kitagawa (1955) introduced the decomposition technique. Wright and Singelmann (1982) and Wright (1997) applied it to the study of social classes.

2. With further algebraic manipulation we can show that the class effect X is equal to $N_1(C_2/N_2 - C_1/N_1) + (N_2 - N_1)(C_2/N_2 - C_1/N_1)$. In this relationship, the first term, the class effect, is expressed with N_1 as the point of reference, instead of N_2, according to our formula in the text. Therefore, here we have the additional term, which is frequently called "interactive" effect, and is no more than the adjustment for changing the point of reference from N_2 to N_1.

Table A.2

Decomposition of Classes: Employment Effect (Y) and Class Effect (X),
1976–1996 (in 1,000s)

| | 1976–1986 | | 1986–1996 | | 1976–1996 | |
	Y	X	Y	X	Y	X
Capitalists	46	113	111	75	120	226
Modern	6	-7	7	45	15	36
Administrative and managerial	3	-7	3	39	8	31
Professional and technical	3	0	5	6	8	5
Traditional	40	120	104	30	104	190
Clerical and related	1	1	1	-2	2	-1
Sales and services	13	-19	15	28	35	4
Agriculture	9	69	37	-26	23	65
Production	17	55	45	39	44	112
Unclassified	0	14	5	-10	1	9
Middle class	119	177	251	467	313	702
Private-sector employees	25	-63	21	134	67	50
Administrative and managerial	4	-11	2	42	9	27
Professional and technical	22	-52	19	92	57	23
State employees: economic and social	94	240	230	334	246	652
Administrative and managerial	1	5	4	122	3	129
Professional and technical	93	235	227	211	243	523
Petty bourgeoisie	703	877	1,425	-616	1,843	545
Modern	9	5	15	101	22	108
Administrative and managerial	0	5	2	32	0	38
Professional and technical	9	0	14	69	22	70
Traditional	695	872	1,409	-717	1,821	438
Clerical	1	3	3	-4	4	0
Sales and services	118	33	201	126	308	170
Agriculture	427	202	757	-891	1,118	-624
Production	148	570	425	68	388	823
Unclassified	1	64	22	-17	3	68

(continued on next page)

Sources: MAI 1980, 1988, 1997.

*Includes rank-and-file workers in administration and defense who are not counted in the total for "working class."

†Included in the other subcategories of political functionaries.

	1976–1986		1986–1996		1976–1996	
	Y	X	Y	X	Y	X
Unpaid family workers	256	-793	157	156	670	-894
Sales and services	3	-7	3	13	9	5
Agriculture	147	-347	125	-18	385	-478
Production	105	-442	26	153	274	-433
Others (includes unclassified)	1	3	2	8	2	12
Working class	885	-1,719	877	953	2,320	-1,323
Private-sector employees	743	-1,903	587	711	1,948	-1,810
Clerical and related	33	-132	11	41	87	-134
Sales and services	74	-211	51	173	193	-106
Agriculture	154	-473	96	26	403	-600
Production	480	-1,128	413	467	1,259	-1,027
Unclassified	3	40	18	4	7	58
State employees*	310	992	824	-624	812	690
State employees: economic and social	142	184	289	243	371	487
Political functionaries	183	937	601	-892	480	349
Administrative and managerial	2	0	4	24	6	24
Professional and technical	13	129	62	-50	33	121
Rank and file	168	807	535	-867	441	203
Military and paramilitary†	97	715	388	-704	253	242
Unspecified	10	407	149	-144	27	395
Total	2,202	0	3,570	0	5,772	0

Table A.3

Upper-Level Work Groups: Urban, 1976, 1986, and 1996 (1,000s)

| | 1976 | | |
	Female	Male	Total
Upper-level work group	172.9	453.0	625.8
Capitalists	2.7	139.5	142.2
Modern	0.4	21.7	22.1
Administrative and managerial	0.1	11.2	11.3
Professional and technical	0.3	10.5	10.8
Traditional	2.3	117.8	120.1
Clerical and related	0.1	2.3	2.4
Sales and services	0.8	49.2	50.1
Agriculture	0.1	8.7	8.8
Production	1.2	56.4	57.6
Unclassified	0.1	1.1	1.2
Modern petty bourgeoisie	1.4	27.3	28.6
Administrative and managerial	0.0	0.0	0.0
Professional and technical	1.4	27.3	28.6
Middle class	168.8	286.2	455.0
Administrative and managerial	1.2	23.1	24.2
State employees★	0.8	10.9	11.8
Private employees	0.4	12.1	12.5
Professional and technical	167.7	263.1	430.8
State employees★	156.4	198.5	354.9
Private employees	11.3	64.6	75.8
State employees★	157.2	209.5	366.7
Private employees	11.7	76.7	88.3

Sources: MAI 1980, 1988, 1997.

★ Includes political functionaries.

| | 1986 | | | 1996 | |
Female	Male	Total	Female	Male	Total
300.7	791.5	1,092.3	541.5	1,509.2	2,050.6
5.5	200.4	205.9	9.1	375.8	384.7
1.7	17.4	19.1	2.8	67.8	70.6
0.1	7.7	7.7	0.9	46.5	47.4
1.6	9.8	11.4	1.8	21.3	23.1
3.8	183.0	186.8	6.3	308.0	314.2
0.4	3.4	3.8	0.1	2.9	3.1
0.9	42.6	43.5	1.9	83.9	85.9
0.6	16.7	17.3	0.5	27.6	28.1
1.2	110.2	111.4	2.7	185.6	188.3
0.7	10.1	10.8	1.0	7.9	8.8
2.9	38.3	41.2	8.1	133.1	141.2
0.0	4.3	4.4	0.8	32.3	33.1
2.8	34.0	36.8	7.3	100.8	108.0
292.4	552.8	845.2	524.3	1,000.4	1,524.7
1.2	26.1	27.3	35.0	168.9	203.9
1.1	19.8	20.8	31.6	126.0	157.6
0.2	6.3	6.5	3.4	42.9	46.3
291.2	526.7	817.9	489.4	831.5	1,320.9
283.1	483.9	766.9	457.8	709.4	1,167.2
8.1	42.8	51.0	31.6	122.1	153.7
284.1	503.6	787.7	489.4	835.3	1,324.7
8.3	49.2	57.5	34.9	165.0	200.0

Table A.4
Lower-Level Work Groups: Urban, 1976, 1986, and 1996 (1,000s)

	1976		
	Female	Male	Total
Upper-level work group	172.9	453.0	625.8
Lower-level work group	287.1	3,199.7	3,486.7
Traditional petty bourgeoisie	38.5	848.1	886.6
Clerical	0.2	4.5	4.8
Sales and services	8.8	355.7	364.5
Agriculture	1.1	121.4	122.5
Production	28.2	363.9	392.3
Unclassified	0.1	2.5	2.6
Working class	191.7	2,303.4	2,495.0
Clerical and related	61.4	326.2	387.6
State employees★	46.4	228.4	274.8
Private employees	15.0	97.8	112.9
Sales and services	53.6	345.6	399.2
State employees★	9.6	151.4	160.9
Private employees	44.0	194.2	238.2
Agriculture	6.0	85.3	91.2
State employees	0.1	18.1	18.3
Private employees	5.8	67.2	73.0
Production	64.2	1,193.9	1,258.1
State employees	4.4	229.0	233.4
Private employees	59.9	964.9	1,024.7
Unclassified	6.4	352.5	358.9
State employees (military/paramilitary)	5.8	345.1	351.0
Private employees	0.6	7.4	7.9
State employees	66.3	972.0	1,038.3
Private employees	125.3	1,331.5	1,456.7
Unpaid family workers	50.7	34.9	85.6
Sales and services	0.9	8.5	9.3
Agriculture	2.8	10.3	13.1
Production	46.7	15.2	61.9
Others (includes unclassified)	0.2	0.9	1.2
Unspecified	6.3	13.2	19.5
Total urban employed workforce	460.0	3,652.6	4,112.6

Sources: MAI 1980, 1988, 1997.

★ Includes political functionaries.

| | 1986 | | | 1996 | |
Female	Male	Total	Female	Male	Total
300.7	791.5	1,092.3	541.5	1,509.2	2,050.6
224.1	4,636.6	4,860.7	450.0	6,299.0	6,748.8
45.1	1,654.4	1,699.5	117.9	2,275.8	2,393.7
0.4	8.6	9.0	0.6	7.7	8.3
11.9	515.0	526.9	28.6	779.6	808.2
4.1	222.3	226.4	7.4	287.2	294.7
27.5	869.8	897.3	77.2	1,163.7	1,240.9
1.2	38.7	40.0	4.1	37.5	41.6
117.1	2,703.2	2,820.9	236.2	3,706.7	3,942.9
41.4	259.6	301.1	93.0	417.6	510.5
36.8	235.4	272.1	73.5	360.9	434.4
4.7	24.2	28.9	19.4	56.8	76.1
22.4	377.1	399.4	42.1	616.9	659.0
15.5	253.7	269.1	26.2	321.9	348.1
6.9	123.4	130.3	15.9	295.1	310.9
2.9	68.3	71.2	6.0	108.0	114.0
0.3	27.3	27.5	0.4	32.7	33.0
2.6	41.1	43.7	5.6	75.3	80.9
28.8	1,247.2	1,276.0	66.4	1,885.2	1,951.5
12.2	487.4	499.6	15.5	539.3	554.8
16.6	759.8	776.4	51.0	1,345.8	1,396.7
21.7	750.9	773.2	28.8	679.1	707.8
20.0	717.5	738.1	21.8	635.1	657.0
1.6	33.4	35.1	6.9	43.9	50.9
84.7	1,721.2	1,806.5	168.0	2,571.4	2,739.4
32.4	982.0	1,014.4	68.2	1,135.4	1,203.5
12.4	34.0	46.5	44.1	68.8	112.9
0.3	8.6	9.0	1.0	21.4	22.4
4.1	8.0	12.0	6.1	15.6	21.6
7.4	14.0	21.4	35.7	27.9	63.6
0.6	3.5	4.1	1.4	3.9	5.2
49.4	245.0	294.4	51.7	247.6	299.4
524.9	5,428.2	5,953.0	991.3	7,808.0	8,799.4

Table A.5
Upper-Level Work Groups: Rural, 1976, 1986, and 1996 (1,000s)

	1976		
	Female	Male	Total
Upper-level work group	20.6	106.7	127.4
Capitalists	2.7	37.4	40.0
Modern	0.0	1.2	1.2
Administrative and managerial	0.0	0.6	0.6
Professional and technical	0.0	0.6	0.6
Traditional	2.6	36.2	38.8
Clerical and related	0.0	0.2	0.2
Sales and services	0.0	2.7	2.7
Agriculture	0.6	26.2	26.8
Production	2.0	6.9	8.9
Unclassified	0.0	0.3	0.3
Modern petty bourgeoisie	0.3	5.1	5.4
Administrative and managerial	0.0	0.0	0.0
Professional and technical	0.3	5.1	5.4
Middle class	17.6	64.3	82.0
Administrative and managerial	0.0	4.2	4.2
State employees★	0.0	2.3	2.3
Private employees	0.0	1.9	1.9
Professional and technical	17.6	60.1	77.8
State employees★	16.9	49.4	66.3
Private employees	0.7	10.7	11.4
State employees★	17.0	51.7	68.6
Private employees	0.7	12.6	13.4

Sources: MAI 1980, 1988, 1997.
★ Includes political functionaries.

	1986			1996		
Female	Male	Total	Female	Male	Total
33.9	241.0	274.8	50.3	327.7	378.2
8.3	127.1	135.4	7.1	135.6	142.8
0.2	3.0	3.2	0.1	3.9	4.0
0.0	0.6	0.6	0.1	2.8	2.8
0.2	2.4	2.6	0.1	1.2	1.2
8.0	124.2	132.2	7.0	131.7	138.8
0.0	0.4	0.4	0.0	0.3	0.3
0.1	3.9	3.9	0.2	5.2	5.4
6.4	89.2	95.6	4.5	91.4	95.8
1.1	25.6	26.8	1.7	32.4	34.3
0.4	5.1	5.5	0.6	2.4	3.0
0.5	5.9	6.4	1.0	21.9	22.9
0.0	0.5	0.5	0.1	5.0	5.1
0.5	5.4	5.9	0.9	16.9	17.8
25.1	107.9	133.0	42.2	170.2	212.5
0.1	2.7	2.7	2.8	21.1	23.9
0.0	2.2	2.2	2.7	16.6	19.3
0.0	0.4	0.5	0.1	4.5	4.6
25.1	105.3	130.3	39.4	149.2	188.6
24.5	99.6	124.0	38.1	136.4	174.6
0.6	5.7	6.3	1.3	12.8	14.1
24.5	101.8	126.3	40.9	153.0	193.8
0.6	6.1	6.7	1.4	17.3	18.7

Table A.6

Lower-Level Work Groups: Rural, 1976, 1986, and 1996 (1,000s)

	1976		
	Female	Male	Total
Lower-level work group	731.4	3,828.1	4,559.5
Traditional petty bourgeoisie	90.5	1,799.1	1,889.6
Clerical	0.0	0.9	1.0
Sales and services	1.8	103.5	105.3
Agriculture	16.7	1,565.3	1,582.0
Production	72.0	127.8	199.7
Unclassified	0.1	1.6	1.7
Working class	189.9	1,523.1	1,713.1
Clerical and related	1.2	38.5	39.8
State employees*	1.0	19.4	20.3
Private employees	0.3	19.2	19.5
Sales and services	8.2	84.1	92.3
State employees*	1.1	35.5	36.6
Private employees	7.1	48.6	55.7
Agriculture	68.0	495.5	563.5
State employees	0.8	21.9	22.7
Private employees	67.2	473.6	540.8
Production	111.7	857.9	969.7
State employees	2.1	73.2	75.3
Private employees	109.6	784.7	894.4
Unclassified	0.8	47.0	47.8
State employees (military/paramilitary)	0.5	44.1	44.6
Private employees	0.3	2.9	3.2
State employees	5.5	194.1	199.5
Private employees	184.5	1,329.0	1,513.5
Unpaid family workers	445.1	490.7	935.7
Sales and services	0.8	3.7	4.6
Agriculture	131.1	442.6	573.7
Production	312.9	43.4	356.2
Others (includes unclassified)	0.3	1.0	1.2
Unspecified	5.9	15.2	21.1
Total Rural Employed Workforce	752.0	3,934.8	4,686.8

Sources: MAI 1980, 1988, 1997.

* Includes political functionaries.

	1986			1996	
Female	Male	Total	Female	Male	Total
416.5	4,357.0	4,773.5	723.6	4,670.3	5,394.1
130.1	2,513.2	2,643.3	220.3	2,421.0	2,641.3
0.0	1.5	1.6	0.1	1.7	1.7
1.9	91.9	93.9	6.6	133.6	140.2
61.3	2,045.0	2,106.3	74.4	1,829.6	1,904.0
66.1	346.4	412.5	133.7	428.5	562.2
0.8	28.3	29.2	5.5	27.7	33.2
70.0	1,459.3	1,528.7	153.9	1,751.1	1,905.1
1.4	36.3	37.7	4.2	63.7	67.9
1.3	31.9	33.2	3.5	55.6	59.0
0.1	4.4	4.5	0.7	8.1	8.9
3.0	99.6	102.5	14.3	171.7	186.0
2.1	73.9	76.0	11.7	104.8	116.5
0.9	25.7	26.6	2.7	66.9	69.5
26.4	260.5	286.9	39.0	327.5	366.7
1.2	35.0	36.2	0.9	30.6	31.6
25.3	225.5	250.8	38.1	296.9	335.1
33.5	651.9	685.4	85.0	841.7	926.7
4.2	186.3	190.6	7.7	165.1	172.7
29.3	465.5	494.8	77.3	676.6	754.0
5.7	411.1	416.2	11.3	346.6	357.9
5.3	392.3	397.0	6.9	325.4	332.3
0.4	18.8	19.3	4.4	21.2	25.6
14.0	719.4	732.8	30.6	681.5	712.1
55.9	739.9	796.0	123.3	1,069.6	1,193.1
197.4	240.1	437.5	322.4	361.9	684.3
0.2	1.6	1.8	0.5	4.7	5.2
149.8	224.5	374.3	155.4	316.9	472.5
46.8	12.3	59.1	161.1	34.4	195.5
0.7	1.7	2.4	5.3	5.8	11.1
19.0	144.5	163.5	27.1	136.3	163.4
450.5	4,598.1	5,048.5	774.1	4,998.1	5,772.2

Bibliography

Abolhasani [Monzer], Ali. 1983. *Shahid Motahhari*. Qum: Entesharat-e Eslami.

Abrahamian, Ervand. 1982. *Iran Between Two Revolutions*. Princeton: Princeton Univ. Press.

———. 1993. *Khomeinism: Essays on the Islamic Republic*. Berkeley and Los Angeles: Univ. of California Press.

Afshar, Haleh. 1982. "Khomeini's Teachings and Their Implications for Iranian Women." In *In the Shadow of Islam: The Women's Movement in Iran,* edited by Azar Tabari and Nahid Yeganeh. London: Zed Press.

———. 1987. "Women, Marriage, and the State in Iran." In *Women, State, and Ideology: Studies for Africa and Asia,* edited by Haleh Afshar. Basingstoke, Hampshire, United Kingdom: Macmillan.

———. 1997. "Women and Work in Iran." *Political Studies* 19, no. 4.

———. 1998a. "Disempowerment and the Politics of Civil Liberties for Iranian Women." In *Women and Empowerment: Illustrations from the Third World,* edited by Haleh Afshar. New York: St. Martin's Press.

———. 1998b. *Islam and Feminisms: An Iranian Case-Study.* New York: St. Martin's Press.

Aghajanian, Akbar. 1991. "Population Change in Iran, 1966–86: A Stalled Demographic-Transition." *Population and Development Review* 17, no. 4.

———. 1992a. "Slow Growth Efforts Renewed in Iran." *Population Today* (October).

———. 1992b. "Status of Women and Fertility in Iran." *Journal of Comparative Family Studies* 23, no. 3 (fall).

Aghajanian, Akbar, Homa Agha, and Andrew B. Gross. 1996. "Cumulative Fertility in Iran." *Journal of Comparative Family Studies* 27, no. 1.

Ajami, Amir I. 2005. "From Peasant to Farmer: A Study of Agrarian Transformation in an Iranian Village, 1967–2002." *International Journal of Middle East Studies* 37, no. 3.

Akhavi, Shahrogh. 1980. *Religion and Politics in Contemporary Iran*. Albany: SUNY Press.

Alavi, I. 2002. "Darbareh-e Nabarabari-ye Touzi'-e Daramad dar Iran." *Aftab,* no. 20.

Alerassool, Mahvash. 1993. *Freezing Assets: The USA and the Most Effective Economic Sanction.* New York: St. Martin's Press.

Algar, Hamid. 1980. *Constitution of the Islamic Republic of Iran.* Translated from the Persian. Berkeley: Mizan Press, 1980.

Alikhani, Hossein. 2000. *Sanctioning Iran: Anatomy of a Failed Policy.* London: I. B. Tauris.

Alizadeh, Parvin. 2000. "The State and the Social Position of Women: Female Employment in Post-Revolutionary Iran." In *The Economy of Iran: Dilemmas of an Islamic State,* edited by Parvin Alizadeh. London: I. B. Tauris.

Alizadeh, Parvin, and B. Harper. 1995. "Occupational Sex Segregation in Iran, 1976–1986." *Journal of International Development* 7, no. 4.

Amirahmadi, Houshang. 1990. *Revolution and Economic Transition: The Iranian Experience.* Albany: SUNY Press.

Amuzegar, Jahangir. 1993. *Iran's Economy under the Islamic Republic.* London: I. B. Tauris.

Amuzegar, Jahangir, and M. Ali Fekrat. 1971. *Iran: Economic Development under Dualistic Conditions.* Chicago: Univ. of Chicago Press.

Anker, Richard. 1998. *Gender and Jobs: Sex Segregation of Occupations in the World.* Geneva: International Labour Office.

Aqevli, Farid. 2004. "Bonyadha dar Yek Negah." *Goft-O-Go,* no. 39.

Arjomand, Said Amir. 1988. *The Turban for the Crown: The Islamic Revolution in Iran.* Oxford: Oxford Univ. Press.

Ashraf, Ahmad. 1969. "Historical Obstacles to the Development of a Bourgeoisie in Iran." *Iranian Studies* 2, nos. 2–3.

———. 1981. "The Roots of Emerging Dual Class Structure in Nineteen-Century Iran." *Iranian Studies* 14, nos. 1–2 (winter–spring).

———. 1982. "Dehqanan, Zamin va Enqelab." In *Masa'el-e 'Arzi va Dehqani, Majmo'eh Ketab-e Agah.* Tehran: Agah.

Assadi, Jamshid. 2003. "Theory-e Eqtesad-e Rantkhari." *Aftab,* no. 24.

Azari, Farah. 1983. "Sexuality and Women's Oppression in Iran." In *Women of Iran: The Conflict with Fundamentalist Islam,* edited by Farah Azari. London: Ithaca Press.

Bauer, John. 1990. "Demographic Change and Asian Labor Market in the 1990s." *Population and Development Review* 16, no. 4.

Bauman, Zygmunt. 1974. "Officialdom and Class: Bases of Inequality in Socialist Society." In *The Social Analysis of Class Structure,* edited by Frank Parkin, 129–48. London: Tavistock Publications.

Baxter, Janeen, and Erik Olin Wright. 2000. "The Glass Ceiling Hypothesis: A Reply to Critics." *Gender and Society* 14, no. 6.

Bayat, Assef. 1987. *Workers and Revolution in Iran: A Third World Experience of Workers' Control.* London: Zed Press.

Behdad, Sohrab. 1988a. "Foreign Exchange Gap, Structural Constraints, and the Political Economy of Exchange Rate Determination in Iran." *International Journal of Middle East Studies* 20, no. 1.

———. 1988b. "The Political Economy of Islamic Planning in Iran." In *Post-Revolutionary Iran,* edited by Houshang Amirahmadi and Manoucher Parvin. Boulder: Westview Press.

———. 1989. "Winners and Losers of the Iranian Revolution: A Study in Income Distribution." *International Journal of Middle East Studies* 21, no. 2.

———. 1994a. "A Disputed Utopia: Islamic Economics in Revolutionary Iran." *Comparative Studies in Society and History* 36, no. 4.

———. 1994b. "Production and Employment in Iran: Involution and De-industrialization Theses." In *The Economy of Islamic Iran: Between State and Market,* edited by Thierry Coville. Louvain, Belgium: Peeters.

———. 1995. "The Post-revolutionary Economic Crisis." In *Iran after the Revolution: Crisis of an Islamic State,* edited by Saeed Rahnema and Sohrab Behdad. London: I. B. Tauris.

———. 2000. "From Populism to Economic Liberalism: The Iranian Predicament." In *The Economy of Iran: Dilemmas of an Islamic State,* edited by Parvin Alizadeh. London: I. B. Tauris.

———. 2001a. "Iran dar Rah-e Esteqrar-e Demokrasi." In *Prostroyka va Eslahat,* edited by Koroush Rahimkhani. Tehran: Jame'eh Iranian. http://www.iran-emrooz.de/archiv/goftgu/1380/behdad800411.html.

———. 2001b. "Khatami and His 'Reformist' Economic (Non-) Agenda." *MERIP Press Information Notes,* no. 57 (May 21). http://www.merip.org/pins/pin57.html.

Behdad, Sohrab, and Farhad Nomani. 2002. "Workers, Peasants, and Peddlers: A Study of Labor Stratification in the Post-Revolutionary Iran." *International Journal of Middle East Studies* 34, no. 4.

Benedict, Richard Elliot. 1964. *Industrial Finance in Iran: A Study of Financial Practice in an Underdeveloped Economy.* Cambridge: Harvard Univ. Press.

Benería, Lourdes, and G. Sen. 1982. "Class and Gender Inequalities and Women's Role in Economic Development—Theoretical and Practical Implications." *Feminist Studies* 8, no. 1.

Blau, Francine D., and Wallace E. Hendricks. 1979. "Occupational Segregation by Sex: Trends and Prospects." *Journal of Human Resources* 14, no. 2.

BMI [Bank Markazi Iran]. Annual. *Economic Report and Balance Sheet.* Tehran: BMI.

———. 1981. *Natayej-e Barresi-ye Kargahaye Bozorge San'ati Keshvar 1359* [Survey of Large Manufacturing Enterprises]. Tehran: BMI.

———. 1984. *Barresi-ye Tahavvolat Eqtesadi-ye Ba'd az Enqelab.* Tehran: BMI.

———. 2003. *National Accounts of Iran 1959/60–2000/01.* Tehran: BMI.

Bozorgmehr, Mehdi, and George Sabagh. 1988. "High Status Immigrants: A Statistical Profile of Iranians in the United States." *Iranian Studies* 21, nos. 3–4.

Breen, Richard, and David Rottman. 1995. "Class Analysis and Class Theory." *Sociology* 29, no. 3.

Brennan, Teresa. 1992. *The Interpretation of the Flesh: Freud and Femininity.* New York: Routledge.

Britton, Dana M., and Christine L. Williams. 2000. "Class, Gender, and Parental Values in the 1990's: Response to Baxter and Wright." *Gender and Society* 14, no. 6.

Brown, Lawrence A., Jennifer L. Mandel, and Victor A. Lawson. 1997. "Development Models, Economic Adjustment, and Occupational Composition: Ecuador, 1982–1990." *International Regional Science Review* 20, no. 3.

Browning, Harley L., and Joachim Singelmann. 1975. *The Emergence of a Service Society.* Washington, D.C.: U.S. Department of Labor.

Carrington, William J., and Enrica Detragiache. 1998. "How Big Is the Brain Drain?" Working paper of the International Monetary Fund (WP/98/12).

Chandler, Alfred D., Jr. 1962. *Scale and Scope: The Dynamics of Industrial Capitalism.* Cambridge, Mass.: Belknap.

———. 1990. *Strategy and Structure: Chapters in the History of Industrial Enterprise.* Cambridge: MIT Press.

Cohen, G. A. 2001. *Karl Marx's Theory of History.* Princeton: Princeton Univ. Press.

Cordesman, Anthony H., and Abraham R. Wagner. 1990. *The Lessons of Modern War.* Vol. 2, *The Iran-Iraq War.* Boulder: Westview Press.

Coville, Thierry. 2002. *L'économie de l'Iran islamique: Entre ordre et désordre.* Paris: L'Harmattan.

Crompton, Rosemary. 1989. "Class Theory and Gender." *British Journal of Sociology* 40, no. 4 (Dec.): 565–87.

———. 1993. *Class and Stratification: An Introduction to Current Debates.* Cambridge: Polity Press.

———. 1997. *Women and Work in Modern Britain.* Oxford: Oxford Univ. Press.

———. 2000. "Class and Stratification." In *Sociology: Issues and Debates,* edited by Steve Taylor. New York: Palgrave.

Crompton, Rosemary, and Jon Gubbay. 1977. *Economy and Class Structure.* London: Macmillan.

Dabashi, Hamid. 1993. *Theology of Discontent: The Ideological Foundations of the Islamic Revolution in Iran.* New York: New York Univ. Press.

DHHD [Daftar-e Hamkari-ye Hozeh va Daneshgah]. 1984. *Daramadi bar Eqtesad-e Eslami.* N.p.: Salman-e Farsi.

Dixon, J. M., and R. E. Mansel. 2000. "Congenital Problems and Aberrations of Normal Breast Development and Involution." In *ABC of Breast Diseases,* edited by J. M. Dixon. London: BMJ.

Erikson, Robert, and John H. Goldthorpe. 1988. "Women at Class Crossroads: A Critical Note." *Sociology* 22, no. 4.

———. 1992. *The Constant Flux: A Study of Class Mobility in Industrial Societies.* Oxford: Clarendon Press.

Esfandiari, A. 2002. "Ravesh-Shenasi-ye Abzarha-ye Andazehgiri-ye Touzi'-e Daramad." *Ettela'at Siyasi-Eqtesadi,* nos. 177–78.

Evans, Geoffrey, and Colin Mills. 1998. "Identifying Class Structure: A Latent Class Analysis of the Criterion-Related and Construct Validity of the Goldthorpe Class Schema." *European Sociological Review* 14, no. 1.

Farzin, Mohammad Reza. 2004. "Ta'amoli dar Jaygah va Naqsh-e Bonyad-e Mostaz'afan va Janbazan dar 'Arseh-ha-ye Eqtesadi." *Goft-O-Go,* no. 39.

Faulkner, Anne H., and Victoria A. Lawson. 1991. "Employment Versus Empowerment: A Case Study of the Nature of Women's Work in Ecuador." *Journal of Development Studies* 27, no. 4.

Ferdows, Adele K., and Amir H. Ferdows. 1983. "Women in Shi'i Fiqh: Images Through the Hadith." In *Women and Revolution,* edited by Guity Nashat. Boulder: Westview Press.

Fischer, Michael M. J. 1980. *Iran: From Religious Dispute to Revolution.* Cambridge: Harvard Univ. Press. 1980.

Foran, John. 1993. *Fragile Resistance: Social Transformation in Iran from 1500 to the Revolution.* Boulder: Westview Press.

Frank, Andre Gunder. 1967. *Capitalism and Underdevelopment in Latin America: Historical Studies of Chile and Brazil.* New York: Monthly Review Press.

Fulcher, James, and John Scott. 1999. *Sociology.* Oxford: Oxford Univ. Press.

Gabriel, J. Satyananda. 2001. "A Class Analysis of the Iranian Revolution of 1979." In *Re/presenting Class: Essays in Postmodern Marxism,* edited by J. K. Gibson-Graham, Stephen Resnick, and Richard D. Wolff. Durham: Duck Univ. Press.

Ganji, Akbar. 2002. *Manifest-e Jomhourikhwahi* [A Republican Manifesto], written in Tehran's Evin Prison, posted at http://www.iran-emrooz.de/iemrooz/ganjimanifest.html.

Geertz, Clifford. 1963. *Agricultural Involution: The Process of Ecological Change in Indonesia.* Berkeley and Los Angeles: Univ. of California Press.

Ghaffari, Reza. 1995. "The Economic Consequences of Islamic Fundamentalism in Iran: The Political Economy of Islamic Republic of Iran, 1979–94." *Capital and Class* 56.

Ghasimi, M. R. 1992. "Iranian Economy after the Revolution: An Economic Appraisal of the Five Year Plan." *International Journal of Middle East Studies* 24, no. 4.

Giddens, Anthony. 1984. *The Constitution of the Society: Outline of the Theory of Structuration.* Cambridge: Polity Press.

Goldenweiser, Alexander A. 1936. "Loose Ends of Theory on Individual, Pattern, and Involution in Primitive Society." In *Essay in Anthropology Presented to A. L.*

Kroeber in Celebration of His Sixtieth Birthday, June 11, 1936, edited by Robert H. Lowie. Berkeley and Los Angeles: Univ. of California Press.

Goldthorpe, John H. 1980. *Social Mobility and Class Structure in Modern Britain.* In collaboration with Catriona Llewellyn and Clive Payne. Oxford: Clarendon Press.

———. 1983. "Women and Class Analysis: In Defense of the Conventional View." *Sociology* 17, no. 4.

Goldthorpe, John H., and Keith Hope, eds. 1974. *The Social Grading of Occupations: A New Approach and Scale.* Oxford: Clarendon Press.

Graham, Robert. 1979. *Iran: The Illusion of Power.* London: Croom Helm.

Gregory, Peter. 1986. *The Myth of Market Failure: Employment and the Labor Market in Mexico.* Baltimore: Johns Hopkins Univ. Press.

Gubbay, Jon. 1997. "A Marxist Critique of Weberian Class Analyses." *Sociology* 31, no. 1.

Habibi, Nader. 1989. "Allocation of Educational and Occupational Opportunities in the Islamic Republic of Iran: A Case Study of Political Screening of Human Capital." *Iranian Studies* 22, no. 4.

Hakim, C. 1980. "Census Reports as Documentary Evidence, 1801–1951." *Sociological Review* 28, no. 3.

Hakimian, Hassan. 1990. *Labour Transfer and Economic Development: Theoretical Perspectives and Case Studies from Iran.* New York: Harvester-Wheatsheaf.

———. 2000. "Population Dynamics in Post-revolutionary Iran: A Re-examination of Evidence." In *The Economy of Iran: Dilemmas of an Islamic State,* edited by Parvin Alizadeh. London: I. B. Tauris.

———. 2001. "From Demographic Transition to Population Boom and Bust: The 1980s and 1990s." ERF working paper 200109.

Hakimian, Hassan, and Massoud Karshenas. 2000. "Dilemmas and Prospects for Economic Reform and Reconstruction in Iran." In *The Economy of Iran: The Dilemma of an Islamic State,* edited by Parvin Alizadeh. London: I. B. Tauris.

Halliday, Fred. 1979. *Iran: Dictatorship and Development.* New York: Penguin Books.

Hamilton, Lord Ernest. 1912. *Involution.* London: Mills and Boon.

Hindess, Barry. 1987. *Politics and Class Analysis.* Oxford: Blackwell.

Hooglund, Eric J. 1982. *Land and Revolution in Iran, 1960–80.* Austin: Univ. of Texas Press.

———. 2001. "Rural Labour in Contemporary Iran." Paper presented at "Twentieth-Century Iran: History from Below," a workshop on Iranian labour history at the International Institute of Social History, Amsterdam, May 25–26.

Horiuchi, Shiro. 1995. "The Cohort Approach to Population Growth: A Retrospective Decomposition of Growth Rates for Sweden." *Population Studies* 49, no. 1: 147–63.

ILO [International Labour Office]. 1969. *International Standard Classification of Occupations.* Rev. ed. Geneva: ILO.

———. 1996. *Yearbook of Labour Statistics*. Geneva: ILO.

———. 2000. *Sources and Methods; Labour Statistics. Vol. 10. Estimates and Projections of the Economically Active Population, 1950–2010*. Geneva: ILO.

Imam-Jomeh, Iraj. 1985. *Petroleum-Based Accumulation and the State Form in Iran*. Los Angeles: Univ. of California–Los Angeles.

IMF [International Monetary Fund]. 1990. "Islamic Republic of Iran Undergoes Profound Institutional, Structural Changes." In *IMF Survey*, July 30. Washington, D.C.: IMF.

———. 2001. *International Financial Statistics Yearbook*. Washington, D.C.: IMF.

Jacobs, Jerry A. 1989. "Long-Term Trends in Occupational Segregation by Sex." *American Journal of Sociology* 95, no.1.

Jacobsen, Joyce P. 1998. *The Economics of Gender*. 2d ed. Malden, Mass.: Blackwell.

Jazani, Bizhan. 1980. *Capitalism and Revolution in Iran: Selected Writings of Bizhan Jazani*. Translated by the Iran Committee. London: Zed Press.

Johnson, Gail Cook. 1980. *High-Level Manpower in Iran: From Hidden Conflict to Crisis*. New York: Praeger.

Kahn, J. S. 1985. "Indonesia after the Demise of Involution: Critique of a Debate." *Critique of Anthropology* 5, no. 1.

Kar, Mehrangiz. 1994. *Zanan dar Bazar-e Kar-e Iran*. Tehran: Roshangaran.

Karbassian, Akbar. 2000. "Islamic Revolution and the Management of the Iranian Economy." *Social Research* 67, no. 2.

Karimi, Zahra. 2002. "Sahm-e Zanan Dar Bazar-e Kar Dar Iran." *Ettela'at-e Siyasi-Eqtesadi*, nos. 179–80.

Karmel, T., and M. Maclachlan. 1988. "Occupational Sex Segregation—Increasing or Decreasing?" *Economic Record* 64, no. 186.

Karshenas, Massoud. 1990. *Oil, State, and Industrialization in Iran*. Cambridge: Cambridge Univ. Press.

Karshenas, Massoud, and Valentine M. Moghadam. 1998. "Structural Adjustment and Women's Employment in the Middle East and North Africa." In *Structural Adjustment, Economic Liberalization, Privatization, and Women's Employment in Selected Countries of the Middle East and North Africa*, edited by Nabil Khoury and Evros Demetriades. Ministry of Finance of the Republic of Cyprus: Printing Office of the Republic of Cyprus.

Karshenas, Massoud, and Hashem Pesaran. 1995. "Economic Reform and the Reconstruction of the Iranian Economy." *Middle East Journal* 49.

Katouzian, Homa. 1981. *The Political Economy of Modern Iran: Despotism and Pseudo-modernism, 1926–1979*. New York: New York Univ. Press.

Kazemi, Farhad. 1996. "Civil Society and Iranian Politics." In *Civil Society and the Middle East*, no. 2, edited by Augustus Richard Norton. New York: Richard Brill.

Kazemi, Farhad, and Lisa Reynolds Wolfe. 1997. "Urbanization, Migration, and Politics of Protest in Iran." In *Population, Poverty, and Politics in Middle East Cities,* edited by Michael E. Bonine. Gainesville: Univ. Press of Florida.

Keddie, R. Nikki. 2000. "Women in Iran since 1979." *Social Research* 67, no. 2.

Khajehpour-Khouei, Bijan. 2000. "Domestic Political Reform and Private Sector Activity in Iran." *Social Research* 67, no. 2.

Khalatbari, Firouzeh. 1994. "The Tehran Exchange and Privatization." In *The Economy of Islamic Iran: Between State and Market,* edited by Thierry Coville. Louvain, Belgium: Peeters.

Khatam, A'zam. 2000. "Sakhtar-e Eshteghal-e Zanan-e Shahri." *Goft-O-Go* 4, no. 28.

[Khomeini, Rohollah]. n.d. *Sahifah-ye Noor.* Collection of speeches, declarations, interviews, and letters of Ayatollah Khomeini. *Rohollah al-Mosavi al-Khomeini.* CD-ROM, 2d ed. Tehran: Zafar Rayaneh.

Khosravi, Khosrow. 1972. *Jame'ehshenasi-ye Roustai-ye Iran.* Tehran: Daneshkadeh Olom-e Ejtema'i va Ta'avon.

————. 1979. *Jame'eh-ye Dehqani dar Iran.* Tehran: Payam.

Khosrokhavar, Farhad, and Olivier Roy. 1999. *Iran: Comment sortir d'une révolution religieuse.* Paris: Seuil.

Kian-Thiébaut, Azadeh. 1998. *Secularization of Iran: A Doomed Failure? The New Middle Class and the Making of Modern Iran.* Leuven, Belgium: Peeters.

Kitagawa, Evelyn M. 1955. "Components of a Difference Between Two Rates." *Journal of the American Statistical Association* 50.

Korpi, Walter. 1978. *The Working Class in Welfare Capitalism: Work, Unions, and Politics in Sweden.* London: Routledge and Kegan Paul.

Ladjevardi, Habib, 1985. *Labor Unions and Autocracy in Iran.* Syracuse: Syracuse Univ. Press.

Lautenschlager, Wolfgang. 1986. "The Effects of an Overvalued Exchange Rate on the Iranian Economy, 1979–84." *International Journal of Middle East Studies* 18, no. 1.

Lawson, Victor A. 1990. "Workforce Fragmentation in Latin America and Its Empirical Manifestations in Ecuador." *World Development* 18, no. 5.

Levy, René, and Dominique Joye. 1994. "What Is Switzerland's Stratification Like: Classes, Prestige Gradation, Professional Categories?" *International Sociology* 9, no. 3.

Li, Jiang Hong, and Joachim Singelmann. 1999. "Social Mobility among Men: A Comparison of Neo-Marxian and Weberian Class Models." *European Sociological Review* 15, no. 1.

Lieberman, Samuel S. 1979. "Prospects for Development and Population Growth in Iran." *Population and Development Review* 5, no. 2.

Lockwood, David. 1958. *The Blackcoated Worker: A Study of Class Consciousness.* London: Allen and Unwin.

Looney, Robert E. 1982. *Economic Origins of the Iranian Revolution*. New York: Pergamon Press.

MacDuffee, Cyrus Colton. 1925. "On the Complete Independence of the Functional Equations of Involution." *Bulletin of the American Mathematical Society* 31, nos. 1–2.

MAI [Markaz-e Amar-e Iran]. Annual. *Natayej-e Tafsili-ye Amargiri az Hazineh va Daramad-e Khanevarha-ye Rousta'i* [Expenditures–Income Survey: Rural]. Tehran: MAI.

———. Annual. *Natayej-e Tafsili-ye Amargiri az Hazineh va Daramad-e Khanevarha-ye Shahri* [Expenditures–Income Survey: Urban]. Tehran: MAI.

———. Annual. *Statistical Yearbook*. Tehran: MAI.

———. 1968. *Sarshomari-ye Omomi-ye Nofoos va Maskan-Koll-e Keshvar, 1345* [Census 1966]. Tehran: MAI.

———. 1977. *Natayej-e Amargiri Keshavarzi, Marhaleh Dovvom-e Sarshomari Keshavarzi 2533* [Survey of Agriculture 1974]. Tehran: MAI.

———. 1980. *Sarshomari-ye Omomi-ye Nofoos va Maskan, Koll-e Keshvar, Abanmah 1355* [Census 1976]. Tehran: MAI.

———. 1981a. *Amar-e Kargaha-ye Bozorg-e San'ati Sal-e 1355* [Survey of Large Manufacturing Establishments]. Tehran: MAI.

———. 1981b. *Amar-e Kargaha-ye Kochak-e San'ati Shahri, Sal-e 1355* [Survey of Small Urban Manufacturing Establishments]. Tehran: MAI.

———. 1988. *Sarshomari-ye Omomi-ye Nofoos va Maskan-Koll-e Keshvar, Mehrmah 1365* [Census 1986]. Tehran: MAI.

———. 1990a. *Amar-e Kargaha-ye San'ati-ye Keshvar, Sal-e 1366* [Survey of Manufacturing Establishments]. Tehran: MAI.

———. 1990b. *Amar-e Kargaha-ye San'ati-ye Keshvar, Sal-e 1366, Dara-ye Panjah Nafar Karkon va Bishtar* [Survey of Manufacturing Establishments with More than Fifty Workers]. Tehran: MAI.

———. 1992. *Sarshomari Omomi-ye Keshavarzi 1367, Natayej-e Tafsili, Koll-e Keshvar, 1* [Census of Agriculture 1988]. Tehran: MAI.

———. 1997. *Sarshomari-ye Omomi-ye Nofoos va Maskan-Koll-e Keshvar, 1375* [Census 1996]. Tehran: MAI.

———. 1999a. *Natayej-e Amargiri az Kargaha-ye San'ati, 50 Nafar Karkon va Bishtar 1375* [Survey of Manufacturing Establishments with More than Fifty Workers, 1996]. Tehran: MAI.

———. 1999b. *Natayej-e Amargiri az Kargaha-ye San'ati, Kamtar az Dah Karkon Keshvar 1375* [Survey of Manufacturing Establishments with Fewer than Ten Workers, 1996]. Tehran: MAI.

———. 1999c. *Natayej-e Amargiri az Kargaha-ye San'ati, 10–49 Nafar Karkon Keshvar 1375* [Survey of Manufacturing Establishments with Ten–Forty-nine Workers, 1996]. Tehran: MAI.

———. 1999d. *Sarshomari Omomi-ye Keshavarzi 1372, Natayej-e Tafsili, Koll-e Keshvar, 1* [Census of Agriculture 1993]. Tehran: MAI.

Majd, M. G., and V. F. Nowshirvani. 1993. "Land Reform in Iran Revisited: New Evidence on the Results of Land Reform in Nine Provinces." *Journal of Peasant Studies* 20, no. 3.

Maloney, Suzanne. 2000. "Agents or Obstacles? Parastatal Foundations and Challenges for Iranian Development." In *The Economy of Iran: Dilemmas of an Islamic State,* edited by Parvin Alizadeh. London: I. B. Tauris.

Marchand, Olivier, and Claude Thélot. 1991. *Deux siècles de travail en France.* Paris: Insee.

Marsh, C. 1986. "Social Class and Occupation." In *Key Variables in Social Investigation,* edited by R. G. Burgess. London: Routledge and Kegan Paul.

Marshall, Gordon. 1988. "Classes in Britain: Marxist and Official." *European Sociological Review* 4, no. 2.

Mata-Greenwood, Adriana. 1999. "Gender Issues in Labour Statistics." *International Labour Review* 138, no. 3.

Mazarei, Adnan, Jr. 1996. "The Iranian Economy under the Islamic Republic: Institutional Change and Macroeconomic Performance (1979–1990)." *Cambridge Journal of Economics* 20, no. 3.

Mehryar, A. H., M. Tabibian, and R. Gholipour. N.d.a. "Changes in the Magnitude and Composition of Annual Expenses of Iranian Households between 1971 and 1993." Working paper no. 6. Research Group on Population and Social Policy, Institute for Research on Planning and Development, Tehran.

———. N.d.a. "Changing Pattern of Household Income in Iran, 1974–1993." Working paper no. 7. Research Group on Population and Social Policy, Institute for Research on Planning and Development, Tehran.

Mir-Hosseini, Ziba. 1999. *Islam and Gender: The Religious Debate in Contemporary Iran.* Princeton: Princeton Univ. Press.

Moaddel, Mansoor. 1993. *Class, Politics, and Ideology in the Iranian Revolution.* New York: Columbia Univ. Press.

Moghadam, Fatemeh, E. 1994. "Commoditization of Sexuality and Female Labor Participation in Islam: Implications for Iran, 1960–90." In *In the Eye of the Storm: Women in Post-revolutionary Iran,* edited by Mahnaz Afkhami and Erika Friedl. Syracuse: Syracuse Univ. Press.

Moghadam, Valentine. 1988. "Women, Work, and Ideology in the Islamic Republic." *International Journal of Middle East Studies* 20, no. 1.

———. 1995. "Women's Employment Issues in Contemporary Iran: Problems and Prospects in the 1990s." *Iranian Studies* 28, nos. 3–4.

Moghissi, Haideh. 1996. *Populism and Feminism in Iran: Women's Struggle in a Male-Defined Revolutionary Movement.* New York: St. Martin's Press.

———. 1999. *Feminism and Islamic Fundamentalism: The Limits of Post-modern Analysis.* London: Zed Books.

Moghissi, Haideh, and Saeed Rahnema. 2000. "Working Class and the Islamic State." *Socialist Register 2001*.

Mojab, Shahrzad, and Amir Hassanpour. 1996. "The Politics of Nationality and Ethnic Diversity." In *Iran after the Revolution: Crisis of an Islamic State,* edited by Saeed Rahnema and Sohrab Behdad. London: I. B. Tauris.

Montazeri, Ayatollah Hosein Ali. 2000. *Khaterat.* Posted on the Internet at http://www.montazeri.com.

Nashat, Guity. 1983. "Women in the Ideology of the Islamic Republic." In *Women and Revolution in Iran,* edited by Guity Nashat. Boulder: Westview Press.

Nomani, Farhad. 1987. "Macroeconomic Trends in the Economic Crisis of Iran." *Mondes en Developpement* 15, nos. 58–59.

———. 2003. "The Problem of Interest and Islamic Banking in a Comparative Perspective: The Case of Egypt, Iran, and Pakistan." *Review of Middle East Economics and Finance* 1, no. 1.

Nomani, Farhad, and Ali Rahnema. 1994. *Islamic Economic Systems.* London: Zed Books.

Olver, Peter J. 1995. *Equivalence, Invariants, and Symmetry.* Cambridge: Cambridge Univ. Press.

Paidar, Parvin. 1995. *Women and the Political Process in Twentieth-Century Iran.* Cambridge: Cambridge Univ. Press.

Pakdaman, Naser. 1987. "Jam'iyat-e Iran: Dirouz, Emrouz, Farda." *Cesmandaz* 2 (spring).

Parkin, Frank. 1971. *Class Inequality and Political Order: Social Stratification in Capitalist and Communist Societies.* London: Macgibbon and Kee.

Parsa, Misagh. 1989. *Social Origins of the Iranian Revolution.* New Brunswick: Rutgers Univ. Press.

———. 2000. *State, Ideologies, and Social Revolutions.* Cambridge: Cambridge Univ. Press.

Pesaran, Hashem. 1982. "The System of Dependent Capitalism in Pre—and Postrevolutionary Iran." *International Journal of Middle East Studies* 14, no. 4.

———. 1992. "The Iranian Foreign Exchange Policy and the Black Market for Dollars." *International Journal of Middle East Studies* 24, no. 1.

Pickthall, Mohammed Marmaduke. 1953. *The Meaning of the Glorious Koran: An Explanatory Translation.* New York: New American Library.

Posusney, Marsha Pripstein, and Karen Pfeifer. 1997. "Islam, Islamists, and Labor Law." In *Islam and Public Policy (International Review of Comparative Public Policy 9),* edited by Sohrab Behdad and Farhad Nomani. Greenwich: JAI Press.

Poya, Maryam. 1999. *Women, Work, and Islamism: Ideology and Resistance in Iran.* London: Zed Books.

Prechel, Harland N. 2000. *Big Business and the State: Historical Transitions and Corporate Transformation, 1880s–1990s.* Albany: SUNY Press.

Raftery, Adrian E., Steven M. Lewis, and Akbar Aghajanian. 1995. "Demand or Ideation? Evidence from Iranian Marital Fertility Decline." *Demography* 32, no. 2.

Rahnema, Ali. 1998. *An Islamic Utopia: A Political Biography of Ali Shariati.* London: I. B. Tauris.

Rahnema, Ali, and Farhad Nomani. 1990. *The Secular Miracle: Religion, Politics, and Economic Policy in Iran.* London: Zed Books.

Rahnema, Saeed. 1992. "Work Councils in Iran: The Illusion of Worker Control." *Economic and Industrial Democracy* 13, no. 1.

Ra'is-Dana, Fariborz. 2004. "Bonyadha az Zavieh-ye Vazayef-e Hemayati va Refahi." *Goft-O-Go,* no. 39.

Ra'is-Dana, Fariborz, Zhaleh Shadi-Talab, and Parviz Piran, eds. 2000. *Faqr dar Iran.* Tehran: Daneshgah-e Olum-e Behzisti va Tavanbakhshi.

Rashidi, Ali. 1994. "The Process of De-privatization in Iran after the Revolution of 1979." In *The Economy of Islamic Iran: Between State and Market,* edited by Thierry Coville. Louvain, Belgium: Peeters.

———. 2002. "Tahavolat-e Sakhtari-e Eqtesad-e Iran." *Ettela'at-e Siyasi-Eqtesadi,* nos. 179–80.

Razzaqi, Ebrahim. 1989. *Eqtesad-e Iran.* Tehran: Nashr-e Ney.

Reid, Ivan. 1981. *Social Class Differences in Britain.* London: Grant McIntyre.

Roemer, John E. 1982. *A General Theory of Exploitation and Class.* Cambridge: Harvard Univ. Press.

———. 1994. *Egalitarian Perspectives: Essays in Philosophical Economics.* Cambridge: Cambridge Univ. Press.

Saffioti, Heleieth I. B. 1978. *Women in Class Society.* Translated by Michael Vale. New York: Monthly Review Press.

Salehi-Isfahani, Djavad. 1989. "The Political Economy of Credit Subsidy in Iran, 1973–1978." *International Journal of Middle East Studies* 21, no 3.

———. 2000. "Demographic Factors in Iran's Economic Development." *Social Research* 67, no. 2.

———. 2001. "Fertility, Education, and Household Resources in Iran, 1987–1992." *Economics of Women and Work in the Middle East and North Africa: Research in Middle East Economics* 4.

Sanasarian, Eliz. 1982. *The Women's Rights Movement in Iran: Mutiny, Appeasement, and Repression from 1900 to Khomeini.* New York: Praeger.

Saunders, Peter. 1990. *Social Class and Stratification.* London: Routledge.

Savage, Michael. 2000. *Class Analysis and Social Transformation.* Buckingham, United Kingdom: Open Univ.

Schirazi, Asghar. 1993. *Islamic Development Policy: The Agrarian Question in Iran.* Translated by P. J. Ziess-Lawrence. Boulder: Lynne Rienner.

Scott, Alison MacEwan. 1986. "Women and Industrialization: Examining the 'Female Marginalisation' Thesis." *Journal of Development Studies* 22, no. 4.

Scott, John. 1996. *Stratification and Power: Structures of Class, Status, and Command.* Cambridge: Polity Press.

Sedghi, Hamideh. 1996. "Women, the State, and Development: Appraising Secular and Religious Gender Politics in Iran." In *The Gendered New World Order: Militarism, Development, and the Environment,* edited by Jennifer Turpin and Lois Ann Lorentzen. New York: Routledge.

Shariati, Ali. 1980. *Marxism and Other Western Fallacies: An Islamic Critique.* Translated by R. Campbell. Berkeley: Mizan Press.

Sherkat-e Sarmayehgozari. 1992. *Gozaresh-e Tahqiqati,* no. 24.

Siltanen, Janet, Jennifer Jarman, and Robert M. Blackburn. 1995. *Gender Inequality in the Labour Market: Occupational Concentration and Segregation.* Geneva: International Labour Office.

Solomos, John. 1986. "Varieties of Marxist Conceptions of 'Race,' Class, and the State: A Critical Analysis." In *Theories of Race and Ethnic Relations,* edited by John Rex and David Mason, 110–30. Cambridge: Cambridge Univ. Press.

Soudagar, Mohammad Reza. 1990. *Roshd-e Ravabet-e sarmayehdari dar Iran, 1342–1357.* Tehran: Sho'leh Andisheh.

Swamy, Subramanian. 1967. "Structural Changes and the Distribution of Income by Size: The Case of India." *Review of Income and Wealth* 1, no. 2.

Tabari, Azar. 1982. "Islam and the Struggle for Emancipation of Iranian Women." In *In the Shadow of Islam: The Women's Movement in Iran,* edited by Azar Tabari and Nahid Yeganeh. London: Zed Press.

Tabari, Azar, and Nahid Yeganeh, eds. 1982. In *In the Shadow of Islam: The Women's Movement in Iran.* London: Zed Press.

Tilly, Charles. 1998. *Durable Inequality.* Berkeley and Los Angeles: Univ. of California Press.

Torbat, Akbar E. 2002. "The Brain Drain from Iran to the United States." *Middle East Journal* 56, no. 2.

Toudeh-Roosta, Mehrdad, and Masoud Ramezani. 2002. "Barresi-ye Tozi'-e Daramad asr Iran." *Ettla'at Siyasi-Eqtesadi,* nos. 177–78.

UNDP [United Nations Development Program]. 1996. *Human Development Report, 1996.* New York: Oxford Univ. Press.

UNHCR [United Nations High Commission for Refugees]. 2000. *The State of the World Refugees, 2000: Fifty Years of Humanitarian Action.* Geneva: UNHCR.

U.S. Bureau of the Census. Annual. *Statistical Abstract of the United States.* Washington, D.C.: Department of Commerce, Bureau of the Census.

Vaghefi, Mohammad Reza. 1975. *Entrepreneurs of Iran: The Role of Business Leaders in Development of Iran.* Palo Alto, Calif.: Altoan Press.

Waldman, Peter. 1992. "Clergy Capitalism." *Wall Street Journal,* May 5.

Westergaard, John, and Henrietta Resler. 1975. *Class in a Capitalist Society: A Study of Contemporary Britain.* London: Heinemann Educational.

Western, John Stuart. 1989. *Social Inequality in Australian Society.* Melbourne: Macmillan.

Wolpe, Harold. 1986. "Class Concepts, Class Struggle and Racism." In *Theories of Race and Ethnic Relations,* edited by John Rex and David Mason. Cambridge: Cambridge Univ. Press.

Wright, Erik Olin. 1985. *Classes.* London: Verso.

———. 1997. *Class Counts: Comparative Studies in Class Analysis.* Cambridge: Cambridge Univ. Press.

———. 2001. "Foundation of Class Analysis: A Marxist Perspective." In *Reconfigurations of Class and Gender,* edited by Janeen Baxter and Mark Western. Stanford: Stanford Univ. Press.

Wright, Erik Olin, Cynthia Costello, David Hachen, and Joey Sprague. 1982. "The American Class Structure." *American Sociological Review* 47, no. 6 (Dec.): 709–26.

Wright, Erik Olin, and Joachim Singelmann. 1982. "Proletarianization in the Changing American Class Structure." *American Journal of Sociology* 88, supp., 176–209.

Index

Page numbers in *italic* type indicate tables and figures.

245

economic liberalization (*cont.*)
    post-Khomeini decade; privatization of
    enterprises
economic reforms, 15, 211. *See also*
    economic liberalization
economic relations, 169–70
economic sanctions, 5, 39, 194, 197
economic systems, 1, 12–13
economy: ad hoc measures, 43–44, 45;
    adoption of floating exchange-rate
    system and, 48, 49–51; crisis in 1998,
    58–59; current conditions, 56; decline
    in Khomeini era, 38–40, 45;
    deinvolution process, 5, 8; effect of oil
    glut/Iraqi War on, 5, 36, 39, 45, 46,
    123, 196; effect on interclass
    movements, 15–16; growth in post-
    Khomeini decade, 56; impact of Gulf
    War on, 47–48; impact on workforce
    participation, 65; Islamic state's
    intervention in, 43–44; in Khomeini
    era, 38–40, *40, 41,* 45, 103–4;
    liberalization policies and, 45–56,
    60–61; non-oil GDP/GNP, 39, *40,* 45,
    48, 56, *57;* postrevolutionary crisis and,
    4–5, 7–8, 33–34; in prerevolutionary
    years, 60; production decline,
    1977–1981, 38; structural involution
    and, 34–36; uncertain restructuring
    plan and, 39, 43; vital statistics for
    1966–2000, *57. See also* investments;
    oil revenues
education: accumulation process and,
    14–15; activity rates and, 131, *131;* class
    location and, 20, 21, *116;* differential
    life opportunities and, 169–70;
    distribution of household expenditures
    and, 184, 202; effect on activity rates,
    81; gender, job stability and, 148;
    impact on labor force, 64–65; income-
    expenditures distribution and, *189;*
    language barriers and, 72–73; life
    opportunities and, 170; of new entrants
    into labor market, 200, 213; public vs.

private sector, 115, 117; state
    requirements for access to, 180;
    unemployment and, 178–79; unpaid
    family workers and, 105; of urban heads
    of households, *189, 190;* women and,
    130–31, 135, 141, 213
embourgeoisement of petty bourgeoisie,
    103–5, 204
employment: categories of in Iranian
    census, 10; classes with increases in,
    171; decomposition of class and, 101–7,
    220–21; economic liberalization and,
    48; in Khomeini era, *158, 159;*
    possibility of and life opportunities,
    170; in post-Khomeini decade, 108,
    158, 159; in prerevolutionary Iran, 157,
    158, 159; in rural areas, 157, *159, 171,
    172, 226–29;* state vs. private sector
    increases in, 171; structural involution
    and, 4; unlevel ground in, 171–75;
    upper-level vs. lower-level occupations,
    171, *172, 222–29;* in urban areas, *152,*
    157, *158,* 171, *172, 222–25;* in various
    modes of production, *158, 159;* wars
    impact on opportunities for, 5–7.
    See also jobs; occupations;
    unemployment
employment effect, 218–19, *220–21*
enterprises: demand for nationalization of,
    3–4; demand for privatization of, 46;
    establishment of small capitalists, 173;
    labor unrest in, 206;
    nationalization/confiscation of, 34,
    37–38, 92, 102, 137, 163, 173–74, 204;
    parastatal enterprises and, 174;
    postrevolutionary crisis and, 4–5, 7–8,
    35, 101, 191; privatization of, 36, 48,
    50, 54, 55, 56, 174–75, 196, 204, 211;
    response of owners to revolution, 33,
    34; size of, *91,* 99–100, 103, 164;
    structural involution and, 44, 46. *See
    also* agriculture; enterprises; industry;
    land redistribution; manufacturing;
    mining; production

post-Khomeini decade (*cont.*)
109–13, *111, 139, 147,* 149–50, 151,
153, *158, 159,* 166, 167. *See also*
deinvolution process; economic
liberalization

postrevolutionary economic crisis: ad hoc
economic policies, 43–44, 45;
characteristics of, 4–5, 7–8; definition
of, 4, 33, 191; disruption of
accumulation process and, 4, 33–34,
36–38, 43, 45; economic policy
debates, 39–40; economy during,
39–40, *40;* fixed capital formation and,
41–43, *42, 43;* growth of agriculture in,
40–41; industry and mining in, 38;
international economic linkages and,
38–39, 41; Iraqi war and, 39;
nationalization of enterprises and,
36–37; in 1998, 58–59; outcomes of,
4–5; periods of, 4–7, 87; production
during, 4; uncertain economic plan
and, 39. *See also* deinvolution process;
economic liberalization; Khomeini era;
post-Khomeini decade; structural
involution

power distribution: class interaction with
gender and, 27, 28, 121, 194; class
structure and, 12–13; gender relations
and, 8; involution/deinvolution and,
156; in Islamic Republic, 22; middle
class and, 18–19; modes of production
and, 156; production relations and, 6–7;
spatial distribution of, 8; wage
determination and, 54

Poya, Maryam, 125

prerevolutionary Iran: activity rates
(male/female combined), 78, *80, 84;*
activity rates for men, *82, 127, 128;*
activity rates for women, *83, 127, 128,
131,* 132, *132, 133, 134,* 135;
administrators/managers in, *136, 144;*
age and women in labor, *132, 133, 134;*
age of population in, 75–77; agriculture
in, *111, 136, 138, 146,* 159–63, *161,*

163, 165; capitalist development in, 1,
88, 157; capitalist production relations
in, 162; capitalists in, 88–93, *89, 136,
144, 158, 159,* 162, 163, *217;* change
ratios/GEEI during, *144,* 145, *146–47,*
152; class structure in, 88–101, *89, 108,
217–18;* Concentration Index for, *104;*
concentration of capital in, 90, 97;
education of urban heads of
households, *190;* expenditures
distribution of workers, *182, 185;*
female social hierarchy of work, *136,
138;* fixed capital formation in, 60;
household income in, *182;* income
distribution and, 201; investments
during, *57;* labor force by gender, *127,
128;* landholdings by size in, *161;* land
redistribution in, 160–62, 165; men in,
127, 128, *128;* middle class in, *136,
144, 158, 159,* 162, 163–64; migration
patterns in, 77–79, *78;* military/
paramilitary in, 164; modern capitalists,
136, 144; modern petty bourgeoisie,
136, 144; modes of production in,
157–64; national expenditures, *57;*
non-oil GDP/capita in, *57;* oil
revenues in, *57;* petty bourgeoisie in,
158, 159, 162, 203; petty-commodity
production, 157, 165; political
functionaries in, 97–98, 100–101, 107,
108, 157, 164; population in, *57,*
77–79; private sector in, *136, 138, 144,
147, 158, 159;* production in, 98, *111,
136, 138, 146, 158, 159,* 162–63;
production relations, 159;
professional/technical workers in, 126,
136, 144; religious groups in, 69–70,
70; revolution in, 1, 3–5, 33–34, 37,
87; secularization of, 122, 124; services
activities in, *111, 144, 146;* service
workers in, *136, 138;* social hierarchy
of work for, *136, 138, 172;* state
employees in, *110, 111, 136, 138, 144,
146,* 157, *158, 159,* 162, 163; state

production, 157; traditional capitalists, *136, 144;* traditional petty bourgeoisie, *138, 146;* unemployment in, *57, 200;* unpaid family workers in, *138, 146,* 157, *158,* 159, *159,* 160, 161–62; urban-rural configuration in, 127, *133, 134,* 156, 157–64, *158,* 159, *159,* 162; women in, 122, 126, *127, 128, 131, 132, 133, 134,* 135, 152; working class in, 98–101, *111, 138, 146, 158, 159,* 163, 164

price controls: capitalists need of, 210; deduction of, 50; elimination of, 48; institution of, 44; resumption of, 51, 56

private consumption, 56, 61

private sector: administrators/managers in, 114, *222–23;* agriculture in, 98; capitalists of, 210, *222–23;* change ratio/GEEI for employees of, *144–45, 146–47;* class composition of, *89, 217–18;* concentration of capital in prerevolutionary period, 97, 195; deinvolution and, 166; distribution of household expenditures in, *185;* economic liberalization and, 48, 56, 109, 197; education of employees, 115, *116,* 117; effect of structural involution, 101, 102, 195, 199; employees of, 109, *158, 222–29;* employment/class effect on workers in, *220–21;* empowerment of women in, 153, 154; gender of employees, 148, 149, 150–51, *222–29;* gross fixed capital formation of, 38, *42,* 43, *43,* 56, *57,* 60–61; household income of, 182–83; income-expenditures distribution in, *185,* 186, 187, 202; industrial employees in, 102; jobs of women in, 142; job stability in, 148, 149, 150–51; in Khomeini era, 60, 102, 164, *222–29;* men employed in, *222–29;* middle class employees, 95, 97, 106, 115, 195–96, 197, 209, *222–23;* petty bourgeoisie in, *222–23, 224–25, 228–29;* in post-Khomeini

decade, 60, 109, *222–29;* in prerevolutionary Iran, 60, 95, 157–62, *222–29;* price controls over, 50, 51; production in, 98, 99, 164; professional/technical workers, 114, *222–23;* reconfiguration of class in, 109; in rural areas, *159,* 164, 165, 171–72, *226–27;* services activities, 98; struggle for advancement, 210; unemployment in, 178, *179;* in urban areas, *158,* 164, 165, 171–72, *222–25;* wages of workers, 53–54; women employed in, 136–37, *136–37, 138–39,* 140, 141, *222–29;* working class in, 98, 102, 111, 195, 206, *224–26, 228–29*

privatization of enterprises: benefactors of, 211; bourgeoisie/public demand for, 46, 196; economic liberalization and, 36, 48, 50; profession/technical workers and, 174–75; progress of, 54, 55, 56. *See also* enterprises

production: capitalists in, 103, *158, 159;* change ratio for workers in, *146–47;* class structure and, 12–13, 158, *159,* 195–96, *217–18;* deinvolution and, 4–5, 8; economic liberalization and, 48, 192; employment/class effect on workers in, *220;* gender and job stability and, 148, 149, 150; gender empowerment/impairment and, 153; IMF–World Bank plan and, 48; impairment of inputs acquisition, 38–39; in Khomeini era, 102, 103, 104, *158, 159,* 163, 164–66, 191; managerial complexity/modernization of class locations, 113–17; middle class in, *158, 159;* modification of and workforce, 6–7; petty bourgeoisie in, 94, 104, 112, *158, 159,* 203; in post-Khomeini decade, 99, 111, 112, *158, 159,* 163, 166, 166–68, 192; in prerevolutionary Iran, 92, 94, 97, 98, 99, 157–64, *158, 159,* 162–63; of private sector, 98, 99, *158, 159;* in rural areas, 98, 158–64,

in, 164; capitalist relations in, 167; construction workers in, 163; economy of, 158–59; effect of deinvolution on workforce of, 167–68; employment in, 108; employment levels by class in, 171–72, *172;* expenditures distribution of workers, *185;* female-male ratios in, 75–76; household income in, 181, *182,* 201; income-expenditures distribution in, 187, 188, 201–2; jobs of women in, 142; in Khomeini era, *128, 132, 134, 159,* 164–66; language divisions in, *73;* male worker activity in, *128;* modes of production in, 158–64, *159,* 197; petty bourgeoisie in, 203; population of, *57, 66;* in post-Khomeini decade, 108, *128, 132, 134, 159,* 166–68; in prerevolutionary Iran, 98, *128, 132, 134,* 157, 158–59, 158–64, *159,* 163; production workers in, 98, 156, *159;* social hierarchy of work in, *172, 226–29;* sources of income in, 181–84; unemployment rate in, *57,* 176, 177, *177;* unpaid family workers in, 104–5, 112; women in workforce in, 127, 128–29, *128, 132, 134,* 135–36; workforce changes in, 156, 164–66, 168; working class in, *159,* 162, 164, 165–66, 167, 172, *226–29. See also* agriculture

rural-urban migration: baby boom and, 60; destabilization of social class by, 15; employment levels as reflection of, 171; land redistribution and, 161, 162; male-female ratios and, 75–76; in 1986/1996, *78;* supply of labor and, 77–79; women in labor market and, 122

Sabagh, George, 67
sales personnel. *See* service activities
Scott, A. M., 120
Scott, John, 12
self-employed proprietors. *See* modern

petty bourgeoisie; petty bourgeoisie; traditional petty bourgeoisie

service activities: baby boom and, 60; change ratio for workers in, *146–47;* change ratio/GEEI for employees of, *144–45;* class composition of, *217–18;* employment/class effect on workers in, *220;* gender and job stability in, 149, 150; in Khomeini era, 35–36, 39–40, *40, 41,* 102, 103, 104; petty bourgeoisie in, 94, 104, 112, 203; in post-Khomeini decade, 109, 113; in prerevolutionary Iran, 90, 92, 94, 98–99; of private sector, 98–99; of the state, 96–97, 100; structural involution and, 4, 34, 101; unemployment in, 178; women in, *138–39,* 140, 142, 152; workers by gender, *222–29;* working class in, 100–101, 102, 111, *111*

service class, 21n. 6
Shariati, Ali, 1–2
skills/credentials: as axis of class concept, 6, 27, 28, 29–31, *30,* 87, 121, 193; class location and, 17–18, 19–21; differential life opportunities and, 169–70; distribution of household expenditures and, 202; employment stability and, 174; gender empowerment/impairment and, 154, 198; job stability and, 148; middle class and, 95; of women, 134–35, *136, 137,* 141

skills rent, 19–20
social hierarchy of work: class-gender nature of, 134–35, 194, 198; data depicted in, 7; of females, 135–43, *136–37, 138–39;* gender relations and, 121, 125; lifelong opportunities and, 169; rationale for, 32; in rural areas, 171–72, *172, 226–29;* structure of, 28–29; in urban areas, 171–72, *172, 222–25*

social inequality, 169
socioeconomic conditions: effect on class structure of labor, 6; fertility rates and,